Urban Space, Identity and Postmodernity in 1980s Spain
Rethinking the *Movida*

LEGENDA

LEGENDA, founded in 1995 by the European Humanities Research Centre of the University of Oxford, is now a joint imprint of the Modern Humanities Research Association and Routledge. Titles range from medieval texts to contemporary cinema and form a widely comparative view of the modern humanities, including works on Arabic, Catalan, English, French, German, Greek, Italian, Portuguese, Russian, Spanish, and Yiddish literature. An Editorial Board of distinguished academic specialists works in collaboration with leading scholarly bodies such as the Society for French Studies, the British Comparative Literature Association and the Association of Hispanists of Great Britain & Ireland.

MHRA

The Modern Humanities Research Association (MHRA) encourages and promotes advanced study and research in the field of the modern humanities, especially modern European languages and literature, including English, and also cinema. It also aims to break down the barriers between scholars working in different disciplines and to maintain the unity of humanistic scholarship in the face of increasing specialization. The Association fulfils this purpose primarily through the publication of journals, bibliographies, monographs and other aids to research.

Routledge
Taylor & Francis Group
LONDON AND NEW YORK

Routledge is a global publisher of academic books, journals and online resources in the humanities and social sciences. Founded in 1836, it has published many of the greatest thinkers and scholars of the last hundred years, including Adorno, Einstein, Russell, Popper, Wittgenstein, Jung, Bohm, Hayek, McLuhan, Marcuse and Sartre. Today Routledge is one of the world's leading academic publishers in the Humanities and Social Sciences. It publishes thousands of books and journals each year, serving scholars, instructors, and professional communities worldwide.

www.routledge.com

STUDIES IN HISPANIC AND LUSOPHONE CULTURES

Studies in Hispanic and Lusophone Cultures are selected and edited by the Association of Hispanists of Great Britain & Ireland. The series seeks to publish the best new research in all areas of the literature, thought, history, culture, film, and languages of Spain, Spanish America, and the Portuguese-speaking world.

The Association of Hispanists of Great Britain & Ireland is a professional association which represents a very diverse discipline, in terms of both geographical coverage and objects of study. Its website showcases new work by members, and publicises jobs, conferences and grants in the field.

www.legendabooks.com/series/shlc

STUDIES IN HISPANIC AND LUSOPHONE CULTURES

1. *Unamuno's Theory of the Novel*, by C. A. Longhurst
2. *Pessoa's Geometry of the Abyss: Modernity and the* Book of Disquiet, by Paulo de Medeiros
3. *Artifice and Invention in the Spanish Golden Age*, edited by Stephen Boyd and Terence O'Reilly
4. *The Latin American Short Story at its Limits: Fragmentation, Hybridity and Intermediality*, by Lucy Bell
5. *Spanish New York Narratives 1898–1936: Modernisation, Otherness and Nation*, by David Miranda-Barreiro
6. *The Art of Ana Clavel: Ghosts, Urinals, Dolls, Shadows and Outlaw Desires*, by Jane Elizabeth Lavery
7. *Alejo Carpentier and the Musical Text*, by Katia Chornik
8. *Britain, Spain and the Treaty of Utrecht 1713–2013*, edited by Trevor J. Dadson and J. H. Elliott
9. *Books and Periodicals in Brazil 1768–1930: A Transatlantic Perspective*, edited by Ana Cláudia Suriani da Silva and Sandra Guardini Vasconcelos
10. *Lisbon Revisited: Urban Masculinities in Twentieth-Century Portuguese Fiction*, by Rhian Atkin
11. *Urban Space, Identity and Postmodernity in 1980s Spain: Rethinking the Movida*, by Maite Usoz de la Fuente
12. *Santería, Vodou and Resistance in Caribbean Literature: Daughters of the Spirits*, by Paul Humphrey
13. *Reprojecting the City: Urban Space and Dissident Sexualities in Recent Latin American Cinema*, by Benedict Hoff
14. *Rethinking Juan Rulfo's Creative World: Prose, Photography, Film*, edited by Dylan Brennan and Nuala Finnegan
15. *The Last Days of Humanism: A Reappraisal of Quevedo's Thought*, by Alfonso Rey
16. *Catalan Narrative 1875–2015*, edited by Jordi Larios and Montserrat Lunati

Urban Space, Identity and Postmodernity in 1980s Spain

Rethinking the *Movida*

❖

Maite Usoz de la Fuente

Routledge
Taylor & Francis Group
LONDON AND NEW YORK

2015

First published 2015 by Modern Humanities Research Association and Routledge

2 Park Square, Milton Park, Abingdon, Oxfordshire OX14 4RN
52 Vanderbilt Avenue, New York, NY 10017

Routledge is an imprint of the Taylor & Francis Group, an informa business

First issued in paperback 2020

ISBN 978-1-909662-44-5 (hbk)
ISBN 978-0-367-60197-3 (pbk)

CONTENTS

	Acknowledgements	ix
1	Introduction: *La Luna de Madrid* and *la movida madrileña*	1
2	*La Luna de Madrid* and the City of Madrid: Reimagining and Reclaiming Urban Space	25
3	*La Luna de Madrid*'s Destabilization of Identity: Gender, Nationality, and the Individual	70
4	Modernity and Postmodernity in and of *La Luna de Madrid*	107
5	Conclusion: Towards a New Critical Approach to *la movida*	145
	Bibliography	156
	Index	161

To my parents and to Gareth, Hannah and Emma
for their enduring and unwavering patience, love, and support.

ACKNOWLEDGEMENTS

I was able to research and write this book thanks to a three-year scholarship from the UK's Arts and Humanities Research Council (AHRC). The Department of Spanish, Portuguese and Latin American Studies (SPLAS) at King's College London provided invaluable support (financial, academic, and pastoral) throughout the three and a half years it took to complete this project.

I am also indebted to a number of individuals who have been essential to the development of this book. First and foremost, Dr Alicia Kent has been wonderful in providing guidance and advice throughout the process, while ensuring that I retained full ownership in terms of the development of ideas and approaches. Her insights in terms of how to read ephemera, on visuality and intermediality have been incredibly helpful — as have her personal interest and investment in this project, and her confidence in my capability to carry it forward. She has been an extremely generous mentor, and remains a great friend.

I would also like to thank Dr Daniel Muñoz Sempere for his willingness to let me 'bounce off' ideas with him, and Professor Catherine Boyle, whose enthusiasm and approachability as Head of Department made SPLAS a great environment to work in. Colleague friends such as Daniela Omlor, Nesrine El-Akel, Gabriela Mejan, Rocío Rødjter, Charlotte Fereday, Rachel Scott and Néfer Muñoz have provided a great informal support network and sounding board for ideas.

Last but not least, I am profoundly grateful to my family for their unwavering support. My parents, who have encouraged me through the years, and Gareth, Hannah and Emma, who have endured with grace and good humour the emotional turmoil that accompanies enterprises of this scale, have helped me stay sane and grounded throughout. For their patience and kindness, this is for them.

London, March 2015

CHAPTER 1

Introduction: *La Luna de Madrid* and *la movida madrileña*

The central aim of this book is to encourage a rethink of the urban youth movement that came to be known as *la movida* through a close textual analysis of the monthly arts magazine *La Luna de Madrid* (1983–1988). Despite the fact that *La Luna* never explicitly aligned itself with *la movida* — nor with any other movement, for that matter — the magazine has come to be seen as one of the movement's most emblematic cultural products. The American scholar Susan Larson, for instance, has described *La Luna* as 'la voz oficial de la *movida*' (2003: 310), and Paul Julian Smith uses the magazine as one of his central objects of study in his 2006 essay, 'La movida relocated: press, chronicle, novel'. Additionally, *la movida*'s emphasis on the present and the experiential suggests that any effort at understanding the movement ought to concentrate on ephemera like *La Luna*, on the periodicals (fanzines, magazines, comics) that provided a relatively unmediated and immediate outlet for the creative energies of those living and working in 1980s Madrid. Because of their serialized nature, such products encourage an understanding of *la movida* as process, rather than as a clearly defined, monolithic entity. Serialization further helps us trace the trajectory of *la movida*, which, as I argue throughout this book, is mirrored by that of the magazine. While retrospective accounts of the period, in the forms of fictionalized approaches such as Luis Antonio de Villena's 1999 *Madrid ha muerto. Esplendor y caos en una ciudad feliz de los ochenta*, the oral testimonies of *movida* participants collected in volumes such as José Luis Gallero's 1991 *Sólo se vive una vez. Esplendor y ruina de la movida madrileña* or Antonio J. Ripoll's *La gloriosa movida nacional* (1988), also contribute to establish a sense of chronology and trajectory for *la movida*, such testimonies can be imbued with a retrospective nostalgia that throws into question their accuracy and reliability. In *La Luna*, by contrast, the temporalized view of *la movida* appears as unmediated, as simply a result of its serialized nature and its contemporaneity with the movement.

The cultural and media landscapes in transitional Spain

The years immediately following General Franco's death have been described as years of *desencanto* or disenchantment. Although the Spanish transition from dictatorship to parliamentary democracy has been heralded as unique and exemplary by a number of historians and political analysts (Payne 1987; Prego 1995;

Tusell and Soto 1996), the process was fraught with uncertainty, terrorist violence, and acute economic problems, with inflation reaching 30 per cent and high levels of unemployment (Payne 1987: 164). The discontent of the old Francoist elite, as well as of those nostalgic of the old regime, was encapsulated in the phrase 'con Franco vivíamos mejor' [our life was better with Franco] (Cebrián 1980: 23),[1] which led to the emergence of the alternative 'contra Franco vivíamos mejor' [our life was better against Franco] in some left-wing circles.[2] Some anti-Francoist activists felt betrayed by the transitional process, which failed (or, arguably, could not afford) to effect a clean break with the immediate Francoist past, opting instead for a *ruptura pactada*, an 'agreed break', which allowed large numbers of Francoist cadres to hold onto positions of power within the new order (Preston 1986: 120).

Spanish critics like Teresa Vilarós (1998) and Alberto Medina (2001) relate the melancholy of *desencanto* to the fact that the possibility of modernization and emancipation coincided, in Spain, with the advent of postmodernism. Thus Medina argues that '[t]ras cuarenta años de espera, la ansiada entrada en la modernidad es simultánea a su cancelación. [...] La posibilidad de emancipación llega cuando ésta no es más que un cadáver' [after a forty-year wait, the longed-for entry into modernity coincides with its cancellation. [...] The possibility of emancipation arrives at a time when it is but a corpse] (Medina 2001: 56). Echoing Medina's diagnosis, the co-founder and editor of *El País* newspaper, Juan Luis Cebrián, has explained how his generation, which came of age in the mid-1960s, was imbued with modernist, Marxist and existentialist principles (Cebrián in Gallero 1991: 313). Their struggle during the years of clandestine opposition had been first and foremost against Franco's dictatorship, but also for a modernist-Marxist project that, by 1975, postmodernism had rendered obsolete. The resulting generational melancholia is thus not difficult to understand, and is palpable in several cultural products of the period, such as Jaime Chávarri's 1976 film *El Desencanto*,[3] or Juan Luis Cebrián's 1980 essay *La España que bosteza [The yawning Spain]*.[4]

Against this generalized sense of crisis and disenchantment, a younger generation emerged, less invested in the political struggle against Francoism and determined to make the most of the freedoms newly available in a democratic Spain. From the mid-1970s, there is a proliferation of comics, fanzines, magazines and events in Barcelona, with the appearance of magazines such as *Ajoblanco* and *Star*; the street performances of the transvestite painter José Ángel Ocaña, alias *La Ocaña*; the emergence of a comics collective known as *El Rrollo*;[5] or the Canet Rock festival (held on the outskirts of the city between 1975 and 1978) as signs of a budding countercultural scene that comes to be known as *el rollo* (Fouce 2002: 15; Alberca 2003: 209).

From around 1977, Madrid became the centre of this type of countercultural activity. The reasons for this geographical shift are not entirely clear, though some have pointed to Catalan nationalism as a possible cause.[6] By 1977, Madrid's Rastro street market had become a hub of countercultural activity. It was here that the *Cascorro Factory*, a collective of artists including the graphic artist and painter Ceesepe and the photographer Alberto García-Alix, edited, copied and sold a range of comics and fanzines, among them some of *El Rrollo*'s titles. Around the same time (1976–1977) another group, known as *La liviandad del imperdible* (later *Kaka de Luxe*), whose members included Fernando Márquez (alias El Zurdo) and Olvido Gara, who, under the alias Alaska, later became one of the *movida*'s most durable icons, set up a stall at the Rastro and soon came into contact with the members of the *Cascorro Factory* (Gallero 1991: 373). The early, underground years of what later came to be known as *la movida* are marked by the close proximity of its members. Borja Casani, the first editor of *La Luna de Madrid*, remarked that 'efectivamente, hay un grupo. Un grupo, además, hiperdogmático y duro. Es el núcleo protagonista de los inicios de la movida, al que yo no pertenezco. El grupo de Almodóvar, McNamara, Costus, Paloma Chamorro, Ceesepe, Ouka Lele, García Alix' [yes, there was a group. A group that, moreover, was hyperdogmatic and tough. It is the core that saw the beginnings of *la movida*, and to which I do not belong. The group of Almodóvar, McNamara, Costus, Paloma Chamorro, Ceesepe, Ouka Lele, García Alix] (Gallero 1991: 2).

Despite the fact that the artists mentioned by Casani did not constitute a cohesive group, inasmuch as they did not release a manifesto or share an explicitly articulated creative or aesthetic programme, they did share numerous vital and creative experiences. Ceesepe, one of the founders of the *Cascorro Factory*, shared a flat with the painter El Hortelano and the photographer Ouka Leele near Madrid's Retiro Park in 1976–1977 (Gallero 1991: 362). Fabio/Fanny McNamara,[7] who duetted alongside Almodóvar in Madrid's bars and appeared in the film-maker's first three feature-length films, lived for some time during the late 1970s at Casa Costus, the home and atelier of painters Enrique Naya and Juan Carrero (alias Las Costus) (Gallero 1991: 319). What Casani identifies as *la movida*'s initial group or nucleus constitutes in fact a network of emerging artists whose shared interests and experiences resulted in fruitful creative collaborations. Pedro Almodóvar's first feature-length film, *Pepi, Luci, Bom y otrás chicas del montón* (1980), for instance, was initially conceived as a story for the adult comic *El Víbora*, a Barcelona-based project in which several former members of *El Rrollo*, such as Mariscal and Nazario, were involved (Strauss 1996: 11). Moreover, the film featured Alaska (Olvido Gara), one of the founders of *Kaka de Luxe*, as one of its protagonists in the role of aspiring punk starlet and sadistic lesbian Bom, and also included a number of illustrations by the *Cascorro Factory*'s Ceesepe.[8] Eduardo Haro Ibars, the only *movida* writer according to the critic and journalist Tomás Cuesta (Gallero 1991: 331), penned many of the lyrics of Javier Gurruchaga's Orquesta Mondragón (Lechado 2005: 279), and his poem 'Pecados más dulces que un zapato de raso' was turned into song by the rock band Gabinete Caligari (Fernández 2005). Photographers such as Alberto García Alix and Pablo Pérez-Mínguez immortalized the period, often using their artist friends as models, and the painter duo Las Costus created their own *movida* iconography through their series *El Valle de los Caídos*, in which they recreated scenes from the Passion of Christ featured in General Francisco Franco's eponymous mausoleum in El Escorial, using figures from Madrid's underground scene as models.

Within this climate of creative countercultural effervescence, ephemera such as comics (cf. *El Rrollo Enmascarado* (1974), *Star* (1974–1980) *El Víbora* (1979–2005), *Makoki* (1982–1993), and *Madriz* (1984–1987), among others), fanzines like *La liviandad del imperdible* (1977), *96 Lágrimas* (1980), and *Lollipop* (1980), and magazines including *Dezine* (1980) and *Madrid me mata* (1984–1985) provided these aspiring artists with an immediate outlet for their work. Interestingly, this proliferation of new titles runs parallel to the disappearance of established publications like *Triunfo* (1962–1982), *Cuadernos para el Diálogo* (1963–1976) and *El Viejo Topo* (1976–1982),[9] independent magazines that, managing to elude censorship, had constituted important fora for the anti-Francoist intelligentsia. This editorial shift can be seen as symptomatic of the wider socio-cultural changes inaugurated by the end of a four-decade dictatorship.

Within this print media landscape, *La Luna* can be regarded as a hybrid, a publication that sought to bridge the gap between the amateur, underground, small-circulation comics and fanzines of its time, and professional, highbrow titles such as *El Viejo Topo, Cuadernos para el Diálogo* and *Triunfo*. Although the influence of the latter titles (in terms of visual style, tone, and content) over *La Luna* is not obvious, the magazine's co-founder Juan Ramón Martínez-Acha has explained how, in 1982,

> nos reuníamos en casa de Borja Casani y hablábamos de la desaparición de antiguas revistas claves de la época franquista como *Cuadernos para el Diálogo* o *Triunfo*, y poco a poco se fueron sumando unos a otros y así fue naciendo *La Luna de Madrid*. (Cadahía 2007: 50)
>
> [we congregated at Borja Casani's house and we talked about the disappearance of some key magazines of the Francoist period, such as *Cuadernos para el Diálogo* or *Triunfo*, and gradually more people became involved and so *La Luna de Madrid* came into being.] (Cadahía 2007: 50)

Martínez-Acha's words suggest that, even if *Triunfo* and *Cuadernos para el Diálogo* did not constitute direct referents for *La Luna*, their demise partly spurred on his group of friends to create their own publication. Moreover, *La Luna*'s editorial ambition and degree of professionalism, evidenced by the magazine's format, length, content, print run, and relative longevity, situate it closer to the 1960s and 1970s anti-Francoist titles than to the amateur and generally short-lived fanzines that exerted a more direct, or at least more visible, influence over the magazine.

La Luna was created, at least in part, out of a necessity to grant visibility to what was happening within Madrid's countercultural scene. As its former editor Borja Casani has remarked:

> Uno de lo grandes objetivos, digamos estratégicos, de toda la cultura madrileña de aquellos momentos era salir a la luz. Alberti aparecía trescientas treinta y tres mil veces en los periódicos, mientras que cosas de real importancia para nosotros no aparecían... (Gallero 1991: 11)
>
> [One of the strategic aims of Madrilenian culture at the time was to gain visibility. Alberti appeared in the press umpteen times, while things which we considered really important did not feature at all...] (Gallero 1991: 11)

These 'cosas de real importancia' that, according to Casani, the mainstream press chose to ignore, were happening at street level. *La Luna* was thus born out of a wish to chronicle the activities of an emerging network of artists, intellectuals and cultural practitioners living in early 1980s Madrid. But behind this relatively humble aim, there was also a latent desire to change the existing cultural landscape. Several founding members of the magazine have referred to the bleak cultural legacy of Francoism, which they describe as ruin (issue 1: 7) and wasteland (issue 15: 7). Casani himself has described the launch of the magazine as 'un acto desesperado' [a desperate act] (Cadahía 2007: 21) in response to the ruinous cultural context in which its founders had grown up; and as an attempt to transform, or at least escape, that context. In the eyes of the magazine's co-founder Pedro Mansilla, the role of *La Luna* in enabling what he terms 'la transición estética' [the aesthetic transition] from Francoism can be seen as analogous to the role of the anti-Franco press of the 1970s, which played a crucial role in facilitating the political process of transition from dictatorship to democracy (Cadahía 2007: 38).[10] The founding members of *La Luna* understood that this 'aesthetic transition' could not, and should not, be a smooth process, and hence conceived the magazine as a 'revista de agitación' [agitation magazine] (issue 34: 3); in other words, as a publication that set out to shake up existing notions of art, culture, and taste.

Critical approaches to *la movida* and *La Luna*

There is a strong strand of criticism, particularly within Spain, that regards *la movida*, the phenomenon *La Luna* purportedly represented, as 'un efecto cultural de superficie' [a superficial cultural effect] (Subirats 2002: 77) with 'la banalidad de lo nuevo' [the banality of the new] (Subirats 2002: 75) at its core. Particularly among Spanish scholars of a certain generation, there is a tendency to characterize the 1980s phenomenon as frivolous, superficial, and ephemeral, and therefore not worthy of critical scrutiny. Figures such as Eduardo Subirats (1993, 2002), José Carlos Mainer (1994, 2000) or Joan Ramón Resina (2000), to cite some of the better-known proponents of this view, insistently and vehemently deny *la movida* any cultural significance. This position is problematic on three accounts: it is often not supported by an in-depth engagement with cultural products of the period, but rather predicated on general impressions; it fails to account for the resurgence of *la movida* at the level of the Spanish popular imaginary since the late 1990s;[11] and it tends to take *la movida* too literally, unquestioningly accepting its self-proclaimed superficiality and frivolity. As the philosopher Javier Sádaba notes in an article for *La Luna*, 'una interpretación no superficial de la frivolidad tal vez nos enseña eso: que se recuperan valores dejados en la sombra, que se rompe con una moral aún excesivamente atada a la teología' [a non-superficial interpretation of frivolity might show us this: that it can lead to the recuperation of values that had been put aside, that it can break with a morality still excessively tied to theology] (22: 8–9). Superficiality and frivolity thus ought not to be too hastily denounced as inconsequential, or used to attack *la movida*, but rather can be seen as strategies that, according to the journalist Tomás Cuesta, were intended to challenge a culture that was 'minada de transcendencia' [undermined by transcendence] (Gallero 1991: 334).

The aforementioned critics also attack *la movida* on the grounds of what they regard as its lack of political engagement; its hedonism and consumerism; its allegiance or affinity with postmodernism; and its failure to produce innovative works and a lasting legacy. While such claims cannot be ignored or flatly dismissed, for there are undoubtedly elements of apoliticism, hedonism, consumerism and postmodernism in *la movida*, such traits need to be carefully considered and contextualized to gain a real understanding of the phenomenon. *La movida's* supposed apolitical nature has been thrown into question by Paul Julian Smith, who claims that the movement 'can be accused of apoliticism only if the political is restricted to formal governance' (2006: 65). Indeed *la movida*'s radical and uncompromising affirmation of the right to difference, its vindication of personal freedoms, and its attempts to enrich everyday life can and ought to be seen as political gestures. It may well be argued that such modest goals — when considered against the broader utopian projects of preceding artistic movements and generations — evidence a selfish individualism. But the limited scale of these goals is also symptomatic of the postmodern realization of the impossibility (and, indeed, the undesirability) of totalising revolutionary change, which, as Jean-François Lyotard notes, inevitably entails a suppression of difference and a 'return of terror' (1984: 81–82).

Teresa Vilarós's 1998 book *El Mono del Desencanto. Una Crítica Cultural de la Transición* inaugurates an alternative trend of critical discourse on the cultural phenomena of the Spanish transition, including *la movida*. Vilarós proposes a psychoanalytical interpretation, seeing Francoism as an 'addiction' for the Spanish social body afflicting even the more radical segments of the opposition, who, with the demise of Francoism, were deprived of a clear enemy. With the death of Franco, the symbolic father, hated and beloved at the same time, Spaniards experience a withdrawal syndrome (*mono* in Spanish slang) that cannot be referenced or elaborated because of the politics of 'borrón y cuenta nueva' that characterized the transition to democracy. Thus, the *mono* becomes a spectral presence in the cultural production of those years, and Vilarós's analysis focuses on the different phantasmatic expressions of this withdrawal syndrome in a selection of Spanish texts from the 1970s to the early 1990s.

Vilarós's analytical model is sophisticated and seductive — indeed, other Spanish critics such as Cristina Moreiras Menor (2002) and Alberto Medina (2001) have since developed similar approaches. The trauma and consequences of the enforced collective amnesia that followed the death of General Franco have only recently begun to generate serious scholarly work, and whilst it remains a key piece in the puzzle that is contemporary Spain, attempting to analyse all cultural texts, or, as in Vilarós's case, a very diverse sample thereof, under its prism inevitably leads to dangerous simplifications and generalizations. The risk of universalizing models such as Vilarós's is that, by conflating very different works and trends under the same theoretical framework, they tend to ascribe to heterogeneous bodies of work one single meaning or explanation. While Vilarós considers both *desencanto* and *movida* as responses to the trauma of the transition, I understand the latter as, at least in part, a reaction to the melancholia of *desencanto*.

Vilarós bases her reading of *la movida* as a traumatic response to Spain's transition to democracy in a dismissal of its celebratory aspects (which she brushes aside as signs of repressed trauma) and in an invocation of the tragic fate of many of its participants, who developed drug dependencies and, in some cases, died prematurely. But what Vilarós posits as a causal relationship (the latent trauma at the heart of *la movida*, hidden underneath the movement's celebratory surface, ultimately leading individuals to the dead-end of 'un tratamiento de metadona' [methadone treatment] (1998: 35), if not worse) is, in my view, in fact a relationship of correlation. Rather than as a manifestation of a latent death wish, as Vilarós argues, the unquestionably high death toll of *la movida* ought to be understood as a result of the fact that its participants belonged to the first generation of Spaniards to be exposed to heroin and AIDS, at a time in which there was little information available on either the drug or the illness.[12]

The past decade and a half has seen the emergence of a third critical position with regard to *la movida*. Susan Larson, Paul Julian Smith, Gema Pérez Sánchez and others have encouraged a revision of the period.[13] Using an analytical model with 'a more sympathetic attitude to the cultural production of the transition' (Smith 2006: 53), these authors have focused on 'themes of life, liberty, and the pursuit of pleasure, if not happiness' (2006: 53). Susan Larson can arguably be seen as inaugurating this trend, with her 1997 article 'Todavía en la luna: A round table discussion with Darío Álvarez Basso, Antonio Bueno, Pierluigi Cattermole Fioravanti, Ignacio Martínez Lacaci, Javier Tímmermans de Palma y José Tono Martíniez', co-authored with Malcolm Compitello. The article brings together two former editors and several former contributors of *La Luna* to discuss *la movida*, the magazine, and, more generally, Spain's cultural landscape a decade after the disintegration of the Madrilenian movement. The participants subscribe to Paul Julian Smith's view that the general mood of the period was a creative, celebratory one (2006), with a hopeful sense that 'había que hacer todo porque todo estaba por hacer' (Larson and Compitello 1997: 163), as Darío Álvarez Basso recalls. Furthermore, participants contest the charge — frequently invoked against *la movida* — that *La Luna* and other cultural products of *la movida* were made possible by the political establishment via *subvenciones* (state subsidies to the arts), and thus, that *la movida's* aims and goals coincided (or were made to coincide) with the cultural renewal programme of Felipe González's Socialist government. In contrast, several participants speak of the government's attempts at appropriation or co-option of projects that had been set up independently. Moreover, they underline the problems created by public subsidies, which contributed to inflate artists' salaries, particularly in the case of musicians, and put those who wished to remain independent, like the editorial team of *La Luna*, at a clear disadvantage.[14]

The work of Larson (2003) and Smith (2006) is novel not only in its more nuanced and more positive valorization of *la movida*, but also in its redefinition of the corpus of works for study, which they broaden to include not only literary, visual and filmic texts, but also retrospective accounts by participants and periodicals, among them *La Luna de Madrid*. Further, these critics use new methodologies (urban and spatial studies; cultural geography) in order to make sense of *la movida*. This book, which borrows from urban studies and lays emphasis on everyday practices, is indebted to this shift and seeks to contribute further to an ongoing re-evaluation of *la movida*.

Gema Pérez Sánchez's 2007 book *Queer Transitions in Contemporary Spanish Culture:*

from Franco to 'la movida', continues the re-evaluation of 1970s and 1980s cultural production initiated by Larson and Smith. The central claim of this work is that

> novelists and artists living at the so-called margins have been central to the consolidation of the contemporary Spanish democracy and that their works have been central to understanding complex changes with regard to gender and sexuality that the Spanish imaginary has undergone — that they and their works enable multiple queer transitions. (2007: 195)

Pérez Sánchez focuses on unveiling the queer content and potential of several twentieth-century texts; but her analysis does not deal exclusively with the period of *la movida*, as four of the seven chapters of her book consider texts from earlier periods, ranging from the 1940s to 1970. The present work differs from Pérez Sánchez's in that its scope is more narrowly defined, in terms of the texts and time frame considered, but broader in terms of the range of methodologies used. In other words, the central concern of Pérez Sánchez's study is not *la movida* itself, but rather the uncovering of queer aspects in a series of Spanish texts of the twentieth century.

More recent studies on *la movida*, such as Nichols and Song's 2014 *Toward a Cultural Archive of La Movida*, offer nuanced approaches to the phenomenon, proposing that neither discourses that dismiss *la movida* as 'a betrayal to the memory of the victims of the dictatorship' (2014: 6), nor narratives that focus on the movement's role in introducing a modern (or postmodern) consciousness in Spain do justice to a phenomenon that they consider far more complex than either of those critical positions would suggest. Like Nichols and Song, I understand *la movida* as an ambiguous and contradictory phenomenon that does not easily yield to interpretation, but which, precisely for that reason, deserves critical attention, and challenges scholars to devise new approaches to make sense of a profoundly eclectic body of works and practices.

Finally, Luis García Torvisco's 2012 article '*La Luna de Madrid*: Movida, posmodernidad y capitalismo cultural en una revista feliz de los ochenta' explicitly addresses the contradictions that characterize *La Luna* and *la movida*, an issue that is central to this book. For García Torvisco, *La Luna*'s hesitant endorsement of both *la movida* and postmodernism is not only characteristic of the magazine's eclectic and heterogeneous editorial line, but also symptomatic of cultural prejudices that are not entirely dissimilar to those of more traditional critics who dismiss *la movida* as merely 'an anachronistic party' fuelled by a 'politically constructed and officially encouraged ludism' (Resina 2000: 98). While García Torvisco's identification of *La Luna*'s wavering between an enthusiastic embrace of and a critical distancing from *la movida* and postmodernism helps reflect the often-overlooked complexity of the publication -and of *la movida* itself-, I do not believe that such oscillations can be simply explained as evidence of the endurance of certain cultural prejudices, but rather testify to an intricate double movement that the *La Luna* collaborator Javier Utray describes in the following terms:

> lo que me parece el alma, el alambre que enhebra la movida [...] responde a la pregunta: ¿cómo puedo hacer lo que quiera y ser crítico con la sociedad, generando un producto que tenga éxito en la sociedad? ¿Cómo me lo puedo

> pasar mejor haciendo una cosa terriblemente crítica y que se convierta en un producto que me es pagado, paradójicamente, por la sociedad? Es decir, sin abdicar en absoluto del radicalismo más crítico ni del radicalismo más infantil. [...] Pero, claro, hay que estar ajustando mucho el motor del coche para tener esas prestaciones. (Gallero 1991: 253)
>
> [what I consider to be the soul or thread that runs through *la movida* [...] is the question: How can I do whatever I want and be critical with society, while generating a product that is successful in society? How can I have most fun while making something incredibly critical, and turn it into a product that is, paradoxically, paid for by society? That is, without renouncing in any way the most critical radicalism, or the most childish. [...] But of course, to achieve that requires a constant adjustment of the car's engine.] (Gallero 1991: 253)

As Utray's words suggest, then, an essential challenge — if not *the* essential challenge — for those taking part in *la movida* (and, as we shall see, for *La Luna*'s editorial team) resided in the parallel undermining of the cultural establishment of its day (through an attack on transcendence, the incorporation of elements of 'low' or popular cultural forms, the mobilization of an often caustically aggressive humour), and the simultaneous aspiration to success (critical as well as commercial) within that very establishment. This double move may appear contradictory, but it can partly be explained by an awareness, on the part of *movida* participants, that any claim of independence or autonomy from the establishment is illusory — a realization that, as will be seen in Chapter 3, is at least partly marked by the postmodern context within which *la movida* emerges. Utray's final sentence concedes the difficulty of engaging in such an operation of attacking the cultural establishment and simultaneously attempting to infiltrate it, which, as *La Luna*'s trajectory illustrates, required a delicate balancing act that could not be sustained over an extended period of time.

La Luna de Madrid

The first issue of *La Luna de Madrid* appeared in November 1983, although the project had been in preparation for well over a year.[15] Its founding members, a group of young artists and intellectuals who gathered regularly around the *tertulias* of Madrid's Galería Moriarty, wanted the magazine to constitute a space for emerging local artists to showcase their work, and an open forum for debate (Cadahía 2007: 13). Though initially conceived as a small-circulation, locally distributed magazine, *La Luna*'s immediate success led to nationwide distribution from its third issue (issue 34: 3), and the magazine soon achieved sales of over 30,000 copies, an unprecedented figure for a publication of its type, according to its co-founder and second editor José Tono Martínez (Cadahía 2007: 13). However, the publication's success was short-lived: the magazine folded in 1988, after 48 issues and a five-year existence marked by a continuing financial struggle to keep the project afloat, and bitter schisms within its editorial team.[16]

Vicente Patón, co-founder of *La Luna*, traces the magazine's beginnings to the failed coup of 23 February 1981:

> Noviembre de 1983 marca la fecha del número 1, aunque la aventura viniese de casi dos años atrás [...], y aunque el pistoletazo de salida fuera realmente el de Tejero, en aquel día de febrero de 1981 en que no consiguió poner la Historia del revés, pero sí logró que a muchos se nos incrementaran las ansias de libertad [...]. (Cadahía 2007: 32)
>
> [The first issue is dated November 1983, but the enterprise had originated almost two years earlier [...], and the trigger was really that of Tejero, in that February of 1981 in which he failed to turn History upside down, but he did succeed in increasing the desire for freedom among many of us [...].] (Cadahía 2007: 32)

The attempted coup not only intensified a generation's desire for freedom, its failure also signalled the irreversibility of the political process — the transition from an authoritarian regime to a parliamentary democracy — set in motion following the death of General Francisco Franco in 1975. This awareness of the irreversibility of political change, further strengthened by the Spanish Socialist Workers Party's (PSOE) electoral victory in 1982, contributed to a shift in emphasis from political to social and cultural change (cf. Casani in Gallero 1991: 8–9).

Central to *La Luna*'s agitation strategy was its irreverent tone, which contrasted with the seriousness and sobriety of other Spanish arts titles of the time, such as *Cuadernos del Norte* (1980–1990). *La Luna*'s irreverence can be interpreted as an attempt to dismantle the transcendental aura that surrounded art and culture in Spain at the time, as well as the reverential attitudes such an aura encouraged, and the exclusions it enabled. Interestingly, this mocking attitude is extended even to iconic underground figures, such as the 'poeta maldito' Leopoldo María Panero,[17] interviewed at the mental health institution he was interned in at the time, who is sardonically presented as 'el último intelectual que se comió el tarro', which can be loosely translated as 'the last intellectual who lost his marbles' (issue 1: 10–12). *La Luna* does not spare itself from this mockery, with the magazine being described within its own pages as 'la revista más pretenciosa de todos los tiempos' (issue 14: 86).

If Madrid's countercultural circles provided the creative ferment which led to the creation of *La Luna*, its founding members procured the economic means that made possible the launching of the magazine. In December 1982, a group of friends led by Borja Casani created Permanyare Producciones S.A. (issue 34: 3). Permanyare was set up as a cooperative-style society, with each of its ten members contributing an equal sum of money (Cadahía 2007: 51).[18] The name of the society, Permanyare, is a phonetic rendering of the Italian 'per mangiare', which literally translates as 'in order to eat', but can also be understood more broadly as 'in order to make a living'. The name is, at least in part, ironic: in its literal rendering, it is reminiscent of the beggar's cry, and can thus be interpreted as a reference to the economic hardship endured by many young artists and cultural practitioners trying to survive in early 1980s Madrid. However, the choice of name also reflects another dimension of the founders' intentions: not only did they hope to make visible the work of artists largely ignored by the mainstream, changing Spain's cultural landscape in the process, they also wanted to make a living out of their activity, both for themselves and for the artists whose work the magazine showcased.

This aim of making a living out of one's creative work is connected to *La Luna*'s aforementioned intention of granting visibility to young and lesser-known artists operating on the fringes of Madrid. Casani and his team understood that '[l]a gente existe a partir de que escribe y es fotografiada en una publicación que dice representar, o que parece que representa, aunque no lo diga, a lo que se está moviendo en Madrid en ese momento' [people exist from the moment that they are photographed and written about in a publication that represents, or seems to represent, even if it does not say so, what is taking place in Madrid at that time] (Casani in Gallero 1991: 8). This awareness of the need to make things visible; to publicize new artists in order to strengthen their ability to support themselves through their work, explains *La Luna*'s editorial ambition. In other words, *La Luna*'s objective of communicating what was taking place within Madrid's underground scene to a wider audience (that is, to an audience beyond that same underground circle) required the magazine to step away from the amateurism characteristic of the underground fanzines that had inspired its creation in the first instance, and to adopt some of the techniques and strategies used by mainstream publications. *La Luna*'s adoption of such techniques can be regarded as a compromise, or even a betrayal, of the underground, countercultural spirit it purportedly sought to communicate. However, the goal of the magazine's founders was not merely to integrate or co-opt underground works into the mainstream, but rather to disseminate those works in order to effect a change within established, mainstream artistic and cultural circles.

Visual style

La Luna's generous size (36cm × 27cm) and length (between 72 and 100 pages per issue),[19] as well as its carefully considered design — the images on the cover printed full bleed, and a wealth of images reproduced inside the magazine — set it apart from the fanzines circulating in Madrid's underground circles at the time. However, the use of rough, poor-quality paper and of unusual, sometimes even chaotic, layouts distinguishes *La Luna* from the more conventional publications of its time, and can be interpreted as a nod to the underground fanzines which provided the creative ferment, in the form of ideas and regular contributors, that made the coming into being of the magazine possible. Visually, the influence of the historical avant-gardes becomes noticeable through the use of futuristic and Dada-like typographies in headings such as that of regular section 'Sombras de la ciudad', as well as through the inclusion of Surrealist-influenced images by artists such as Ouka Leele (Figure 1.1). Further influences include the aesthetic of the 1950s and 1960s sci-fi and underground comics movement, traceable, for example, in the heading for Pedro Almodóvar's Patty Diphusa section (Figure 1.2).

The visual eclecticism within *La Luna* is announced by its covers, which feature an original design by a different artist every month.[20] The only unchanging element on the covers is the masthead, created by José Luis Tirado, artistic director of the magazine until 1985. The covers feature photos and photographic montages, abstract and geometric graphic creations, figurative and semi-figurative drawings, portraits, and collages. The styles of these covers range from the glamorous, with

FIG. 1.1 (above). Escuela de Romanos (1983) © Ouka Leele

FIG. 1.2 (below). Heading of Patti Diphusa section © Vicente Patón

fairly conventional glossy portrait photographs in the last three issues, to the expressionistic and abstract.

La Luna's content is made up of diverse materials: opinion pieces, features and articles, reviews, drawings, photographs, comics, poetry, short stories, urban chronicle, and more. The content is structured in several ways, grouped into sections that cover a range of topics (music, fashion and design, visual arts, literature, film and theatre, sport, and more), or into regular contributions that are independent from these sections (for instance, Almodóvar's Patty Diphusa column in issues 1–9/10 and 14–15; and Ramón Mayrata's 'Sombras de la ciudad' in issues 1–9/10, among others). Additionally, there are occasional contributions — in the form of drawings, photographs, comics, graphic arts, poetry, short stories, and opinion pieces — that may or may not be framed within a generic section.

The magazine's pages combine a range of different formats (text, drawings, photographs) and layouts: conventional straight columns of text coexist with diagonally tilted columns, or loose, floating blocks of text. Images are interspersed in a variety of ways: at the side of the text; surrounding the text; in the centre, above or below the text; and often placed at an angle. This eclectic mix does not make for a chaotic or improvised look; rather, it results in a highly distinctive visual style, characterized by the sparse use of colour — limited, particularly in the early issues, to a few accents in bold colours (acid pink, orange and yellow), as well as to one or two colour reproductions of works; and by a compressed layout, with narrow page margins that are frequently transgressed, with images (and more rarely, headlines) undercut by one of the ends of the page. These features may suggest an austere, if innovative, visual style, in accordance with the founders' stated intention of establishing a magazine that was, above all, 'muy utilitaria' (Tímmermans in Gallero 1991: 173). However, the playful combination of conventional and unusual layouts, and the wealth of visual elements cleverly integrated within the magazine result in a visually exciting ensemble. Moreover, despite the near total absence of colour in the early issues, the visual is granted enormous relevance from the start: there are non-textual elements (whether drawings, photos, or symbols) on virtually every page of every issue of the magazine. Even the page numbers are accompanied by a small-size version of the masthead logo (a half-moon). In some cases, in the absence of images, the text itself is laid out in separate blocks of different shapes, sizes and/or shade of background, thus enhancing its visual impact. Arguably, the visual is granted a greater autonomy than the textual, inasmuch as the former is often presented unmediated (that is, allowed to stand by itself), whilst the latter is generally punctuated by images or illustrations of some sort, when not itself becoming a visual motif.

Images are not merely used to illustrate texts, although this function is preserved in certain cases, with photographs frequently used to illustrate articles within the fashion and architecture sections of the magazine. In some cases, images are used ironically. For instance (and as will be discussed in more detail in Chapter 3) the regular women's section 'Luz de Boudoir' is frequently accompanied by old photographs of 1950s and 1960s models and pin-ups, who embody the type of clichéd femininity parodied by the articles within the section. Images are also used

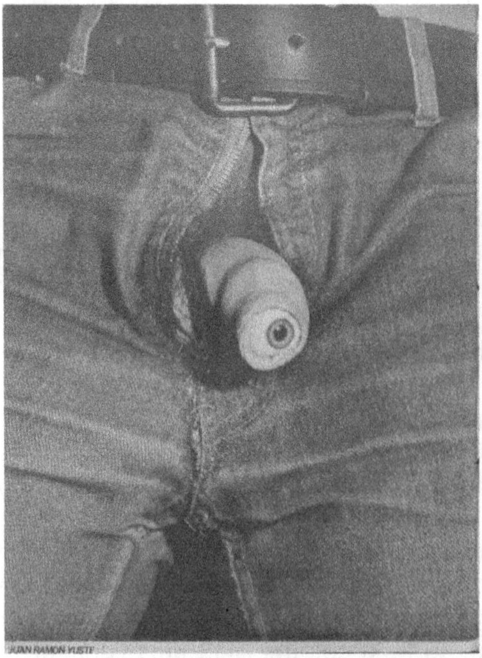

FIG. 1.3. Eyed penis © Juan Ramón Yuste

to establish sharp contrasts between text and image, or to effect breaks between textual blocks: for instance, a striking photographic montage by Juan Ramón Yuste depicting an eyed penis (untitled and occupying an entire page) is printed alongside the book review section (issue 3: 50, Figure 1.3), one of the visually more sedate sections of the magazine. Its shock potential is thus reinforced by the stark contrast that emerges between the image and the conventionally laid-out text on the following page. Aside from the often equivocal relationships that emerge between text and image, the fragmentation of texts — whether through the interspersion of images, or through the reproduction of texts in unusual, broken up or scattered layouts — challenges linear reading practices and encourages readers to jump from one fragment of text to another, in a sequence of their own choosing. These practices lead to an inflation of the visual and a fragmentation of the textual, and thus result in a complex web of sometimes conflicting or discordant meanings. For the reader, the overall impression is of great visual and content density, if not saturation, in other words, a sense of information overload. In this respect, the experience of flicking through *La Luna*'s pages is reminiscent of (and may have been influenced by) audiovisual and digital means of information dissemination.

La Luna's distinct style does not, however, remain static, but develops over the course of the magazine's five-year existence: the presence of colour becomes more habitual, with pages and motifs in a range of colours replacing the original black, white and grey; and layouts gradually grow more streamlined. This development, which can be regarded as a 'glossification' or standardization of the magazine's original style, owes much to economic and editorial factors. The use of colour is likely to have been determined, at least in the magazine's beginnings, by its implications in terms of printing costs; thus the increase of colour is indicative, in the first instance, of *La Luna*'s commercial success. The proliferation of colour in later issues, though enabled by the magazine's success, is also the result of an editorial decision. Indeed, these two aspects (the economic and the editorial) cannot be entirely disentangled. In the same way in which *La Luna*'s initially limited resources must have conditioned some editorial decisions, the magazine's eventual success, which led to its gradual transformation into a highly influential style guide, must have had an impact on the editorial team's ability (or willingness) to take risks.

La Luna's emphasis on the visual goes some way towards the inversion, or, at least, the redefinition, of the traditional relationship between the visual and the textual in print media, which tends to subordinate the former to the latter. Additionally, the foregrounding of the visual suggests a concern with design on the part of *La Luna*'s editorial team that is confirmed by the extensive coverage granted to the different aspects of this discipline (fashion, architecture, furniture and graphic design) within the magazine's pages. This preoccupation with the visual does not run counter to the magazine's utilitarian aim, but rather reflects the editorial team's necessity to establish not only a textually defined editorial identity, but also one defined by the development and deployment of a new and distinct visual style. *La Luna* in fact resisted defining its own editorial identity textually, publishing a notice that read '*La Luna* no tiene opinión editorial' on the index page of every issue. *La Luna*'s refusal explicitly to align itself with any movement, ideology, opinion or group is a sign of the magazine's founders' desire for independence, as well as a testimony to their eclectic tastes and interests. This absence of an explicitly formulated editorial line not only facilitated the development of an innovative visual style, allowing the magazine's pages to fluctuate between different looks and influences, but also made the formulation of a distinct visual style all the more relevant. Rather than telling its readers what *La Luna* stood for, sought to represent, or wanted to become, the magazine strove to show them, through the deployment of a highly distinctive visual style.

Influences and referents

La Luna modelled itself on two American publications: *Interview*, a monthly magazine founded in 1969 by Andy Warhol and John Wilcock; and *The Village Voice*, a New York newsweekly founded in 1955 by Ed Francher, Dan Wolf, John Wilcock and Norman Mailer. The influence of Andy Warhol's *Interview* is clearly visible in the format of *La Luna*: in its size, in the use of rough paper, and in the display of a bold and distinctive visual style. The fashion designer and former contributor Pedro Mansilla has also pointed to *Interview*'s influence on *La Luna*'s 'exquisita consideración con la moda' [exquisite treatment of fashion] (Cadahía 2007: 40), a field often ignored or dismissed as frivolous by other arts publications. Several other former members of *La Luna*'s editorial team have remarked upon Warhol's influence, and have described how the magazine's offices sought to emulate the legendary Factory (Cadahía 2007: 11). *La Luna*'s inclusion of barely edited or unedited transcripts of conversations, round table discussions and interviews is another feature probably inspired by *Interview*, since Warhol's magazine heavily relied on this type of content, which conveys a strong sense of immediacy to the reader, a sense of unmediated access to the words someone spoke, as they spoke them.

Another aspect of *La Luna* in which Warhol's influence is felt is the Patty Diphusa section, written by Pedro Almodóvar. Patty, a perpetually optimistic, frivolous and narcissistic porn star who shares her adventures with readers in a regular section,[21] is a character inspired at least in part by the films of Andy Warhol and Paul Morrisey (Almodóvar 1991: 11).

The other key referent for *La Luna* was New York's *The Village Voice*. Borja Casani, first editor and co-founder of *La Luna*, has described its influence:

> [L]a base sobre la que yo pensé *La Luna*, es la del *Village Voice* de Nueva York. O sea, un periódico [...] lleno de letras de principio a fin, que combinara tanto artículos de fondo potentes como el lanzamiento de propuestas que pudieran morir a los diez minutos, haciendo un gran hincapié en la ciudad y en el espectáculo que la ciudad está generando en ese momento. (Gallero 1991: 13)

> [The basis upon which I conceived *La Luna* was that of New York's *Village Voice*. That is, a newspaper [...] filled with letters from beginning to end, that combined both powerful articles with the launch of proposals that might last ten minutes, and with a strong focus on the city and on the spectacle that the city is generating at that particular time.] (Gallero 1991: 13)

The imprint of *Voice* thus appears to have been mainly conceptual, reflecting for instance in the strong focus on the city of Madrid. In terms of format and periodicity, it differs from *La Luna*: *Voice* was, and remains, a weekly arts tabloid, whilst *La Luna*'s format was larger, and it was published monthly.

Though *La Luna*, like *Interview*, announces and reviews events taking place in Madrid, the magazine is much more than just a chronicle of Madrid's nightlife and cultural activities. Each issue of the magazine focuses on a specific topic, to which its initial pages are devoted. The topics chosen range from the theoretical (postmodernity in issue 1, simulation in issue 13); to the playful and celebratory (carnival in issue 2, lust in issue 7); to the ironic or irreverent, with titles such as 'Contra la juventud' (issue 11) or 'El fin de la lampancia' (issue 6). Contributors respond to the suggested themes in very different ways; balanced opinion articles coexist with manifesto-like proclamations, drawings, short stories, and humorous pieces. Despite the diversity of the material included and the often irreverent tone in which even the more serious topics are considered, this thematic focus provides the magazine with a solidity that sets it apart from *Interview*. *La Luna*'s content density — a mix of thematic pieces, topical sections (music, film, plastic arts, and more), interviews, and showcased art — places it closer to *Voice*. However, its design, with its unconventional layout of text; its playful use of multi-style typography; and the inclusion of a wealth of heterogeneous non-textual elements, is far more daring than that of *Voice*, which, at least visually, remains anchored to traditional newspaper design conventions.

La Luna's self-modelling upon two foreign publications may seem surprising, given the magazine's focus for what was happening at a local level in Madrid. The magazine's first editor, however, explains this looking outwards as a response of sheer necessity, given the cultural wasteland that Francoism had left behind (Casani in Ripoll 1988: 21–24). In any case, a comparative reading of *La Luna* and the two American titles that exerted a more direct influence over it shows not only what the Spanish publication borrowed from its referents, but, more importantly, the ways in which it diverged from *Interview* and *Voice*, thus succeeding in establishing a distinct editorial identity. *La Luna* was not merely a Spanish version of either American title; in fact, its combination of eclectic and often provocative commentary and visually striking materials in an innovative editorial format (part respectable arts title, part irreverent and amateurish fanzine) arguably made it more radical and more daring than either of its models.

Trajectory

La Luna's five-year existence is marked by tensions derived, at least in part, from its constant renegotiation of a series of ambiguous positions. As we have seen, the publication was, in origin and spirit, close to the underground fanzines that circulated in Madrid in those years, which also inspired some of its features. However, from the outset the magazine appears as a far more professional venture, with an established and stable editorial team and a regular series of contributors. In other words, the magazine is simultaneously an independent project set up by a group of friends with little or no prior editorial experience, and a fairly ambitious venture, as suggested by its carefully articulated visual style, its range and density of content, and its distribution well beyond Madrid's underground scene of Rastro stalls, cafés and bars. Such ambiguity also manifests itself in the position occupied by *La Luna* with regard to other classificatory binaries. The magazine seeks to communicate to a wider audience what is taking place at an underground level, within Madrid's countercultural circles, and can be therefore seen to straddle the underground/mainstream divide. Its pages often mock and parody cultural icons, as in the case of the poet Leopoldo María Panero, while simultaneously testifying to a genuine curiosity and passion for cultural and artistic manifestations of every kind, from the often highly intellectual and intellectualized pieces of its opening pages, to the literary experiments of writers such as Eduardo Haro Ibars or Juan Madrid, to the visually striking photography of Juan Ramón Yuste and Ouka Leele or the graphic work of Rodrigo Muñoz Ballester.

The first 20 issues of *La Luna*, under the editorship of Borja Casani, succeed in maintaining a precarious balance between the many contradictions that plague the magazine, including its fierce defence of individualism and individual expression within what is ultimately a collaborative project. But within less than two years of its launch, in the spring and summer of 1985, the publication suffers an internal crisis that culminates in the departure of Casani and other members of the editorial team, and from which *La Luna* never fully recovers. Casani sees professionalization as central to that crisis, which he extends beyond his magazine to *la movida* as a whole: 'El principio de contabilidad es el que empieza a matar a las compañías discográficas independientes, a Ediciones Libertarias, a todo el mundo [...]. No porque la gente quiera dinero, ni aprovecharse de las circunstancias, sino porque, mentalmente, empieza otra etapa' [The principle of accountancy is what kills the independent record companies, the publisher Ediciones Libertarias, everyone [...]. Not because those involved want money, or to take advantage of the circumstances, but because, mentally, it marks the start of a new phase] (Casani in Gallero 1991: 78).

For Casani, then, the success of *La Luna* and other *movida* products contains the seeds of its demise, for it is the movement's success that leads its participants to realize they can make a living out of their artistic and cultural activities; but this realization leads, according to Casani, to a change of mindset that entails the neutralization of the original 'aspecto radical y suicida' [radical and suicidal side] (Casani in Gallero 1991: 28) of the magazine (as well as of other *movida* initiatives). Casani's words can thus be read as an insider's account of the familiar (and perhaps inevitable) process of co-option and/or institutionalization undergone by any countercultural, underground or avant-garde movement that attains a sufficient degree of visibility beyond its immediate sphere of action.[22] At this turning point for *La Luna*, the question arises of what to do with the magazine, of where to take it next, but finds no unanimous answer amongst its editorial team. While there are incomplete versions of the reasons and the process that led to the editorial schism of the summer of 1985,[23] retrospective accounts suggest that, for Casani and others, *La Luna*'s success rendered it redundant, unnecessary; or else they were not willing to witness the taming of its initial 'espíritu cavernícola' [caveman spirit] (Casani in Gallero 1991: 78). Be that as it may, textual evidence within the magazine in the issues that follow the departure of Casani suggest the split was acrimonious, and further, that his intuition with regard to the inevitable and progressive neutralization of the more radical aspects of the magazine was not misplaced.

After Casani's departure, *La Luna* co-founder José Tono Martínez takes over as editor. This second phase of the magazine sees its progressive standardization or glossification, a process that is occasionally referred to within the magazine itself: 'Un amigo de los del "glam" lo expresaba de otro modo: "*La Luna* está muy bien"... Bueno, no sé. Pero lo que importa es saber si viste o no viste colocarla en el recibidor' [A friend from the "glam" world put it differently: "*La Luna* is great"... Well, I don't know. But what matters is whether or not it is fashionable to place it in your hallway] (Tono Martínez in 25: 6). While Tono Martínez's intention in this editorial is to denounce the superficiality of such attitudes, to attack those who see in *La Luna* an object useful primarily for coffee-table display, he is nonetheless forced to acknowledge that, by this point (early 1986) his publication was regarded, at least in some circles, precisely in such terms. Over the course of Tono Martínez's editorship, *La Luna* evolves from what Libbie Rifkin terms the performative (that is, a cultural product that contributes to shape and effect change in its field) to the constative, merely reflecting and reproducing what is taking place (if not what has already taken place) (Rifkin 2000). By the time Javier Tímmermans steps in as editor at the end of 1987, the publication is in its death throes: 'La última época es patética. El caserón que teníamos, el chalet, parecía la casa Usher. Todo estaba muy deteriorado, no teníamos ya ni colaboradores' [The last period is pathetic. The house we had was like the house of Usher. Everything had deteriorated, we didn't even have contributors any more] (Tímmermans in Gallero 1991: 177). The absence of contributors is reflected in the contents of the final issues, which increasingly rely on photographic snapshots of celebrities and aspiring celebrities of the period and noticeably shorter and more anodyne features on films, bands and exhibitions. The heterogeneous and quasi-amateur messiness of the early issues, central to *La Luna*'s identification with underground culture and its ensuing success, is completely obliterated from these last issues, characterized by their streamlined style and their rather unchallenging contents.

During its five-year existence, *La Luna* captured the public's attention like no other magazine of the period. According to Juan Ramón Martínez-Acha, the first number, with a print run of 10,000 copies, sold out so quickly that a second print run had to be ordered (Cadahía 2007: 50). At its peak, the magazine sold over 30,000 copies,[24] an unprecedented figure, according to Tono Martínez: 'Esto no tenía precedentes en el pasado, puesto que nuestras vanguardias históricas habían sido siempre muy elitistas' [This had no precedents in the past, as our historical avant-gardes had always been very elitist] (Cadahía 2007: 13). Despite its success in terms of circulation and influence, the tensions at work within the magazine, as well as its failure to develop a sustainable business model (cf. Tímmermans in Cadahía 2007: 55), led to its disappearance in 1988.[25] *La Luna*'s end, though caused, in the first instance, by the aforementioned problems, can also be seen as resulting from, or at least symptomatic of, the gradual fizzling out of *la movida*, the climate of urban creative effervescence that *La Luna* was created to document.

The city, the self, and postmodernity

Despite the wealth and range of materials incorporated in *La Luna*, its contents are centred around two broad and intersecting thematic poles: the city, and the possibilities it offers for the creative exploration and de- and reconstruction of identity (or rather, identities in the plural). The focus on the city is evident from the magazine's title, which refers directly to Madrid. As Borja Casani, co-founder and first editor of *La Luna*, explained, the publication's focus was on the city and on the spectacle it generated at the time (cf. Gallero 1991: 13). Javier Tímmermans, co-founder and third editor, expressed a similar view, stating that the founders' aim was to establish 'una revista muy madrileña' [a very Madrilenian magazine] (Gallero 1991: 173).

The first chapter of this book considers *La Luna*'s engagement with urban space and urban motifs. As we shall see, the magazine's focus on the city of Madrid is not motivated by chauvinistic sentiment; there is no claiming that the Spanish capital is superior to other cities, but rather a sense of relief that it has finally caught up with the times: 'un ponerse a la altura de los tiempos de efectos liberadores' [a catching-up with the times that has liberating effects], according to Borja Casani (Gallero 1991: 0).[26] The city is celebrated not for its history or for its particular identity or essence, but rather because it grants the space necessary for the expression of one's individuality, because it allows individuals to explore and play with different identities. In a sense, the celebration of Madrid within *La Luna*'s pages is also a celebration of urban space in general, and the recognition of its creative potential. Issues 16, 17, 18 and 19 incorporate the section '*La Luna* en las ciudades', which includes an in-depth feature on one city (Bilbao, Rome, Venice, and Palma de Mallorca, respectively), as well as several shorter articles about other cities (Johannesburg, New York, and Buenos Aires, for example), reflecting an interest in urban life that is not limited to the city of Madrid.[27] However, as a magazine made by Madrilenians and originally conceived for distribution solely within Madrid, *La Luna* contains numerous local references and many details that speak of contributors' affection for their city: for instance, there is a cut-out section which features a different area of Madrid every month, allowing readers to create a miniature replica of the city. These cut-outs feature famous buildings, statues and squares, but include also the lottery and chestnut vendors and traffic wardens that make up Madrid's cityscape. The inclusion of these 'minor' elements reveals a keen eye for detail, and, perhaps more importantly, an appreciation of the city as a living entity; that is, as a space that is alive and changing, defined not only by its architectural landmarks, but also by its inhabitants.

La Luna's vindication of Madrid is related to the fact that, as one of the magazine's founders later stated, the city was at that time (early and mid-1980s) still in the process of becoming modern (Olivares in Cadahía 2007: 43). This process led to the discovery of the freedom and the creative potential that the modern city could offer; to the realization, in Javier Olivares's words, that 'la modernidad era diseño, arte, música y libertad de ser, de vestir y de entender la vida como una performance individual de primera calidad sin necesidad de salir en el *Art News*' [modernity meant design, art, music, the freedom to be, to dress and to understand life as a first-class individual performance, without the need to appear on *Art News*] (Cadahía 2007: 43). The (post)modern city grants individuals the necessary space and freedom to play with different identities, to perform different roles, whilst at the same time providing a shared spatial framework that opens up the possibility of interaction and fruitful collaboration between individuals. Thus the city is perceived as more than a mere stage or backdrop: it is seen as that which furnishes the necessary conditions for creative exploration; as an agent that enables and encourages creative and existential experimentation.

The space granted to the city and city life within *La Luna* also bears witness to a linking of the creative and the experiential, two aspects that those working on the magazine regarded as inseparable and interchangeable. In the climate of change and effervescence of 1980s Madrid, life and art became conflated; or rather, life took precedence over art: living artistically, leading a creative life, was regarded as more important than actually making artworks. Such an attitude is not new; as Peter Bürger has noted, the attempt to organize a new life praxis from the basis of art is central to the project of the historical avant-gardes (Bürger 1984).

In the case of *La Luna*, the attempt to merge art and life manifests itself primarily in the magazine's exploration of individual and collective identities, as the second chapter of this book illustrates. In a context in which living and being is more important than the products that may result from creative activity, the key question becomes not what one does, but who, and how, one is. In *La Luna*'s pages, identity is understood and treated as something fluid and performative, rather than as an unchangeable essence received at birth, or fixed from a given point in one's life.

As we shall see, such a notion of identity comes to the fore in the magazine's self-portrait section (issues 1–12), in its women's section *Luz de Boudoir/Somos unas señoras* (issues 1–14), and in the *Patty Diphusa* series (published intermittently in the first 20 issues), as well as in the treatment of popular culture elements associated with a traditional and somewhat folkloric Spanishness, such as flamenco and bullfighting, which are re-signified in the magazine's pages through parody and re-contextualization.

La Luna's emphasis on urban experience and on identity and self-definition — two themes that are understood to be interrelated, as the city offers the necessary space for personal and creative exploration —, alongside its penchant for parody, for irreverent re-articulations of old ideas, images and clichés, helps explain the magazine's (and, more broadly, *la movida*'s) recurrent association with postmodernism, considered at length in Chapter 4. As I argue there, one problem of the simple equation of *movida* with postmodernism is that such an operation posits both concepts as stable notions with transparent meanings, rather than as processes that are still the subject of much academic debate and controversy. Additionally, by aligning a localized movement such as *la movida* with a global phenomenon such as postmodernism, there is a danger of overlooking, or indeed obliterating, the contextual specificities of the former.[28] While I do not seek to deny or minimize the influence of postmodernism over *la movida* as a whole, and over *La Luna* in particular, it is essential to trace the elements of postmodernism that *La Luna* incorporates, and those which it questions, if we are to make any sense of its labelling as postmodern. In the final chapter, I clarify the magazine's evolving understanding of and engagement with postmodernism through a close textual analysis of *La Luna*'s editorials, which feature such postmodern themes as chaos and carnival (issue 2) or simulation (issue 13). My analysis underlines the complex and evolving nature of *La Luna*'s engagement with postmodernism, thus problematizing the received wisdom that posits the Madrilenian phenomenon as simply a localized postmodern manifestation.

Notes to Chapter 1

1. Translations are mine, unless otherwise specified.
2. The phrase seems to have been coined by Manuel Vázquez Montalbán in his 1981 novel *Asesinato en el Comité Central*. In that novel, the sentence is uttered with ironic intent by a Communist Party activist and former ETA member (cf. Vázquez Montalbán 1981: 227). In a 1992 interview published in *El País*, Vázquez Montalbán explained that he proposed the sentence tentatively, as a question rather than as a statement, 'porque temía que era el criterio de cierta izquierda conservadora [...] que no superó esa situación de vivir contra el franquismo' [because I feared that that was the sentiment amongst a conservative left that was unable to get over life against Francoism] (Moret 1992).
3. *El Desencanto* has come to be regarded as a particularly emblematic cultural product from this period, attracting considerable scholarly attention. The film, a documentary constructed from a series of interviews with the widow and three sons of the Falangist poet Leopoldo Panero (1909–1962), portrays a dysfunctional family in the process of disintegration, and the haunting absence-presence of Panero senior in the film has invited psychoanalytical readings that posit Panero as a patriarchal figure within his family analogous to that of General Franco within Spain (cf. Vilarós 1998: 48).

4. Cebrián's essay constitutes a strong critique of the shortcomings of the transitional process: it denounces the corruption and nepotism within public institutions and political parties; it decries de survival of authoritarian and anti-democratic practices within the judiciary, the police and security services; and it laments the lack of political courage to address popular demands for greater personal freedoms, citing for instance the delays in legalizing divorce, or the failure to widen access to contraception. The central argument of this essay is that the focus on changing the old regime's juridical nature during the transitional process has failed to acknowledge the need for deeper institutional, cultural and social changes.
5. *El Rrollo* was formed by Nazario Luque, Javier Mariscal, Francesc Capdevilla (alias Max), and Miquel and Josep Farriol (alias Farry and Pepichek, respectively). The collective edited and distributed adult comics, with titles such as *El Rrollo Enmascarado, Purita* or *Nasti de Plasti. La Piraña Divina,* the group's most provocative work, authored by Nazario and released in 1975, attracted the interest of the police, a circumstance that led to the dissolution of the collective.
6. For instance, in a series of conversations with Frédéric Strauss originally published by *Cahiers du Cinéma in France* in 1994, Almodóvar argues that Catalan nationalism isolated Barcelona from the rest of Spain, thus encouraging the consolidation of Madrid as cultural and countercultural capital (Strauss 1996: 1).
7. Fabio McNamara's was Fabio de Miguel's artistic alias, and Fanny McNamara, the name of his drag persona.
8. Ceesepe's illustrations appear with the initial credits, and are also inserted in the film, accompanied by text, as devices reminiscent of a narrative strategy common in silent films. Almodóvar later explained that the use of such a device allowed him to make explicit the influence of comic strips over the film and to 'describe the action in a dramatic and condensed manner' (Strauss 1996: 13).
9. *El Viejo Topo*, however, reappeared in 1993, after over a decade's absence, and is still in existence at the time of writing (2014).
10. For more on the democratizing role of the anti-Francoist press, see Ignacio Fontes and Manuel Ángel Menéndez. 2004. *El parlamento de papel. Las revistas españolas en la transición democrática* (Madrid: Anaya y Asociación de Prensa de Madrid).
11. This resurgence of *la movida* over the past two decades has manifested itself in the release of music compilations such as *La Edad de Oro del Pop Español* (2001); the premiere, in 2005, and continued success of the musical *Hoy no me puedo levantar*; the DVD release of the cult 1980s TV programme *La bola de cristal* (2004); or the opening of the *movida* museum-bar *Madrid me mata* in Malasaña in 2012.
12. The film-maker Iván Zulueta, who featured heroin addiction in his cult film *Arrebato* (1980), and whose substance dependency lasted until his death in 2009, referred to the fact that his generation was naïve about the dangers of heroin because they had been brought up in fear of sex, homosexuality, masturbation and marijuana. Hence, when warned about the effects of heroin, he and many of his contemporaries simply assumed this was yet another lie (cf. Gallero 1991: 172).
13. I am thinking, for instance, of Héctor Fouce's doctoral thesis "*El futuro ya está aquí". Música pop y cambio cultural en España. Madrid 1978–1985* (Universidad Complutense de Madrid); Tatjana Pavlovic's 2003 *Despotic Bodies and Trangressive Bodies. Spanish Culture from Francisco Franco to Jesús Franco,* which considers how themes such as femininity, sexuality, and national identity intersect and become embodied in a series of Spanish cultural texts from the second half of the twentieth century; Germán Labrador's 2009 *Letras Arrebatadas. Poesía y química en la transición española,* which analyses the discourses of drug use, rapture and disappearance in poetic texts of the 1970s and 1980s; or Michael Preston Harrison's 2009 doctoral thesis *Comics as Text and Comics as Culture: Queer Spain Through the Lens of a Marginalized Medium* (University of California, Irvine).
14. In her own analysis of *la movida,* Gema Pérez Sánchez makes an interesting counter-argument in favour of state subsidies, arguing that 'by allowing the [publicly] financed artistic products not to have to compete on an equal footing with other products in the capitalist market, official subsidies open up a mainstream space for women and queers to tell their stories in ways that can be much more influential than the explicit, supposedly underground representations of gay male

life in Nazario's comic book story *Anarcoma*' (2007: 193). Thus, for Pérez Sánchez public subsidy can in fact grant emerging or marginalized artists a degree of independence from commercial considerations and constraints.

15. An issue 0 of *La Luna* appeared earlier in 1983. It was intended as a means to present the project and help attract advertising, but only 500 copies were printed, and it is virtually impossible to locate a copy. None of the collections of the magazine held at public institutions have a copy of this issue, but founding members of *La Luna* have mentioned its existence (Cadahía 2007: 32), corroborated also by Susan Larson (2003).
16. This figure of 48 issues does not include issue 0, which was not released commercially.
17. Leopoldo María Panero is the second son of Falangist poet Leopoldo Panero and Felicidad Blanc. He featured alongside his brothers José Luis and Michi and their mother Felicidad in Jaime Chávarri's aforementioned 1976 documentary film *El Desencanto*.
18. Founders of the magazine give conflicting accounts of the amount of money each member contributed. Founding member and third editor Javier Tímmermans says that members paid 25,000 pesetas each, which he describes as an insignificant sum (Gallero 1991: 173). But co-founder Juan Ramón Martínez-Acha states that each member in fact contributed 50,000 pesetas, a considerable amount of money at the time (Cadahía 2007: 51).
19. Issue 34 (December 1986) was even longer, at 136 pages, as it included a 40-page special feature entitled 'Los 87 del 87' (see *La Luna de Madrid*, 34: 96–106).
20. Every magazine cover is showcased in Emma Cadahía's *La Luna de Madrid y otras revistas de vanguardia de los años 80*, a catalogue for an exhibition of the same title held at Madrid's Biblioteca Nacional in 2007.
21. The Patty Diphusa section appears in issues 1–9/10, is discontinued after the issue 9/10 (July-August 1984), and appears again in issues 14, 15, 16, 18 and 19 of *La Luna*. Patty makes her last appearance in the magazine in issue 20, but instead of the usual chronicle, in this number she interviews her author. These texts appeared in book format in 1991 under the title *Patty Diphusa y otros textos* (Barcelona: Anagrama). Note that in the section heading within *La Luna*, Patty's name is spelt Patti, although within the text it is always given as Patty.
22. It is worth noting that, by 1985 Madrid and its *movida* had become something of an international sensation, and were attracting international press coverage, with *Rolling Stone*, *Newsweek*, *The New York Times*, *Time*, *Le Monde*, *Le Soir* and *Le Nouvel Observateur* all featuring articles on the city's (counter)cultural resurgence in that year. Additionally, *National Geographic* published the extensive feature 'Madrid: The Change in Spain' by John J. Putman in February 1986 (pp. 142–80).
23. The issue of the schism is broached by some former members of the magazine's editorial staff in José Luis Gallero's volume on *la movida*. Here, Javier Tímmermans and Juan Carlos de Laiglesia point to the magazine's failure to translate its success into economic viability and the clash of personalities between Casani, Tono Martínez, and others, as two of the key factors that led to the split (cf. Gallero 1991: 174–76).
24. By comparison, cultural magazine *Cuadernos del Norte* had a print run of 12,000 in 1983, according to a review of that publication which appeared in *El País* in 1983.
25. It seems that *La Luna*'s disappearance happened abruptly: there is no warning about the discontinuation of publication in the magazine's final issue (no. 48, May 1988). Additionally, the creation of the blog <http://lalunademadrid.wordpress.com> in late 2011 by former editorial staff members Javier and Juan Carlos Melero, points to the suddenness of the magazine's dissolution: the purpose of the blog is to find the original authors of photographs, drawings and collages which were left behind when the magazine collapsed, so that these works can be returned to their rightful owners.
26. The page numeration is not a printing error: José Luis Gallero's volume of oral history of *la movida*, made up of a series of transcripts of conversations amongst *movida* participants, starts in the book jacket — a detail that, for Paul Julian Smith 'suggests that the movida, like the city, was not a thing, but a process, which has always already begun' (Smith 2006: 64). It is worth noting that *La Luna* also has an issue 0.
27. This section first appeared in the same issue in which the editor Borja Casani called for a move towards 'otras ciudades, otras ideas, otras lenguas, otros signos' [other cities, other ideas, other

languages, other signs] (issue 16: 7), published in March 1985; the section was discontinued following Casani's departure from *La Luna* in the summer of 1985.

28. Paul Julian Smith warns of this danger when he writes that 'Spanish versions of such concepts [as postmodernism] must be carefully and sensitively localized, read for their individualities, if they are to give up their true meaning' (2006: 60).

CHAPTER 2

La Luna de Madrid and the City of Madrid: Reimagining and Reclaiming Urban Space

Urban space and, more specifically, Madrid's cityscape constitutes one of the thematic axis around which the content of *La Luna* is articulated. The present chapter investigates the ways in which urban space is treated, represented and imagined within *La Luna*'s pages, as well as *La Luna*'s own role in 'space production' — namely, through the magazine's establishment of a space of its own. Following the French sociologist Henri Lefebvre, a conception of space as produced and constructed, rather than as a natural given, underpins this chapter. As Lefebvre argued in his influential *The Production of Space*, space is understood here not merely as a transparent void in which objects find themselves, but rather, as an entity shaped by relations of power, and one which, dialectically, further contributes to the shaping of such relations (Lefebvre 1991). Lefebvre's theorization of space is relevant to my analysis because *La Luna*'s treatment of urban space does not merely consider the ways in which the city conditions the experiences and interactions of its inhabitants; it is also concerned with how citizens' perceptions, use and appreciation of the spaces they inhabit contribute to their transformation.

The first part of this chapter will examine the ways in which urban space is de- and reconstructed within *La Luna*'s pages. Lefebvre's concepts of *representations of space* (space as objective and mappable, as seen by architects and planners) and *representational spaces* (spaces as imagined by its inhabitants) provide the methodological framework and structuring principle for this segment. In *La Luna*, apparently objective representations of space (photographic reproductions of buildings, floor plans and models of building projects) coexist with the representational spaces in which urban chronicles, short stories and comics reproduced in the magazine are located, and from which different images of the city emerge.

The second part of this chapter is concerned with a reading of *La Luna* itself as space. The magazine not only offers glimpses of a possible, imagined Madrid; it also opens up an editorial-textual space, becoming a virtual meeting-point for its readers. *La Luna*'s success in what Paul Julian Smith terms the 'self-conscious creation of a community' (2006: 58) is related both to the magazine's recreation of and 'locatedness' in Madrid -with the city providing a shared spatial framework for readers-, and to the magazine's own emergence as what Foucault defined as a heterotopic site, a space in which 'all the other real sites that can be found within the culture, are simultaneously represented, contested, and inverted' (Foucault 2002: 231). My reading of *La Luna* as heterotopic space will help explain the magazine's simultaneous creation of a community of readers and its refusal of and resistance to definition. Moreover, the characterization of *La Luna* as a heterotopic site ties in with the magazine's exploration of individual and collective identities, which will be discussed in Chapter 3, for, as Fincher and Jacobs have noted, space formation stands in a complex and dialectical relationship to identity formation (Fincher and Jacobs 1998: 2).

The third part of the chapter considers the spatial practices — that is, the ways of engaging with urban space — which *La Luna* seeks to simultaneously portray and encourage through the articulation of a new urban imaginary. Additionally, I analyse the ways in which the Spanish magazine's approach to urban everyday practices may have been influenced by previous avant-garde movements, as well as the ways in which it differs from them. Finally, the closing section situates *La Luna*'s attempts to reimagine and reclaim the city of Madrid within its socio-historical context, tracing the areas of overlap, but also the significant differences, between the magazine's project and the urban renewal program of Madrid's municipal administration.

Urban space in *La Luna*

Madrid's cityscapes, as well as other urban spaces, occupy a central role within *La Luna*'s pages: issue 1, for instance, opens with a section entitled 'Sombras de la ciudad' (1: 4–5), by the writer Ramón Mayrata, which chronicles life (or rather, survival strategies) in the city, and which is a regular fixture of the magazine until issue 9–10. The first four issues of the magazine contain a specific 'Madrid' section, distinct from other topical sections such as 'Diseño', 'Cine' and 'Literatura', and which not only details the cultural and nightlife events taking place in the city, but includes also reflections on the city like Gregorio Morales's 'Erótica de Madrid' (1: 60) and Lourdes Ortiz's 'Elogio de la Metrópoli' (1: 65). From issue 5, this section disappears, but some of its contents are granted a section of their own, whilst others are integrated within the magazine's listings section, 'Guía de Madrid' (issues 1–8), and, later, within 'Post' (issues 28–41), a review and listings magazine within the magazine.

Since it would be impossible to consider individually the hundreds, if not thousands, of items within *La Luna*'s pages with a focus on the urban, I have chosen instead to concentrate on a limited number of particularly representative examples. I have further divided these samples into two categories: items which seek to reproduce or map the city of Madrid in, at least apparently, objective terms; and items in which the city is recreated or imagined in subjective terms. The first group is concerned with the architectural, material make-up of Madrid, whilst the second is primarily preoccupied with the experiences that take place in the city; or rather, with the experiences that urban space (which is not always identified with, or identifiable as, Madrid) makes possible. In spite of the difference in emphasis, both approaches are intimately related, and thus need to be considered in conjunction.

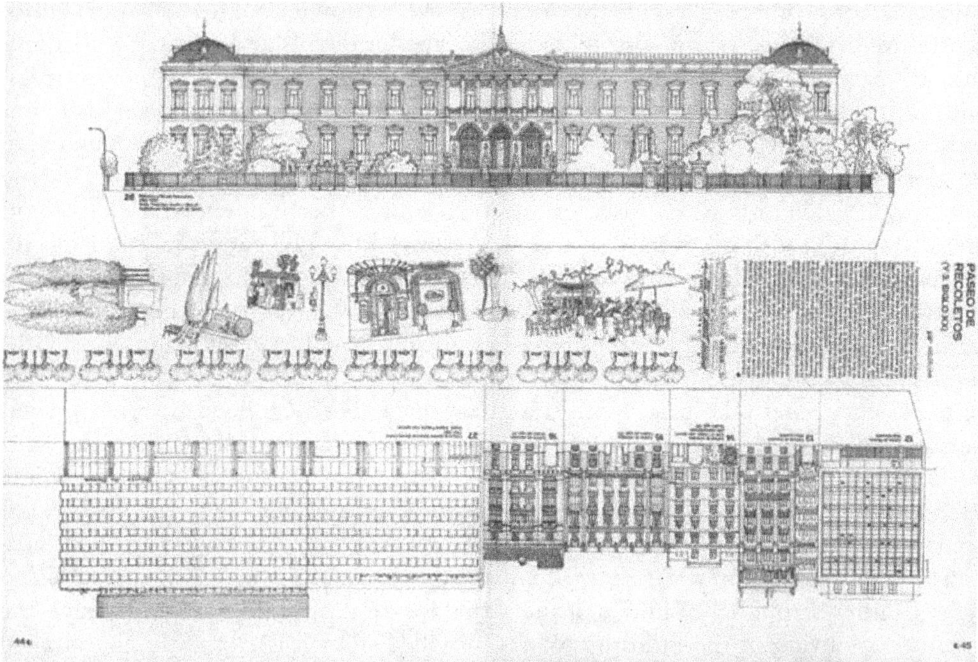

Fig. 2.1. Recortables section: Paseo de Recoletos © Vicente Patón

The attempts at mapping, or re-mapping, Madrid are permeated by individual and subjective appreciations of the city, whilst the experience of Madrid's built environment underlies even the more inventive urban re-imaginings. In both instances, the focus is upon spatial practices, in other words, upon space as lived: at the heart of the pieces that deal with the material make-up of the city is a concern with the experiences that different spaces facilitate or impede; whilst the more subjective and imaginative recreations of cityscapes usually arise from narratives of urban life, from events that are made possible, and, to some degree, shaped by their being located within an urban environment. Given the centrality of spatial practices to both approaches, my analysis will seek to establish the types of urban practices that shape *La Luna*'s urban imagery, and the extent to which such practices resemble (or distance themselves from) those of previous avant-garde movements.

Representations of space: Mapping Madrid

La Luna's concern with what Lefebvre terms 'representations of space' — the material make-up of the city and the ways in which it is rendered in maps and plans — is most evident within the magazine's 'Recortables' [cut-outs] section (issues 1–18; Figure 2.1), in which different landmarks of Madrid are reproduced as cut-outs, allowing readers to create their own miniature replica of different areas of the city. These cut-outs represent areas which are key to Madrid's commercial and social life: Plaza Callao, with its wealth of shops and cinemas; the transport hub and city crossroads of Puerta del Sol, and the nightlife node of Glorieta de

Bilbao, among others. Despite the focus on well-known squares and corners of central Madrid, this section also includes the smaller details and everyday elements that are part of Madrid's cityscape: the lamp-posts, phone booths, benches, trees, and kiosks that contribute to give an area its specific character. Further, it is not only objects that are depicted within this section; the inhabitants and frequenters of these sites (lottery and chestnut sellers, pensioners feeding pigeons, couples sitting on the odd patch of grass, florists, groups of youths gathering next to a metro exit) are all reproduced here as part of the city's street life. The representation of city space within this section thus echoes Lefebvre's theorization of space as a triad consisting of built environment, experienced, and imagined space. In this case, the meticulously reproduced buildings represent the city's material environment, whilst the figures seen engaging in different activities offer an insight into the repertoire of experiences that take place within a given space. Readers need to rely on their personal mental mapping of the city in order to be able to construct the cut-outs. Although a number system is provided to guide readers so that they know where each building should be located, these indications are not very specific, and do not apply to the additional, non-built elements provided. Additionally, the cut-outs constitute an invitation to readers to embark on personal re-imaginings of familiar spaces, either through a reshuffle of the actual location of buildings, or through the creative colouring of the building blocks provided, which is explicitly encouraged in issue 14 (81).

The aims of this section are multiple. On one level, the section has a clear informative or pedagogic finality: the tab under each reproduced building contains a two- or three-line summary detailing its year of construction, the architect or architects who designed it, and the style it was built in, or sought to emulate. These details suggest a desire to encourage readers to take an interest in the history and the architectural make-up of their city — a desire that becomes more explicit within the architecture section discussed below, within which the last three instalments of the 'Recortables' (issues 16–18) are framed. The cut-outs are further accompanied by short texts that summarize the spatial history of the sites reproduced, offering an insight into the different uses and meanings these familiar settings had over the ages. These historical overviews do not simply intend to broaden *madrileños*' knowledge of their local history, but rather are concerned with the ways in which the past has shaped these sites, and the ways in which certain traces of that past may still be visible or noticeable in the current shape and feel of certain spaces. For instance, writing about the historical evolution of Madrid's Puerta del Sol, the author notes

> resulta curioso observar que [en Sol] se conserva ese aire de zoco o mercadillo popular y bullanguero, lugar de cita de gentes de paso, tahúres, desocupados y menesterosos que tuvo hace ya varios siglos. Como si la ciudad, mecanismo con vida propia, guardase tácitamente sus propias, inalterables claves, superando en el tiempo los dictados de la política o de la economía. (issue 3: 63)[1]

> [it is curious to note that [at Sol] that air of souk or loud and popular market has been preserved, a meeting place for those on the go, gamblers, the unoccupied or lazy, that it already had centuries ago. As if the city, a mechanism with a

> life of its own, had implicitly saved its own, unchanging codes, overcoming through time the dictates of politics or of the economy.] (issue 3: 63)

The author marvels here at Madrid's capacity to retain its character, at least in specific areas, and wonders (his use of the subjunctive suggests this is not a certainty) about the city's power to withstand time, as well as economic and political pressures. Further, the description of the city as 'mecanismo con vida propia' implies a degree of independence of city life from political and economic constraints. However, this ability of the city and the life it fosters to resist such imperatives is later put into perspective, as the author laments the transformation that has taken place in other parts of the city, such as Plaza San Martín and Las Descalzas (15: 75) — a transformation largely driven by economic motives which the city, in this instance, has not been able to withstand. It is precisely this consciousness of the city's positive but limited capacity to resist economic and political pressures that drives the authors of the section, who seek to boost the city's ability to resist by encouraging new, more engaged ways of thinking about and living in the city among its readers. Underlying this is a belief that a city is not shaped only, or even primarily, by those in positions of economic and political power, but by the citizens that inhabit it, whose habits, attitudes and actions can contribute significantly to the city's form and feel.

This goal of encouraging readers to participate more actively in city life is mirrored in the strategy used in the section to achieve it. Readers are expected to engage actively with the material offered (cutting out the buildings, colouring them, and pasting them onto a street grid) rather than to passively consume a cultural product. Like the city, this section of the magazine presents itself to readers as an unfinished work in progress that requires their input in order to achieve its full potential. This participatory nature of the section is what renders it effective. By involving readers in this small-scale reconstruction of the city, the 'Recortables' not only transform the relationship of readers with the magazine, but, in so doing, they also create a sense of empowerment amongst readers, who are promoted here to the role of co-creators of the city model, which they can adapt or transform at will. This change of role further encourages feelings of ownership, as the model becomes for readers a project they have invested time and effort in. Although readers are presented with objective-realistic building blocks to recreate the city, the resulting model will inevitably be not simply Madrid, but *their* Madrid — a repertoire of cityscapes, each invested with the individual and subjective vision of every reader. These feelings of empowerment and ownership, though effected through readers' participation in the section, can then be symbolically transferred to the object of their modelling: the city of Madrid itself. The ultimate aim of this section is thus not merely informative or pedagogic: through the projection of a city imagery that is not only dependent upon its built features, but is also made up by the collection of objects, plants, animals and people that inhabit it, and through the involvement of readers in the creation of a miniature city model, this section manages to instil in readers the belief that they are part of the city, and that, as such, they have the right and the power to contribute to its shaping.

The architecture section of the magazine (issues 1–20 and 23–24), which dissects and discusses Madrid's lesser-known and new buildings, as well as urban development projects for the city and surrounding areas, is another key feature in *La Luna*'s 'mapping' of Madrid. The authoritative commentary of Vicente Patón, editor of the section and author of most of these pieces,[2] as well as the wealth of elements used to illustrate the section (photographs, reproduction of plans, sketches of different angles and views of the buildings discussed) lend the section an air of detached objectivity. However, underlying this appearance of objectivity is a personal understanding of the role of contemporary architecture as a means to seamlessly encourage the active engagement of the city's inhabitants with their surroundings. This awareness of the relationship between built environments and human interactions echoes Lefebvre's theorization of space as a product, and simultaneously as producer and reproducer, of social relationships (Lefebvre 1991).

From the first issue, buildings and projects are considered not only in terms of how they respond to their assigned function, or how they look; the dialogues buildings establish with their surroundings, and the effects of such dialogues, are also taken into account. For instance, referring to the large windowed balconies of a new block of flats, Patón writes

> Aquí la vida se hace transparente al exterior conectando con una de las características del modo de ser urbano, es decir la falta de privacidad y por tanto, no están ausentes del proyecto la exhibición y la provocación que esa forma de vida conlleva. (1: 35)
>
> [Here, life becomes transparent to the outside, thus connecting with one of the features of the urban mode of being, that is, the lack of privacy, and thus, the provocation and exhibition that such a form of life entail are not absent from the project.] (1: 35)

Patón interprets the large windowed balconies not in terms of their obvious function (allowing for a luminous interior), but rather, as representative of one of the characteristics of urban life (lack of privacy). Interestingly, lack of privacy is not considered in negative terms here, but is linked to the exhibitionism and provocation that, for the author, are inherent to the urban way of life. Indeed, in this instance the lack of privacy that may result from the large balconies — which is also referred to, in more positive terms, as transparency towards the exterior — is celebrated, for it is seen as an element which allows the building to insert and assert itself within 'el modo de ser urbano'.

The link between architecture and city life is again made explicit in issue 3, in what is the clearest articulation of Patón's aims for his section:

> Únicamente llevando a la calle el debate sobre la nueva arquitectura (la terminación de un edificio debe ser un ACONTECIMIENTO en la ciudad), se podría integrar ésta en un proceso de cultura popular que haga inviable la construcción especulativa e indiscriminada. (3: 34).
>
> [Only by taking the debate about new architecture to the street (the finalising of a building must be an EVENT in the city) might we be able to integrate architecture within a popular culture process that makes indiscriminate and speculative building unfeasible.] (3: 34)

Patón wants to move the debate about architecture from the closed, specialist fora for architects and urban planners onto the street. Such a move involves raising the profile of architecture within public consciousness ('la terminación de un edificio debe ser un ACONTECIMIENTO en la ciudad'). This double objective -raising public awareness about architecture, and encouraging open public debate on the subject- stems from the author's obvious interest in and love for his discipline, but it also has a political dimension: protecting urban space from 'la construcción especulativa e indiscriminada', in other words, from uncontrolled market forces. Fundamental to this desire of protecting the city from speculative and indiscriminate development is a conception of the city as 'gran deidad protectora que acoge en su seno las actuaciones más diversas, gran escaparate de los vicios y sueños de una cultura [...]' [great protective deity that shelters the most diverse interventions, great showcase of the vices and dreams of a culture] (issue 5: 38). Patón's wish to protect Madrid from ruthless forms of development is thus not merely concerned with the preservation of architectural landmarks, even if these are recognized as a central element of the city's cultural heritage.[3] For Patón, the threat posed by certain developers transcends the city's material make-up, and extends to the city's capability to foster and protect the rich diversity of its inhabitants' dreams and vices.

The articles published within the architecture section do not only attack the careless, chaotic developments that resulted from Spain's rapid modernization and economic growth from the early 1960s onwards. There is also a critique of modernist architecture, based on a questioning of its insistence on the functional segregation of spaces, as seen, for instance, in the separation of residential units from shops and services in city centres, which, it is argued, has led to the emergence of 'espacios sombríos de uso improbable' [sombre spaces of improbable use] (issue 19: 77) in the places within residential areas once occupied by shops and cafés. Although the section's focus on the city as lived space and its conception of the urban as a site of diversity and difference are reminiscent of theorizations of space associated with postmodern criticism, such as those of Lefebvre (1991) and Foucault (2002), postmodern architecture is not embraced as an alternative. In fact, the durability of its results is thrown into question: 'Lo que hoy nos puede parecer tan irónico, atractivo, lúdico o divertidamente frívolo, ¿no será tan sólo empachoso y polvoriento decorado en la Nochevieja Fin de Siglo?' [That which, today, seems so ironic, attractive, playful, or joyfully frivolous... might it not, in fact, become merely an over-the-top and dusty set by the end of this century?] (issue 23: 66). Though the fall of the modernist school, in part facilitated by the emergence of a postmodern movement, is celebrated as liberating, as inaugurating 'un momento de gozosa dispersión' [a moment of joyful dispersion] (issue 19: 66), postmodern architecture is taken to task for its ornamental and technological excesses, which, it is argued, ultimately lead to 'una destrucción del concepto de **lugar**. Esto es, del espacio donde podemos vivir, relacionarnos o convivir' [the destruction of the concept of **place**. That is, of the space where we can live, mix with others, coexist] (issue 12: 76; emphasis in the original). Further, Vicente Patón unmasks what he regards as a regrettable continuity between the modernist and the postmodern architectural schools:

> En el fondo si analizamos ese movimiento, tan bobo, que ahora suscita tanto interés, como es el posmodernismo, [...] lo que encontramos es una especie de nostalgia por parte de un grupo de arquitectos norteamericanos que no protagonizaron la Revolución formal, ética, visual y estética que significaron los años veinte y treinta en Europa. (12: 78)
>
> [In essence, if we analyse the foolish movement that is postmodernism, which is currently generating so much interest, [...] what we find is a sort of nostalgia on the part of a group of American architects who did not live through the formal, aesthetic, ethic and visual revolution of the 1920s and 1930s in Europe.] (12: 78)

The nostalgia that Patón refers to in this segment is not nostalgia for modernist architecture itself, against which the postmodern architectural school in fact defines itself, at least in formal terms. For Patón, the postmodern break from the modernist tradition is not radical enough because it does not question the legitimacy of modernism's once privileged position within the field of architecture; rather, it seeks to usurp its hegemony. According to Patón, it is this dominant position within the field, and the privileges it entails, that postmodern architects long for. As he notes elsewhere in the same article, the very existence and legitimacy of such positions of hegemony within the field are justified by the notion of the architect as revolutionary, visionary genius with the power single-handedly to change the face of the earth, a notion which he himself denounces as 'una interiorización completamente reaccionaria de la actividad profesional' [a completely reactionary internalisation of professional activity] (12: 78). For Patón, this concept of the architect as genius is not only reactionary, but also dangerous, for it allows architects to ignore environmental, communal, and functional concerns in the name of their superior vision — the result being spectacular buildings that, at best, fail to engage their supposed users or dwellers; and, at worst, threaten or tear through the existing urban, social and personal-sentimental fabric of the city. The shift from modernist architecture's functionality to the postmodern school's ironic or re-historicising ornamentation and spectacularization is problematic because, in the author's view, both constitute dogmatic approaches and, as such, tend to ignore users' needs and legitimate concerns. Rather than a postmodern architecture, then, what is favoured in this section is a revised form of modernism or postmodernism, based on case-by-case interventions that take into account the needs and views of local residents. Architecture is thus regarded as a discipline that is, or should be, subordinate to the requirements of city life and the needs of its inhabitants. In order for such an approach to become widespread, it is necessary to create truly participatory public debate on the subject, a goal that this section aspires to help realize.

The very decision to publish these pieces within a general arts magazine like *La Luna*, rather than in a specialized publication, already points to the authors' ambition of facilitating and encouraging more inclusive discussions of Madrid's built environment. Despite the profusion of technical elements (architects' drawings, floor plans), used to illustrate articles, the tone of the section is very accessible, conceived to appeal to a non-specialist readership. The section's focus is not upon Madrid's architectural landmarks, or upon spectacular new projects, but upon buildings whose most salient features are generally their seamless integration into their surroundings and their habitability. Buildings and projects featured in this section include, for instance, the restoration of an old residential block in Madrid's Lavapiés district (5: 38–39); a building intended to house a day centre for the elderly residents of Carabanchel (11: 64–65); and a social housing development in the historical area of La Latina (13: 32). The focus on the everyday elements of the city becomes particularly noticeable in Manuel Bueno's discussion of street furniture within the section 'Mis Horrores Favoritos' in issue 14. Here, Bueno despairs at the lack of attention paid to 'esos objetos que amueblan nuestras ciudades [...], uniformando y en cierto modo contribuyendo a definir la calidad del panorama' [those objects that furnish our cities [...], which standardize and, in a way, contribute to define the quality of the panorama] (14: 60), and calls on Madrid's municipal authorities to undertake an overhaul of the design of phone booths, bins, fences, plant pots and bus stops. This attention to the less obvious aspects of Madrid's urban make-up is coherent with the authors' view of architecture as indelibly linked to city life and the experience of the city. Additionally, this novel focus on everyday elements serves two further, interrelated purposes: broadening readers' notion of architecture, so that they come to regard it as a discipline concerned with matters close to their own experiences and interests; and pushing forward the idea that contemporary, thoughtful architecture should not be a luxury reserved for a few flagship projects, but a right that extends to every aspect of the urban environment. This notion of a 'right to architecture' echoes Lefebvre's vindication of the 'right to the city', that is 'the right of citizens not to be excluded from the city's centrality and its movement' (Lefebvre 2003: 150).

In line with its authors' notion of the city as lived and liveable space, this section seeks not only to inform readers about changes to Madrid's cityscape, but also to encourage their participation in city life. Most, if not all, articles constitute an implicit invitation for readers to embark upon 'paseos', leisurely, often aimless strolls, as a means to discover or rediscover different areas of their city. This invitation is made explicit in issue 15, where Vicente Patón writes that the section's focus on 'los olvidados', hidden or forgotten architectural gems, hopes to incite readers to 'fijarse en ellos durante un paseo' [take note of them whilst on a stroll] (15: 61). This reference to the street walk as a means to discover concealed aspects of the city is reminiscent of Baudelaire's notion of *flânerie*, the dandy's aimless, idle wandering through the metropolitan streets. Indeed, Patón himself could be cast in the role of the Baudelairean *flâneur*, which Heinz Paetzold describes as a 'cultural worker' who 'communicates his experiences in the streets within the cultural apparatuses of journals, magazines and radio stations' (Paetzold 2000: 216). However, there are some important differences: as Benjamin notes, a pedestrian only becomes a *flâneur* by virtue of his/her separation of, or displacement within, the urban masses (Benjamin 1999: 169), a dissociation which affords the *flâneur* a certain distance from the turmoil of the city. It is this distance or isolation from the masses that explains the emphasis on the *flâneur*'s subjectivity, a subjectivity that is, at the same time, the pre-condition for the *flâneur*'s detachment from the crowd. Baudelaire's modern *flâneur* is still able to regard him- or herself as separate from the urban masses and the cityscape they inhabit. By contrast, the authors of *La Luna*'s architecture section are not concerned with their separation from or distinctiveness within their surroundings; rather, they are interested in the ways in which citizens, a collective of which they consider themselves part, simultaneously shape and are shaped by the space they inhabit. Underlying this shift is a postmodern problematization of the modern *flâneur*'s privileged position of exteriority with respect to the anonymous urban masses. After all, one of the most significant insights of postmodern theory, a current of thought with which *La Luna*'s editorial team was familiar,[4] is its uncovering of individuals' perceived autonomy from their social, cultural, linguistic and spatial contexts as illusory.[5] Unlike the modern *flâneur*, who failed to include him- or herself in the picture of the city s/he depicted, thus absolving him-/herself from considering the position s/he occupied within the city's social, economic and cultural orders, those working in *La Luna* were aware of the inevitably limited and partial nature of their views.

The resort to city walks as a way to discover not only the city's architectural make-up, but also the particular rhythms of the life it fosters, also echoes the French Situationists' notion of *dérive*, a drifting through the city aimed at uncovering what they called its psychogeography, that is, 'the exact laws and precise effects of the geographical environment, consciously organized or not, acting directly on the affective development of individuals' (McDonough 2002: 45). As noted above, *La Luna*'s architecture section is not merely concerned with the material features of buildings and projects, but considers also the effects of such features on the surrounding environment and on the community of users or residents — thus demonstrating an awareness of the relationship between built environment, personal and communal development that resonates with the Situationist concept of psychogeography.[6] Once again, however, there are some significant differences: whilst the Situationists offer a grand solution to the question of urban space and planning through the formulation of what they term 'unitary urbanism', those writing for *La Luna* refrain from promoting an analogous master plan. Indeed, they plainly state their wish to steer clear from any revolutionary ambitions:

> Un edificio, actualmente, debería ser producto única y exclusivamente de una arquitectura del sentido común y de la lógica constructiva, nada que vaya a cambiar la faz de la tierra. Al final no es más que un testimonio como el llanto de un poeta, o el grito de un herido, no se puede pretender hacer de él una bandera de conquista. (issue 12: 78)
>
> [At present, a building ought to be solely the product of common sense architecture and of building logic, and not something intended to change the face of the Earth. Ultimately, it is nothing more or less than a form of testimony, like the cry of a poet, or the scream of a wounded person, and it cannot become an emblem of conquest.] (issue 12: 78)

This abdication from more radical goals may seem striking. Nevertheless, the apparent humility of this statement is made understandable when considered against the Situationist alternative of a unitary urbanism. Constant Nieuwenhuys, one of the movement's co-founders and arguably the main proponent of unitary urbanism, defined it in 1959 as 'urbanism made to please' (Constant in McDonough 2002:

96). This definition leaves open a key question, namely, whom this new urbanism ought to please. In a later, 1974 formulation of the concept, it becomes apparent that 'unitary urbanism' is intended to fulfil the needs of *homo ludens*, the ludic man of the future who, liberated by technology from mechanical and repetitive activities, can explore and develop his full creative potential (Constant in McDonough 2001: 97). Unitary urbanism is thus conceived as both the driving force and the result of a wider shift from *homo sapiens* to *homo ludens*. The conception of a unitary urbanism as part of a wider revolutionary programme is problematic, as it calls into question its applicability, which becomes dependent upon the attainment of as yet unrealized technological conditions. Further, this form of urbanism involves a homogenization of the needs and traditions of different communities, their differences obliterated in order to fit a vision of society and the city promulgated by a minority (the Situationists). Constant's New Babylon project (1956–1974), an attempt to model a Situationist city on the principles of unitary urbanism, illustrates the limitations of such an approach. The project envisaged a global metropolis consisting of a vast, layered, sheltered structure, supported by pillars and covering the entire Earth.[7] New Babylon remains interesting as artwork, inasmuch as it queries different ways in which we could live in the future (and thus also, by implication, the ways in which we live at present), but, in its utopian nature and scale, it does not address the everyday problems and needs of city dwellers. Its radicality not only made it inapplicable in practice, but also alienated ordinary citizens, who failed to engage with its futuristic vision of an endless, all-encompassing, multiple-level city.[8]

La Luna's approach was entirely different: instead of formulating a radical blueprint for urban transformation based on structural and material alterations to the city, it set out to change the city by transforming its readers' perception of Madrid. As its second editor José Tono Martínez wrote retrospectively, one of the key aims of the magazine was to have readers join in the belief that Madrid could rid itself from its 'complejo de Villa y Corte rancia y franquista' [complex as a rancid and Francoist town and court] and become 'esa gran ciudad abierta, plural y divertida que todos estábamos buscando' [that great, open, diverse and fun city which we were all looking for] (Cadahía 2007: 11–12). In line with this general objective, the representations of space within the magazine discussed above encouraged readers to conceive of Madrid's built environment as more than a mere accidental and accessory backdrop; it invited them to look at buildings in new ways, suggesting, for instance, that readers consider the ways in which spaces condition people's behaviours and interactions. Unlike the ambivalent Baudelairean *flâneur*, both fascinated and shocked by the sights and sounds on display in the modern city, those writing in *La Luna* are entirely at home within the urban landscape, which they feel all *madrileños*, and particularly local residents, have a right to claim as their own, and reinvent according to their particular needs and desires. Indeed, *La Luna*'s refusal to formulate an alternative urban development programme is underpinned by the belief that no top-down intervention can be truly radical; those working on the magazine saw the tendency to ignore local requirements and traditions in the name of a greater, often utopian vision as the central flaw of both modernist and postmodern architecture. Thus, rather than at the level of representations of space, a field to which traditionally only a small number of technical experts and public officials have access, *La Luna*'s editorial team saw urban transformation as necessarily taking place, first and foremost, at the level of representational spaces, that is, of the ways in which citizens thought of and imagined their city.

Representational spaces: the imagined city

In order for Madrid to become the city that *La Luna*'s founders longed for it to be — open, diverse, fun, but as yet non-existent (cf. Cadahía 2007: 44) — it was necessary for readers to be able to imagine what Madrid might become; to conceive of other possible cities lurking beyond its present incarnation. In an article by Alberto Humanes published in issue 28, and invoking Ortega's notion of 'las ideas como realidades que integran nuestro mundo' [ideas as realities that are part of our world] (28: 65), the author defends the view that 'entre los materiales con que se construyen los edificios y las ciudades están también los recuerdos, los deseos, los miedos, los sentimientos...' [memories, desires, fears and feelings are also amongst the materials with which cities are built] (28: 66). In accordance with this view of memories, desires, fears and feelings as integral to the city's material constitution, *La Luna* attempted not only to transform the ways in which its readers perceived and engaged with Madrid's cityscapes, but also to offer them a glimpse of the many possible cities -possible inasmuch as imaginable- that Madrid could be.

Manuel,[9] a serialized graphic narrative published in the first 16 issues of *La Luna*, offers some particularly fascinating representations of the city as imagined by its author, Rodrigo Muñoz Ballester.[10] *Manuel* is an autobiographical tale of unrequited homosexual love, as Muñoz Ballester explained in an interview in issue 7 (22–24). However, it is much more than that: following the protagonist's pilgrimage through the city, readers are presented with highly original visions of Madrid, which is depicted in minute detail from unusual perspectives and impossible angles. Readers are confronted with images of their city that are familiar and recognisable, yet at the same time strange, thus producing a sense of discovery and of the uncanny. The themes of homosexual love and lust are articulated through a refiguring of Madrid's cityscapes that, in turn, affects the comic's own spatial configuration.[11]

In the first instalment of the story we see the unnamed protagonist, an alter ego of the author, leave his flat and head for Noviciado metro station in Madrid (issue 1: 40; Figure 2.2). The frame that depicts the metro entrance offers a conventional and detailed perspective of the curving street: its shops, buildings, road and street signs. Even for those readers unfamiliar with this area of the city, the metro sign on the right-hand side of the frame is immediately recognisable and roots the narrative firmly in Madrid. By contrast, the frame immediately below presents readers with a view of the city that they will have never seen: a cut across the different subterranean levels that lead to the metro platform. The unusual construction of this frame not only offers us, as readers, a perspective that we could never experience otherwise; it also allows us to follow the movements of the protagonist as he enters the station and descends the stairs and escalator. The use of the metro's passages, escalators and platforms as frame structuring elements allows the author to create an impression of temporal sequencing within a single frame. Further, the transversal cut invites

Fig. 2.2. *Manuel*: Noviciado metro station © Rodrigo Muñoz Ballester

readers to rediscover a sense of wonder and surprise about everyday elements and spaces of city life, such as Madrid's metro, which many might have grown to take for granted. Although the protagonist does nothing unusual or particularly exciting in this sequence -he descends to the platform and waits for his train- the unconventional perspective used lends the whole scene an air of adventure, with the protagonist seemingly burrowing his way deep into the city's underbelly. Since this scene is of little consequence to the development of the plot, its main function seems to be to encourage readers to approach everyday practices, such as commuting, with a sense of adventure. This vindication of the rich experiential possibilities that everyday city spaces and practices can offer is echoed in the author's description of Madrid's metro as 'una auténtica orgía de sensaciones' [a veritable sensorial orgy] (issue 7: 23). The sensorial possibilities of the city are further celebrated as the protagonist arrives at the public swimming pool and dives in for a swim.

Within *Manuel*, there is a focus on what Foucault terms heterotopic sites, that is, places in which 'all the other real sites that can be found within the culture, are simultaneously represented, contested, and inverted' (Foucault 2002: 231). The swimming pool, which provides the setting for the protagonist's first encounter with Manuel (issue 1: 39–40), is a prime example: as Thomas van Leeuwen notes, the pool is 'the product of a paradoxical play of nature and artifice' (1998: 8); a place that allows for both exercise and recreation; and the swimmer's embrace of the water is a sensuous-erotic, yet also potentially dangerous experience. This wealth of superimposed meanings extends to the different uses associated with the specific example depicted here (the public swimming pool at Casa de Campo in Madrid), which in the late 1970s (the action of *Manuel* is set in 1977) functioned as both a popular recreational spot for families, and as an informal meeting point for gay men.

The nightclub depicted in the second instalment (issue 2: 38–39) is another example of heterotopia: it is linked to a specific temporality or 'heterochrony', in Foucauldian terms. The club exists only at certain times (at night, on some week nights); and it operates according to rules that contest or contradict the conventions that apply to other spaces. For instance, here social and physical contact amongst strangers is not only allowed, but encouraged. The codes of behaviour within the club, moreover, seem fluid enough to allow for different forms of interaction. For example, the sequence of three frames that depict the club's interior (2: 39) starts with Manuel approaching several women, ostensibly to ask them to dance, and ends with an unsuccessful Manuel giving up on the ladies and taking to the dance floor with his male companion. Despite this being a 'straight' club, that is, a venue conceived to encourage meetings between heterosexual men and women, the looseness of the rules that apply to this space also allow for two men (the protagonist and Manuel) to dance and flirt with each other.

The most obvious example of this focus on urban heterotopias can be found in issue 11, as the protagonist, who has been rejected by Manuel, embarks on a tour of Madrid's gay scene (issue 11: 72–77). The fact that in 1977, when the action is set, the Francoist Ley de Peligrosidad y Rehabilitación Social, which allowed the legal prosecution of homosexuals, was still in force,[12] supports a reading of the gay

Fig. 2.3. *Manuel*: Inconsistent cityscapes © Rodrigo Muñoz Ballester

venues featured here as heterotopic sites, since those frequenting them were not only contesting social mores, but also challenging the existing legal framework and thus risking prosecution. Such an interpretation is further reinforced by the fact that, whilst the gay venues are portrayed in a realistic-naturalistic manner, the frames featuring other spaces (the entrance lobby of the gay porn cinema, the traffic-clogged street, the park) are sketched in a distorted manner, as if, following Foucault, the protagonist's contact with the heterotopic realm of Madrid's gay scene had operated 'a sort of simultaneously mythic and real contestation of the space in which we live' (Foucault 2002: 232), conferring upon everyday city spaces an air of unreality and inconsistency (Figure 2.3).

These heterotopic sites are not, however, depicted in an unequivocally positive or sympathetic manner. The opening frame in issue 11 shows the protagonist receiving oral sex at a porn cinema, whilst a barely visible man at the side (only his waist and flaccid penis are visible) awaits his turn. The scene's stark realism contrasts with the lyric style of previous instalments, and the general impression is one of seediness, rather than of conspiratorial secrecy, liberation or solidarity. The portrayal of a gay club's dark room (issue 11: 74–75; Figure 2.4) is similarly unsympathetic: an initial frame shows a series of shadows huddled in groups, barely recognisable as human forms; the following frame depicts the same scene, this time lit up to reveal several distorted figures engaging in different sex acts. By contrast, the public bath and sauna (issue 11: 76) are represented in more positive terms; their glamorous interiors filled with scantily clad men enjoying the opportunity to socialize and to gaze openly at, and touch, each other's bodies. Whereas the cinema and the dark room appear as sinister spaces in which sex becomes a hurried and mechanical exchange, the bath and sauna are portrayed as sites of a more subtle and laidback eroticism. This ambivalence towards Madrid's gay scene echoes the author's view:

> No me imagino que existan sitios específicos para encontrar sexo, para encontrar cuelgues o para encontrar amor. Eso en el curso cotidiano de tu vida, ya se va dando. Tan inverosímil me resultan los sitios de señoritas pupés y caballeros muy machos ellos que las sacan a bailar, como las barras en las que abres la puerta y ya te están despelotando galanes con cueros. [...] No sé por qué tiene que haber tanta localización de las cosas así, a priori. (issue 7: 23)
>
> [I cannot conceive of specific places to find sex, to become infatuated, or to find love. That already happens in the course of everyday life. I find places full of dolled-up ladies and very macho gentlemen who take them out to dance as unreal as those bars where, as soon as you open the door, you are confronted by leathered hunks trying to strip you of your clothing. [...] I don't understand the need for such a specific, a priori localization of things.] (issue 7: 23)

Muñoz Ballester's reservations with respect to gay venues seem to stem from the fact that these sites, though challenging established social and legal norms, are prescriptive in their own way, open only to certain types of encounters and interactions, namely those of a sexual or sexualized nature. Further, the author's allusion to the a priori 'localización de las cosas' suggests he regards gay venues as, at least to an extent, confining gays to a restricted, localized space at the margins, and thus arguably rendering them invisible within the city's everyday life. Instead,

Fig. 2.4. *Manuel*: Dark room © Rodrigo Muñoz Ballester

Muñoz Ballester argues that encounters leading to sex or love should and do occur 'en el curso cotidiano de tu vida', that is, in an everyday which, both for the author and for the protagonist of the narrative, is firmly rooted in the city of Madrid. Indeed, the narrative's focus on urban heterotopias -even in those instances in which they are approached critically- underlines the city's role in fostering diversity and granting individuals the freedom to embark in existential and creative explorations such as the ones undertaken by the protagonist of *Manuel*.

Within *Manuel*, the city constitutes the site in which the erotic and the creative converge. The link between the urban and the erotic is made explicit in the final, full-page frame of the series' second instalment, which provides readers with the first close-up of Manuel's face (issue 2: 40; Figure 2.5). Here, Manuel's head appears framed by a series of lamp posts that not only help create a sense of perspective, but also provide a halo of light around his head. This halo confers an aura on Manuel presumably intended to reflect the protagonist's subjective view of and feelings for the character. This construction is particularly interesting because the motif used to create a garland with which to decorate the object of love is highly unconventional: rather than candles, stars, or flowers, Manuel's face is framed by rather ordinary street lights. Such a choice not only reflects the urban nature of this love story, but also establishes a direct connection between the city and the protagonist's object of desire. This saintly representation of Manuel finds echo in the opening frames of the narrative, in which the protagonist is seen lying in bed and surrounded by votive candles (issue 1: 38). In both instances, Muñoz Ballester manages to confer a quasi-mystical aura upon urban and everyday objects and situations. The influence of religious art becomes apparent elsewhere in the comic, through the incorporation of Pedro de Mena's *Magdalena Penitente* (1663–1664), a replica of which can be seen in the protagonist's studio (issue 5: 55). The author explained this inclusion as a reflection of his aspiration to become an *imaginero* [image-maker or image painter] in the tradition of de Mena, but as he readily conceded, 'en más *country*' (7: 24), that is, no longer concerned with divine subjects, but devoting his craft to decidedly (and, one might add, proudly) quotidian objects.

The connection between the erotic or experiential and the creative is established at the level of the plot: the comic is concerned with the love story between the protagonist and the eponymous Manuel, a story largely based on the author's own experience of unrequited love. This basic plot line soon becomes complicated by the protagonist's decision to make a statue of Manuel — a creative activity which is both inspired by his lived experience, and approached as a means to transcend, or at least compensate for, the protagonist's disappointment following Manuel's rejection. This link between the experiential-erotic and the creative is further underlined through the intertextuality (or rather, intervisuality) found in the third instalment of the narrative. Here, we find two frames drafted in a remarkably different visual style to that of the rest of the narrative, and which are revealed as the work of two other comic artists.[13] The inclusion of these works is due not only to Muñoz Ballester's admiration for their authors, but also to the fact that they were his friends. As the author explained elsewhere (issue 7: 24), since this segment of the

Fig. 2.5. *Manuel*: Close-up of title character
© Rodrigo Muñoz Ballester

Fig. 2.6. *Manuel*: Intervisual collaboration by Nuevo
© Rodrigo Muñoz Ballester

story is concerned with the protagonist's friends' reaction to his news about Manuel, he decided that those friends of his who also happened to be comic artists should be given the chance to present their views in an unmediated way, through the integration of their drawings into the narrative. Thus in this instance intervisuality serves as a means to underline the autobiographical character of the story, with the testimony or reaction of the author's friends becoming confused with that of the protagonist's friends.

Additionally, the integration of these frames — the schematic, harshly geometric shapes of Nuevo and the comparatively imprecise, soft and naïve elements by Plasti (issue 3: 40–41; Figure 2.6) — establishes a stark contrast with Muñoz Ballester's elaborately detailed reproduction of the protagonist's day-to-day life in the city. Muñoz Ballester's drawing style is realistic, though often destabilized by the adoption of unusual perspectives, or through the inclusion of out-of-place motifs, the distortion of scale, or the juxtaposition of elements, frames, spaces, times or dimensions. The effectiveness of the author's visual language resides precisely in the lack of correspondence between his naturalistic drawing style and the imaginative, non-realistic scenes he constructs. Though the vast differences, arising in part from the fact that the medium used here offers very different possibilities from that of conventional painting, should not be overlooked, this deliberate incongruity between naturalistic style and non-realistic choice of motifs, perspectives and compositions has Dalinean echoes, not least in terms of its uncanny effect upon the viewer/reader. The influence of Dalí can be felt particularly in a full-page image in which the protagonist is seen binge-eating the contents of a tray of cakes whilst gradually becoming transformed into a runny, amorphous blob reminiscent of Dalí's melting figures (issue 12: 72; Figure 2.7);[14] as well as in the partial reproduction of the Surrealist painter's 1949 'Leda Atómica' within the final segments of the narrative (issue 14: 77), characterized by frequent discontinuities and by the collapsing of several spatial and temporal settings into one frame. In the same instalment of the comic, we find an image that is particularly striking for its wealth of disparate references (issue 14: 78; Figure 2.8). Placed within an Escherian composition structured by beams, staircases, and irregular perspectives, are a series of figures that allow readers a glimpse into the very diverse network of visual and cultural references that populate Muñoz Ballester's creative universe. The 1960s child star and Spanish popular icon Marisol appears in the foreground, flanked by a part-reproduction of Velázquez's *Las Meninas* (1656), rotated onto its side; the promotional poster for Víctor Erice's 1983 film *El Sur* is reproduced on the bottom right-hand corner; and a playful, inverted portrait of the French composer Erik Satie occupies the top left-hand corner.[15]

The incorporation of such a range of visual intertexts and citations works on several levels. In the case of the contributions by Plasti and Nuevo, the inclusion of work by artist friends underlines the autobiographical dimension of the story and points to the existence of a creative community shaped both by close personal contact and by artistic collaborations; its emergence and survival made possible, at least in part, by the conditions of the spatial-temporal framework its members shared, that is, by early 1980s Madrid. Although these graphic intertexts establish a

FIG. 2.7. *Manuel*: Melting Figures
© Rodrigo Muñoz Ballester

Fig. 2.8. *Manuel*: Escherian frame with multiple visual citations
© Rodrigo Muñoz Ballester

break with Muñoz Ballester's detailed, naturalistic drawing style, they nevertheless integrate successfully within the comic because the author's visual language is precisely characterized by its disregard for linearity and continuity. The citations not only give us an idea of the diverse figures that influence Muñoz Ballester's work as a visual artist; the combination of such disparate figures (Spanish and non-Spanish, old and new, popular and canonical) within a built environment which, like many of the author's reproductions of iconic Madrid landmarks (Gran Vía, Metrópolis building) defies perspectival conventions can also be read as an analogy of the layering of styles, symbols, times, uses and meanings that characterizes the (post)modern city.

Madrid's urban landscape is creatively destabilized and reimagined within *Manuel* — the author's original use of perspective and composition presents readers with a new, yet familiar and recognisable, view of their city. The author's de-familiarization strategies challenge the notion of city space as a stable, unchanging reality, suggesting instead that our view of the city is determined by our experiences, as well as by the position we occupy within it. This awareness of the wealth of possibilities lurking beneath any one actualization of the city does not only affect the way in which the city is portrayed; it also infiltrates the narrative structure of the comic. The action becomes increasingly confused, particularly in the second half of the series, by frequent discontinuities and by the collapse of several spatial and temporal settings within one frame. The consummation of the protagonist's and Manuel's relationship depicted in issue 15 (69–71) is ambiguous, and the question of whether the sexual encounter featured here is real or whether it is a fantasy or dream of the protagonist is left open. The final frame of the story (issue 16: 82) shows the protagonist leading another man towards his statue of Manuel. This man could be Manuel himself, but once again, the narrative resists closure, and the man's face remains unseen, his back turned to the reader. If we opt for a reading that identifies the faceless man with Manuel, a plausible, but by no means certain interpretation, then this ending can be understood as a coming together of two of the central motifs of the story: the erotic-experiential, represented by the flesh-and-blood Manuel, is brought before the creative, the statue of Manuel. Though it is the protagonist who acts as the mediator in this encounter, the city of Madrid can be shown to play an equally relevant, if less obvious, role in enabling the kind of transferences between lived experience and creative activity which constitute the subject matter and the driving force of *Manuel*. Indeed, the fact that the comic's erotic theme unravels through a depiction of heterotopic sites such as the swimming pool, the park, the nightclub or Madrid's gay clubs and saunas, and through a parallel destabilization of some of the city's landmarks (Gran Vía, Metrópolis building, Plaza Dos de Mayo) suggests a connection between urban space and sexuality, in line with Henning Bech's theorization of the city as the space in which sexualities (and, particularly, homosexual sexualities) can be materialized:

> the city is not merely a stage on which a pre-existing, preconstructed sexuality is displayed and acted out; it is also a space where sexuality is generated. What is it about the city that stimulates? Surely that altogether special blend of closeness and distance, crowd and flickering, surface and gaze, freedom and danger. (Bech 1997: 118)

The pre-eminence of urban space in *Manuel* underscores the generative potential noted by Bech, but in the comic, such potential is not conceived of solely in sexual terms, it is also harnessed creatively, leading to the emergence of a polysemic, multi-layered narrative that, like the city itself, resists interpretative closure.

The reconstruction of the city within *Manuel* seems to be telling its readers that there are many possible cities, but they are all contained in this one — echoing the motto of the *La Luna*'s editorial team, 'Hay muchos mundos pero están en éste' [There are other worlds, but they are in this one].[16] This aim of uncovering other worlds lurking beneath the apparently objective material surface of everyday objects, spaces and experiences resonates with the Surrealists' goal of exploring and bringing to light unconscious thoughts and desires. Indeed, *La Luna*'s motto seems to have been unwittingly borrowed from Paul Éluard,[17] who is reported to have stated that 'There exists another world. But it is assuredly in this one' (Walker 2002: 79–80).[18] Both *La Luna*'s motto and Éluard's phrase suggest a pragmatic, optimistic view of the realities we inhabit. However, whilst Éluard speaks of 'another world' in the singular, those working on *La Luna* use the plural ('otros mundos'), a small but significant detail, which points to a wider shift. The Surrealists still operated in dichotomous terms, such as conscious-unconscious; material-spiritual; real-imagined, and while these dichotomies were frequently challenged, for instance, through the incorporation of oneiric elements or imagery into otherwise realistic scenes or descriptions, one half of the dichotomy (the unconscious, the spiritual, the imagined) was generally favoured over the other, held as more meaningful and more powerful than its opposite. The Surrealists recognized that the unconscious, the imaginary and the spiritual can affect and transform the conscious, the real and the material, but the premise on which such influences and transferences between conscious and unconscious, real and imagined, and spiritual and material were predicated was precisely the existence of a (relatively) clear demarcation between domains: if the unconscious could be seen as intersecting with or irrupting into conscious thoughts and actions, it was because it was regarded as fundamentally separate from the conscious, as its 'other'. It is this implicit view of the conscious and the unconscious, the real and the imagined, as separate and distinct realms that underlies the Surrealists' efforts to integrate both planes in the quest for a human totality. In *Manuel*, however, distinctions between the real and the imagined, the experienced and the created or creative, become blurred and complicated, giving way, as we have seen, to a multiplicity of hybrid or in-between planes where the real can no longer be disentangled from the imagined, and vice-versa. This view of human experience as determined by a multiplicity of merging planes of perception and meaning, echoed in the plural ('otros mundos') of *La Luna*'s motto, is symptomatic of a shift away from the Surrealists' search for totality, which is also a search for meaning, and towards what the American critic Richard Sheppard describes as postmodernism's (and Dada's) 'nondespairing acceptance of flux [...]; play amid irreconcilable opposites and shimmering, ambivalent surfaces; and the concomitant renunciation of any quest for meaning and final answers' (Sheppard 2000: 361–62).

In contrast to the overwhelmingly positive view of the city as a site of diversity, freedom, and creative exploration mediated in *Manuel*, Juan Madrid's urban chronicle in his section *La Jungla de Madrid* offers a very different view of the urban landscape.[19] As the title indicates, the city is portrayed here as a jungle, that is, as a lawless site of struggle and violence. However, the title also introduces a note of ambiguity, as it lends itself to different readings: the prepositional construction, literally 'the jungle of Madrid', could be taken as metaphorically associating the city of Madrid with the jungle, but also as indicating authorship (the jungle created by the author Juan Madrid), ownership (the jungle belonging to the author Juan Madrid), and even belonging (the jungle in which the author Juan Madrid lives). The semantic polyvalence of the title suggests that the city of Madrid may be a dangerous and inhospitable place, but that it nonetheless remains the author's own jungle, a space which he simultaneously creates and inhabits.

This column takes the form of a fictional 'crónica de sucesos', as the use of this epigraph in issue 37 (50) explicitly acknowledges. This news category, which focuses on human interest stories, crimes of passion, and other events considered too small-scale, isolated, or exotic to fit into other rubrics of a newspaper, is akin to the French 'fait divers', a category appropriated by the Surrealists and incorporated into reviews such as *Littérature*, *La Révolution Surréaliste* and *Le Surréalisme au Service de la Révolution.*[20] The existence of a Surrealist precedent to Juan Madrid's use of the 'suceso' or 'fait divers' may be just a coincidence: there is no evidence to suggest that Madrid was aware of the aforementioned Surrealist examples. Nevertheless, Madrid's approach to and intentions with respect to the 'suceso' share some of the traits of its Surrealist antecedents.

One of the means used by the Surrealists in order to subvert the 'fait divers' form was to celebrate its protagonists, often perpetrators of violent crimes, as Surrealist anti-heroes, as in the case of the Papin sisters (see note 19) or of the anarchist Germaine Berton, who murdered the French Action League member Marius Plateau in 1923, and whose photograph was featured in the first issue of *La Révolution Surréaliste* in December 1923. *La Jungla de Madrid* is similarly sympathetic to some perpetrators: in several instances, events are retold through the perspective of the 'criminal', a narrative strategy that encourages readers to identify with the perpetrator, who is ultimately revealed as the victim of an unfair social order. This approach is taken for instance in issue 2 (61), which features the story of a Filipina immigrant who, after losing her job as a maid following her employer's sexual advances, throws herself in front of a train at Tirso de Molina station. Though events are told by a third-person narrator, rather than by the suicide herself, they are seen through her eyes: we are told about the initial happiness of her life in Madrid, about her previous life in Manila, of her love for Plaza Tirso de Molina, where she spends several hours every Sunday; and as the incident that leads to her sacking is described, it is conjured in the confused terms in which the protagonist herself, who appears not to have realized what was taking place, experienced it. In *La Jungla de Madrid*, this adoption of the perpetrator's perspective is favoured in those cases where the protagonist can be considered a struggling figure at the margins of society — and it is thus perhaps not surprising that many of the characters featured fit the 'type' of the anti-heroic outcast: retired or amateur boxers, prostitutes (male and female), exploited and impoverished workers, petty criminals... However, not all the instalments of the series consider the violent outbursts described within them as the product of social inequality. The other side of that paradigm is the uncovering of the dark secrets hidden behind respectable bourgeois appearances. In issue 3, for example, we find the story of an apparently respectable old lady, wife of a high-ranking military officer, who in her old age decides to take revenge on her husband for years of marital abuse and infidelity by confining him in the house and torturing him for several years (3: 61). In this case, the perpetrator of the crime has not been pushed over the edge by social inequality, but rather by the rigidity and hypocrisy of a social order that makes marriage an indissoluble union, even when it is an unhappy, unhealthy one, and that stipulates that any abuse, transgression or violence which occurs within it is to remain a private matter, to be dealt with behind closed doors. Although the wife can be seen as a victim of the established social order, her status as victim is made less clear than that of other perpetrators within the series. For one thing, the narrative is not recounted through her eyes, but through those of her neighbours. Further, the graphic description of her husband's emaciated body and the closing scene, in which she is caught putting out her cigarettes on what remains of her husband's testicles (issue 3: 61) dissipates any sympathy readers may have felt for her up to that point. This difference in treatment appears to stem from the fact that, unlike the outcasts of other instalments, who have either chosen or been forced to live outside the dominant social order, her crime does not seek to challenge that order, but in fact, to maintain it. Indeed, the wife manages to maintain her crime undetected, keeping up an appearance of bourgeois respectability for several years. Rather than a desperate, violent, unpremeditated attempt to break free from the shackles imposed by the social order, her crime constitutes a role reversal (the formerly abused wife becoming the abuser of her husband) that reverses the power (im)balance within the marital order, but does not destroy it. The title of this column, 'Viva el amor', ironically refers to the ideal of marriage as an unconditionally indissoluble union, a notion stretched here to the extremes of mutual abuse and torture.[21]

As these two examples make clear, the violence of the 'sucesos' in *La Jungla de Madrid* does not always emanate from an unfair and rigid social order: it is also occasionally revealed as a mechanism that helps maintain that very order. Whilst the disenfranchised resort to violence, a violence often turned against themselves, as a last, desperate attempt to escape an intolerable situation, others in more privileged positions use violence as a means to survive and hold on to their (relative) privileges within the existing order. Whilst both sets of characters can ultimately be regarded as victims of the prevailing social order, the author's sympathies are more clearly aligned with the first group. Juan Madrid's column, much like the Surrealists' use of the 'fait divers', contributes to uncover the violence and brutality hiding behind the everyday. However, Madrid's critique, though more nuanced, goes further than that of the Surrealists, for he reveals the violence of the 'suceso' or 'fait divers' not only as an outburst brought about by untenable socio-economic, familial and psychological pressures, but also as a response that can be redirected and used to ensure the survival of the very conditions that contributed to its appearance in the first place. The clearest example of this form of 'suceso' can be found in issue 38 (46), in which a foreign multinational executive tortures a prostitute and then throws her from his hotel room window. The reconstruction of the crime is interspersed with the executive's impressions of Madrid and his thoughts on marketing strategies and ideas for growth, a juxtaposition that creates the impression in readers of a highly functional and successful individual, rather than of a desperate or crazy figure. The title of the column, 'Coma hamburguesas', is reminiscent of the direct, laconic style of old-fashioned advertising slogans, and it not only refers to the perpetrator's job, but also suggests a link between his successful professional activity and the crime recounted within the column. The haunting power of this story lies not so much in the unmasking of an apparently respectable businessman as sadistic torturer and murderer, as in the possibility that his professional activity may be in some way linked to his criminal activity, his criminal acts perhaps constituting an outlet for the pressures and stress accumulated at work, and his success thus maybe deriving, in part, from his criminal exploits.

Writing on the ethical dimension of the Surrealists' appropriation of the 'fait divers', Dominique Perrin notes that, from the Surrealists' perspective, the 'fait divers' is the domain of those with no access to the symbolic realm, its violence constituting the sad privilege of those without access to language (André, Boyer-Weinmann et al. 2008: 142). This conclusion also applies to Juan Madrid's column, through which the author attempts to give a voice to the voiceless, like the Filipina in issue 2, whose poor command of Spanish limits her ability to understand and communicate with those around her. In the last instalment of the series, published in issue 41 (44), we find an explicit example of exclusion from the linguistic-symbolic realm. Here, a middle-aged accountant facing redundancy arranges a meeting with his company's director to plead to be kept in his job. Despite having memorized and rehearsed what he wants to say to his boss, once in his presence, the accountant becomes unable to express it in any articulate form: 'Tengo cincuenta años... señor director -balbuceó Tomás- Y... quiero decir... que...' [I am fifty years old... sir -Tomás babbled- And... I want to say... that...] (issue 41: 44). After the boss refuses to reinstate him, the accountant blames the refusal on himself, for having forgotten to mention his six children. When the accountant makes a final attempt to make his case to the director's wife, he fails even more dramatically, as the woman's screams in response to the unexpected confrontation by a stranger drown his attempts to explain his predicament. As the boss recognizes him and tries to pull him away, the desperate and disturbed accountant resorts to the only means left to him: he pulls out a kitchen knife and attacks his boss. Both men are killed, the boss by the stab wound inflicted by the accountant, the accountant shot dead by a security guard. In a final ironic twist, the security guard claims the accountant was a thief and his crime an unfortunately blotched mugging attempt, a version of events that obscures the true motivations for the violent act, and deprives it of its symbolic meaning. Similarly, the Filipina's suicide in issue 2 is retrospectively described as an accident (2: 61). The inability or unwillingness of others to acknowledge the nature and context of these violent acts underlines and reinforces their perpetrators' exclusion from the symbolic realm, and reveals their attempts to be heard and noticed, even at their most dramatic, desperate and violent, as ultimately futile.

While the Surrealists regarded violence as the only means for 'outsiders' (the destitute, the insane) to counter the violence exercised upon them by the existing order, and therefore celebrated individual acts of violence (particularly when irrational and spontaneous) as symbolic acts of resistance or contestation to institutional and institutionalized forms of violence, Juan Madrid's treatment of the 'fait divers' offers a more negative view of individual acts of violence, which, as we have seen, are not always portrayed as desperate responses to the unbearable pressures imposed by an unfair system, but are also seen as mechanisms to reinforce that very order. Indeed, some of the most vicious and gratuitous acts of violence featured in Madrid's section are committed by those in positions of power (executives, policemen, and businessmen) and in those instances their crimes tend to go unpunished, either because they are not identified as the culprits, or because they manage to excuse or cover up their acts by offering a 'rational' explanation — alleging, for instance, that they acted in self-defence.[22] Juan Madrid, unlike the Surrealists, no longer regards irrational outbursts of violence as potentially liberating and transgressive, in the sense that they offer a temporary break with or inversion of the existing, repressive order. Instead, his stories suggest that the established socio-economic order in fact always uses violence to its advantage: in those cases in which aggression is aimed at reinforcing or perpetuating the system, it either remains undetected, or is excused; and in the instances in which the violent act constitutes an implicit or explicit challenge to the existing order, it is misconstrued so as to obscure its true causes and meanings.

The city that emerges from Juan Madrid's *La Jungla de Madrid* stands in stark contrast to the Madrid depicted in *Manuel*. Urban space is no longer the site of erotic and creative explorations, as in *Manuel*, but a harsh, unequal, and potentially dangerous and violent environment. However, this negative view of the city coexists with more positive renderings; some of the characters cherish specific corners of Madrid, like the Filipina in issue 2, who loves to sit in Tirso de Molina square. And it is not the city that is held responsible for the violent events described in the column, and largely located within it, but the unequal power relations that simultaneously shape it and are challenged by it. Though individuals are regarded as incapable of escaping or transforming such power relations, the column's ambiguous title, which, while likening the city of Madrid to a jungle, also underlines the author's role in inhabiting and thus contributing to the making of that space, suggests a more nuanced, indeed more hopeful view. Ultimately, Juan Madrid's column is not only a portrayal of the violence inherent to the (post)modern city, but also an exercise in storytelling that seeks to establish a space for alternative voices and narratives often silenced by dominant discourses.

La Luna as space

As the previous pages have made clear, the treatment of urban space in *La Luna* is less clear-cut than it might appear at first sight. On the one hand, the city is recognized as the space that allows individuals to embark on creative and experiential journeys; its capacity to foster diversity and its ability to withstand political and economic pressures are celebrated. At the same time, however, there is an implicit recognition that the city is a permanently threatened environment — threatened by market speculation, by ruthless or unwise planning initiatives, but also by social and symbolic exclusion, which lead to outbursts of violence, its precarious balance sustained primarily by the active involvement of its inhabitants in all aspects of city life. This section considers the extent to which *La Luna*'s own emergence as space was influenced by the magazine's treatment and view of the city, and the characteristics and implications of the publication's spatial constitution — that is, in Lefebvrian terms, of its status as a trialectics consisting of the magazine's material make-up, the reading practices it encouraged, and the different readings or actualizations of the magazine effected by its readers.

As has been seen in the Introduction, the magazine is characterized by its large format (tabloid A3); its use of poor-quality paper, its considerable length (between 72 and over 100 pages); the sparse presence of colour, at least in its first 20 issues; as well as its eclectic mix of formats (incorporating text, photos, drawings, comics, reproductions of paintings, collages and graphic creations), layouts (conventional columns and blocks of text coexist with unusual, broken-up or scattered arrangements of text), and visual styles (with Futurist and Dada-style typographic experimentation found alongside typographies reminiscent of the style of 1950s and 1960s American comics, and Surrealist-influenced imagery appearing next to abstract, geometric or graphic visual creations). In that discussion, *La Luna*'s material constitution (its size, length, quality of printing paper, use of colour and images) was considered solely in terms of its role in enabling the magazine to establish a unique and distinct visual style and editorial identity that set it apart both from the *zines* from which it draw many of its ideas and contributors, as well as from the more conventional arts and culture titles of the time, whose often normative views *La Luna* set out to challenge. Here, I want to consider how these features encouraged a series of specific reading practices.

La Luna's large size and considerable length did not make the magazine easily portable. This, coupled with the frequent use of compressed layouts and a relatively small font size, suggest that the magazine sought to invite reflective reading practices, rather than a casual and quick flicking through the pages. However, such reflective readings are unlikely to have been linear or continuous: *La Luna*'s diversity and density of contents point to fragmentary reading practices, that is, to individual readers choosing personal itineraries through the magazine's pages, as well as to discontinuous readings — with readers likely to have engaged with different sections or parts of the magazine at different times. For example, readers would have checked the magazine's listings section 'Guía de Madrid' (issues 1–8) as and when they wanted to find out about the different activities taking place in the city. The review sections for music, books, films and plays played a similar referential role, offering readers an overview of new releases. The inclusion within the magazine of very diverse sections, ranging from literature to architecture, sport, and 'women's issues', and materials (listings, reviews, interviews, short stories, photography, reproductions of paintings, collage and more) further supports the argument that *La Luna* was read in non-linear and fragmentary ways, since it seems likely that individual readers would prioritize certain sections or elements of the magazine over others, which they may have either skipped, or to which they may have returned at a later stage.[23] But such non-linear, fragmentary readings of *La Luna* derived not only from the juxtaposition of heterogeneous sections and materials, but also from the unconventional and at times chaotic layouts of some of the magazine's pages, which required readers to find their own way of navigating content.

La Luna's generous format and the fact that it could be read in a variety of ways over a period of time (its contents, beyond the listings section, were not time-sensitive, and its publication at monthly intervals reinforces the theory that the publication was meant to last, if only until the next issue was due), could lead to the conclusion that the magazine was conceived and perceived as a 'coffee-table' publication, that is, as a respectable, luxuriously put-together arts title which conferred a certain sense of status to its buyers. While there are suggestions that *La Luna* eventually came to be regarded in those terms, such a definition does not apply to the magazine in its initial phase under the editorship of Borja Casani (1983–1985). On one level, the magazine's use of poor-quality paper, the initial near-total absence of colour, and the inclusion of deliberately controversial, shocking and irreverent materials contests such a label. More importantly, *La Luna* was not conceived as a finished, static product. Rather, readers were explicitly encouraged to interact with the magazine, to the point of threatening its physical integrity: for example, in the 'Recortables' section discussed above, readers were invited to cut out the reproduced buildings. Similarly, the calendars that appear in issues 1, 2, 3, 5, 6 and 8 of the magazine include blank spaces for readers to fill in. Unlike coffee-table titles, which, as their name suggests, are often bought not so much to be read as to be displayed, *La Luna* was intended, at least initially, to be read and put to use by readers, with some of its pages conceived to be completed, or dismantled and re-assembled, by readers.

La Luna's experiential nature, manifested in the aforementioned inclusion of interactive elements, and rendered explicit, as Susan Larson noted (2003: 316), in the phrase that appears in the calendar of issue 1, 'Léete la revista y búscate la vida' [Read the magazine and make your own way] (issue 1: Guía V), as well as its heterogeneity and refusal of interpretative closure — the diversity of its contents and the relationships and dialogues arising from their juxtaposition allowing and, indeed, inviting, multiple and sometimes contradictory readings — suggest that the magazine sought to place itself in a role analogous to that of the city. *La Luna*, like the Madrid portrayed within its pages, wanted to become a shared spatial-temporal framework characterized by its openness and dynamism, and thus able to foster a heterogeneous community of readers. There are several factors that suggest that the magazine succeeded in its aim of establishing such a space, at least during its initial phase (1983–1985).

Firstly, the magazine's founders managed to attract a wide and diverse range of contributors, from complete unknowns like the illustrator Fernando Vicente, to emerging talents such as the film-maker Pedro Almodóvar and the photographer Ouka Leele (both of whom later came to be regarded as *movida* icons), to respected thinkers such as José Luis Aranguren and Fernando Savater. Although many of those contributing to *La Luna* retrospectively became associated with *la movida*, partly because of their age, partly because of their involvement in the magazine, and, in some cases, because of their creative eclecticism, it should be noted that many of those writing within its pages had little to do with that movement. Aranguren, for instance, was at the time in his seventies, and his age and reserved character mean it is highly unlikely that he would have been aware of what was taking place within Madrid's countercultural circles. Other contributors such as Juan Madrid, Fernando Savater and Eduardo Haro Ibars were closer to the previous generation of 1960s *progres* in terms of their age and political militancy, although their status as dissidents within their own generational group might explain their sympathy towards *la movida*, a movement that emerged, in part, as a response to the solemnity and dogmatism of the 1960s generation. The common trait shared by *La Luna*'s contributors is thus neither their adherence to *la movida*, nor their belonging to a particular set or generation of artists; rather, they are linked by their heterodoxy, by their unusual trajectories and views,[24] in short, by their status as (relative) outsiders, whether from their own generational group, as in the case of some of the older contributors, or from the cultural field altogether, as in the case of younger contributors. The diversity among the magazine's contributors (their shared heterodoxy applies to different fields and is manifested in a variety of ways) reflects upon its contents, which are similarly heterogeneous.

Secondly, this polyphony of voices within *La Luna*, which reflects the polyphony of the (post)modern city, is further sharpened by the non-hierarchical and often apparently discordant juxtaposition of contents within the magazine. Although every issue of *La Luna* has a contents page, this feature does not impose or suggest a discernible hierarchy of contents or an order of reading; and it is, as will be seen below, of limited use when navigating the magazine. The contents page can be seen as analogous to the map of a city. Like the map, the contents page does not include every element within the magazine, but rather focuses on the main sections and articles, interviews and graphic contents. The artworks and other items interspersed between sections often do not get a mention within the contents page,[25] just as some of the alleys and passageways of a city are not shown on a map. Like the map, the contents page is not entirely reliable, as there are inaccuracies in terms of page numbers, with the number given in the contents page not always matching the actual page in which an item appears, and contents' titles, with the title of a piece not always matching its entry on the contents page.[26] But more importantly, the contents page, like the map, creates an illusion of space as a distinct and finalized entity that can be neatly parcelled into smaller separate and clearly demarcated units (whether city districts or magazine sections), thus failing to reflect the relationships and dialogues that arise between different, neighbouring elements and spaces — or, in the case of the magazine, between different, juxtaposed formats and contents. By presenting the space of *La Luna* (or of the city) as a finite and finalized whole, both map and contents page ignore the nature of magazine and city as ongoing, unfinished processes; and thus the usefulness of both map and index in terms of navigating space, urban or editorial, is limited to offering some basic orientation. Despite the appearance of order and containability that both map and contents page help create, a tour through the magazine's pages, like a walk through the city, soon dispels such an impression. *La Luna*'s heterogeneity and the complex relationships that emerge from its juxtaposition of very diverse contents leave it open to a wealth of possible readings on different levels: the magazine can be considered a review of Madrid's cultural life, a showcase for new and emerging artists; a forum for intellectual debate, a *revista de tendencias*, that is, a publication that aimed to keep track of and report on the latest trends in art, design and lifestyle, or even a practical joke waged by a group of friends (the magazine's founders) upon Spain's cultural and intellectual establishment. *La Luna* is simultaneously all and none of these things: while none of these definitions manages to entirely capture the magazine's ambiguity and complexity, there are elements of all of them within it.

Thirdly, *La Luna*'s diverse contents and its openness to multiple readings suggest that the magazine sought to attract as wide and diverse a readership as possible. Though it is impossible to establish with any degree of certainty what the magazine's readership was like, its focus on the city and identity, as well as the space granted to formats traditionally associated with youth culture, such as comics and pop music, suggest that its readers were, or considered themselves, young and urban. This basic profile remains, however, very broad, as both 'young' and 'urban' are diffuse and subjective terms: the urban can be taken to include suburban areas, as well as smaller regional centres, whilst young can be used to describe a wide age range, roughly encompassing those in their teens to those in their early forties, and, arguably, beyond, as some would contend that youth is defined by attitude and state of mind, rather than by age. Thus what Paul Julian Smith describes as *La Luna*'s 'self-conscious creation of a community' (2006: 58) was based upon readers' participation, rather than upon the formulation of a homogeneous -and thus potentially exclusive- editorial identity with which readers could identify. Participation was sought both at the level of readers' engagement with the magazine, required not only to navigate and make sense of its pages, but also to complete or actualize certain sections, such as the 'Recortables' discussed in the first part of this chapter; and at the level of readers' involvement in city life, which they were encouraged to explore in full through wanderings through Madrid, as well as through their attendance to the myriad of concerts, exhibitions, parties, and other events listed within *La Luna*'s pages. This community-building through participation, rather than identification, allowed the magazine to remain, at least for some time, a diverse, open, heterogeneous space that celebrated difference and resisted definition. *La Luna*'s space, in many ways analogous to that of the (post)modern city which the magazine simultaneously imagined, celebrated and contributed to create within and through its pages, proved, however, a fragile environment. The magazine's early success, particularly in terms of the influence it soon wielded,[27] and its co-option by, or at least collusion with, the political and cultural establishment, which will be discussed in the final section of this chapter, led to differences and tensions within its editorial team that culminated in an editorial schism in 1985 that saw the departure of the first editor Borja Casani, as well as several other members of the team. From mid-1985 onwards, *La Luna* became increasingly ossified, gradually losing its edginess and ambiguity, and with it a significant proportion of its readers, until its final demise in 1988.

Spatial practices: (re)discovering the everyday

The creation and dissemination of new urban imaginaries is perhaps the most salient aspect of *La Luna*'s attempt at reimagining and reclaiming Madrid. However, implicit in these new visions of the city is a set of spatial practices, that is, a series of new ways in which the city's inhabitants are shown, and the magazine's readers are encouraged, to interact with the surrounding urban space. If the city is portrayed as a site for personal and creative experimentation (as, for instance, is the case in *Manuel*), such explorations are not depicted as epic adventures, but rather are seen as happening at the level of everyday practices: through walks in the city, commuting, or the enjoyment of public spaces such as the pool, the park, the street, the theatre, and the bar or nightclub. This emphasis on the everyday extends also to other sections of the magazine: the architecture section focuses primarily, as we have seen, not on Madrid's landmarks, but on small-scale projects and little-known or forgotten corners of the city; and the 'Recortables' feature not only well-known buildings, but also the minute details and characters that contribute to give an area its particular look and feel: the lamp-posts, benches, vegetation, and the figures that frequent such spaces — flower and lottery vendors, school children, dog walkers, etc. Even Juan Madrid's *La Jungla* column, whose characterization as 'crónica de sucesos' might seemingly set it apart from the everyday, inasmuch as it appears to chronicle singular occurrences, events that are defined against the norm, ultimately shows, through the author's treatment of its subject matter, that violence is not exceptional, but an inherent part of the (post)modern city's everyday.

The spatial practices depicted in and promoted by *La Luna* are characterized by participation, with readers implicitly encouraged within the architecture section to embark on city walks, and explicitly invited through the listings section to take part in Madrid's cultural and social life. Urban participation is sought not only via *La Luna*'s exploration of its many facets and possibilities, which can take the form of a factual review of an exhibition or that of the fictional accounts of Patty Diphusa's crazed urban adventures, discussed in detail in the following chapter, but also by encouraging readers to take on a more active role with relation to the magazine itself. The magazine's incorporation of a range of interactive features (most notably the 'Recortables' section), its frequent requests for readers to send in contributions, for example, within the sections 'Mis horrores favoritos' (7–19) and 'Madrid Insólito' (4–5), and its calls for readers to take part in the competitions and parties organized by *La Luna* bear witness to the magazine's attempts to forge a more participatory role for its readers. Participation in city life is thus not only encouraged through *La Luna*'s reimaginings of the city or via the promotion of cultural initiatives and activities taking place in Madrid, but also through the pursuit of a more active role for its readers, who are encouraged to interact with and intervene in the magazine.

Movement also defines the spatial practices featured in *La Luna*. The main characters of the urban fictions featured in the magazine, particularly the protagonist of *Manuel*, and Patty Diphusa, are shown almost constantly on the move. Their travelling through Madrid is not always a means to reach a specific destination; for instance, in one occasion Patty gets into a taxi and asks the driver to take her anywhere, via the longest possible route (issue 4: 11), and it is occasionally depicted even though it is of no consequence to the story's narrative development, as in the first instalment of *Manuel*, which features a frame showing the protagonist entering a Madrid metro station (issue 1: 40). Such examples suggest that movement is valued in its own right, as a process that, owing to its transitional nature and because it can lead to unforeseen encounters and experiences, may help one find oneself, as Patty explains in issue 4 (11). These dynamic practices also reflect upon the magazine and its contents: as shown in the analysis of *Manuel*, the movement portrayed within the narrative also affects its structure, with destabilizing effects, and *La Luna*'s non-linear, non-hierarchical juxtaposition of contents requires readers to establish their own itinerary through its pages.

Enjoyment permeates the spatial practices portrayed in and encouraged by *La Luna*. Many of the movements and activities undertaken in the city by the characters of the magazine's urban fictions have no other purpose than their procuring an immediate (and often ephemeral) sensorial pleasure. In *Manuel*, for example, the public spaces of the city (streets, bars and cafés, the park or the pool) are shown as sites of pleasure and social interaction, whereas the private space of the protagonist's flat is depicted as the place in which he works and reflects. The experience of urban space is thus not portrayed as a productive practice, at least in the conventional sense of the term, resulting in a product with use and exchange value. Rather, the practices featured in the magazine tend to exhaust themselves in their realization, leaving nothing behind — nothing, that is, that can be seen or made tangible. Urban spatial practices are, however, shown to be productive in other ways: they play an important role in the processes of identity exploration and (re)configuration that can be seen taking place within and through *La Luna*'s pages; and they are key to the formation of creative networks — both in terms of allowing individuals to meet, interact and collaborate with each other, and in terms of establishing new meanings, of resignifying existing concepts and practices.[28]

Participation, movement and the pursuit of pleasure, at the level of readers' interactions with both their city and the magazine, are thus key strategies in the process through which *La Luna* sought to (re)discover the city's everyday. *La Luna*'s focus on the everyday is not trivial. As Michel de Certeau argued in *The Practice of Everyday Life*, it is precisely through the types of everyday urban practices highlighted in the magazine that ordinary citizens can appropriate the images, discourses, and practices determined by the grid of local socio-economic constraints that they live in, opening a path for subversion even in the face of increasingly sophisticated and seamless technological means of population surveillance and control (cf. de Certeau 1984: 201). De Certeau acknowledges that such forms of rebellion offer only limited scope for action, constituting, as he recognizes, 'a common and silent, almost sheeplike subversion' (de Certeau 1984: 200). However, in the socio-historical context in which he is writing and in which *La Luna* appeared (a context marked by a global loss of faith in utopian revolutionary ideals, their totalitarian dangers made manifest by the lack of freedoms and the prevalent climate of fear in Soviet block countries, as well as by a generalized scepticism with regard to the viability of the Enlightenment project, its belief in human reason and scientific and technological progress as vehicles for the emergence of a better world and a better society undermined by the twentieth century's legacy of horror and destruction), de Certeau's everyday, with its focus on practice at the micro- rather than the macro-level, nevertheless credits subjects with 'the ability to impact on and alter the systems with which they engage', as Michael Sheringham notes in his comprehensive study of the *quotidien* within the French tradition (2006: 232). We find a very similar valorization of the everyday within *La Luna*, where José Tono Martínez writes, in an article entitled 'El Espacio Radical'

> intentar una postura radical que inmediatamente no sea absorbida por el discurso de legitimación del poder es casi imposible. [...] Tal vez sólo nos quede la ilusión radical mínima, aquella que afecta a la vida cotidiana (si es que eso existe) no manifestada en discurso alguno, en el terreno de lo desapercibido [...].' (issue 12: 6)

> [it is virtually impossible to attempt a radical stance and not be immediately absorbed by the power-legitimising discourse. [...] There only remains, perhaps, the minimal radical hope, which concerns everyday life (if, indeed, such a thing exists), not uttered in discourse, at the level of the unnoticed [...].] (issue 12: 6)

Like de Certeau, Tono Martínez sees in quotidian everyday practices that go largely unnoticed the potential to resist, or at least defer, the co-option and integration mechanisms of the establishment. Martínez's tone is cautiously hopeful, as he tentatively suggests that 'la vida cotidiana' might, by virtue of its inconspicuousness, perhaps constitute a last realm for radical action, though what such radical attitudes and practices may entail is not elaborated upon.

La Luna's preoccupation with the everyday also links the magazine, and, by extension, *la movida*, to the historical avant-garde movements. As Michael Sheringham argues, Surrealism, with its emphasis on experience and process, played a central role in the emergence of a creative and critical body on (and of) the everyday. Though Sheringham acknowledges the existence of precursors concerned with the (re)discovery of the everyday (citing Baudelaire and Rimbaud, among others), he nonetheless assigns the Surrealists a foundational role in a tradition of twentieth-century discourses on and approaches to the everyday.[29] For Sheringham, Surrealism's engagement with the everyday is inextricably linked to the movement's focus on the urban, on its view of the city street as a site of potential adventures. Further, he argues that the Surrealists' focus on the everyday simultaneously results from and leads to the emergence of experience as the central dimension for the movement; and, because human experience cannot be reduced to one single form of knowledge, Surrealists favour multidisciplinary approaches that combine art with philosophy, psychiatry, ethnology, science and linguistics (cf. Sheringham 2006: 67). The diversity and heterogeneity of the intertwined domains of the everyday and human experience lead also to a questioning of the traditional notion of genre, often expressed through a crossing of traditional generic boundaries and through hybridization. In this context, the emergence of practices such as montage and collage in the early twentieth century can be seen, following Sheringham, as linked to a wider tradition of the everyday which, in the latter part of the century, leads to the proliferation of discourses and forms which blur disciplinary and generic boundaries, such as experimental ethnology or autofiction, and other forms of life writing.

Sheringham convincingly argues that the everyday constitutes a common element underpinning a wide range of critical and creative practices and discourses in France throughout the past century. His work traces the echoes and influences of Surrealism (and, to a lesser extent, Dada), through their pioneering focus on the everyday, on later movements such as conceptual and minimalist art, without, however, proposing a rigid, linear, successive genealogy of movements, which would risk obliterating the differences that distinguish them, ignoring their nuances and simplifying their complexity. *La Luna*, with its enduring and comprehensive engagement with the urban and its focus on the minute, quotidian elements and practices of city life, can be seen as part of the tradition of the everyday charted by Sheringham. While his work is primarily concerned with approaches originating in France,[30] a cultural and geographical distance from the Spanish phenomenon that should not be overlooked, some of the key features he identifies in relation with discourses and practices of the everyday also apply, in some degree, to *La Luna* and *la movida*. For the Spanish magazine and movement, as for the Surrealists and the Situationists, the everyday spaces and practices of the city are not merely subject matter for art works and theoretical discussions; rather, the urban everyday constitutes the realm within which and through which a transformation of existing realities may take place — changing, in the first instance, the creative process itself and its resulting products, which reflect and contain within them the urban everyday's indeterminacy, ambiguity and resistance to closure.

However, despite the common focus on urban everyday practices and the existence of some shared traits, the differences between *La Luna* and *la movida* and the earlier explorers of the everyday should not be overlooked. The Surrealists' and the Situationists' projects still had totality at their core; their desire to restore man's totality, freeing him from alienation, ultimately sought to change humanity and society. Thus, though based in the first instance on the transformation (through rediscovery) of everyday spaces and experiences, their projects also had wider, utopian goals that transcended, and hence arguably betrayed, the everyday, which nevertheless served as the platform from which both movements launched their offensives. By contrast, *La Luna*'s goals seem relatively modest: the magazine did not intend to change the existing political, economic and social orders. Instead, its aim of creating and disseminating a new urban imaginary that would encourage *madrileños* to reclaim the city's streets for their own enjoyment remained circumscribed to the level of the everyday, not only because the scope of this change did not go beyond the habitual uses of urban space, but also because the means by which such change ought to be achieved was seen to be at the level of the everyday, too, in the pursuit of such quotidian activities as walking through the city, going to a concert, or reading a magazine. *La Luna*'s comparatively small-scale ambitions in relation to the transformative and transgressive power of the everyday is explained by the socio-historical context within which the magazine emerged, a landscape marked by a global loss of faith in revolutionary utopias arising from the failures to realize such utopian visions, exemplified by the experience of May 1968 in France; and in Spain, by the left's relinquishing of many of its ideals during the transition to democracy that followed General Franco's death in 1975.[31]

La Luna's reinvention of Madrid within its socio-historical context

La Luna's attempts to reinvent the city of Madrid as an open, dynamic, diverse and (post)modern metropolis, a spatial model upon which the magazine modelled itself, did not take place in a vacuum, but rather, within a specific socio-historical context which needs to be considered. As Hamilton Stapell (2010) has noted, following the death of Francisco Franco in 1975 and the subsequent process of transition to democracy, Madrid needed to reinvent itself; to establish a new image that distanced the city from its previous incarnation as the drab, bureaucratic capital of a highly centralized state, and as the centre of Francoist power and repression.[32]

During Enrique Tierno Galván's tenure as mayor of Madrid (1979–1986),

Madrid's municipal administration embarked upon a radical transformation of the city. Although Tierno's plans for the city, articulated in the *Plan Especial Villa de Madrid* (1980) and in the *Plan General de Ordenación Urbana de Madrid* (1985), included alterations to Madrid's built environment, through, for instance, the renovation and recuperation of historical buildings and monuments, the transformation sought by these plans, as Stapell has noted, transcended the mere physical transformation of the city, serving 'a more fundamental purpose: "the social recuperation of the city"' (2010: 49). This broad and ambitious aim, stated in the 1985 *Plan General*, required not only the improvement of the city's infrastructures, but also a transformation of the ways in which its inhabitants engaged with and thought of their urban environment. Madrid's local authorities soon realized that the best way to achieve such a change was through citizens' participation in the city's cultural life. In order to promote a culture of participation and a participatory notion of culture, Tierno's administration favoured two particular strands of cultural expression largely ignored, if not repressed, during Francoism: 'fiestas populares' or popular street festivals such as carnival and the Feria de San Isidro,[33] and the wide range of youth and countercultural manifestations of *la movida* (Alberca García 2003). The mayor's emphasis on cultural activity and participation not only contributed to the forging of a new sense of identity for Madrid and *madrileños*, it also helped project a new image of the city as modern, diverse and culturally dynamic at the national and international levels. The support of Tierno's administration for popular festivals and *la movida* (two phenomena which often intersected, with prominent *movida* figures often at the centre of concerts and events organized within the framework of street festivals) was financial, either through direct sponsorship of events and publications or, as in the case of *La Luna*, through advertising. Further, Madrid's local authorities actively promoted youth culture activities through the sponsorship of competitions such as the rock contest *Concurso Rock Villa de Madrid* and the organization of events such as the 1984 exhibition *Madrid, Madrid, Madrid* (1974–1984), which charted Madrid's cultural life over the space of the preceding decade with a focus upon manifestations of youth and popular culture.

The support of Madrid's local authorities to *la movida* during the 1980s was motivated not by sheer altruism, but by the political elite's desire to use the movement as a means to implement its own programme of urban and cultural change within the city. *La movida* appeared useful to local politicians for several reasons. Firstly, by promoting an essentially cultural or countercultural, rather than a political movement, and by making it the symbol of a new Madrid, the city's local authorities were able, as Stapell argues, to present their plans for urban and cultural renewal as non-partisan initiatives (2010: 78). Unlike most Surrealists, who were members of, or associated with, the Communist Party, *movida* participants rarely engaged in party politics. *La movida*'s lack of explicit political engagement along party-political lines did not, however, prevent the movement's manipulation for political ends, but in fact facilitated it within the context of consensus politics that marked Spain's transition to democracy.[34] Secondly, *la movida*'s emphasis on the present, manifest in *La Luna*'s 'absolute contemporaneity' (Smith 2006: 57), was celebrated by politicians keen to distance themselves and the city they governed from the recent Francoist past. Thirdly, *la movida* was attractive to local authorities for its optimism and dynamism, for its belief that 'había que hacer todo porque todo estaba por hacer' [we had to do everything as everything remained to be done] (Compitello and Larson 1997: 163) — an optimistic attitude and a creative energy that the municipal administration sought to project upon itself and upon the city of Madrid, a move made explicit in the incorporation of the gentilic adjective 'madrileña' to the term *movida*. Finally, and most importantly, *La Luna*'s project to transform Madrid into a freer, more habitable, more accessible and more fun city coincided, in some of its aims, with the urban renewal programme formulated by Madrid's local government: both initiatives wanted to effect change not merely, or even primarily, through intervention at the level of representations of space, that is, of the physical make-up of the city, but rather by altering the ways in which inhabitants perceived and engaged with their city.

The differences in motivation, approach and scope between *La Luna*'s attempts to transform Madrid and those of Tierno's administration should not, however, be overlooked. *La Luna*'s desire to change Madrid stemmed from cultural and lifestyle imperatives; at heart, it represented the desire by a generation of *madrileños* of, as contributor Javier Olivares put it, 'no querer perder un año más de vida en una ciudad premoderna' [not wanting to waste another year of life in a premodern city] (Cadahía 2007: 43). While this longing to live in a city that allowed its inhabitants the space and freedom to experiment and lead creative lives had political implications, for instance, in terms of individual freedoms and the right of access to and use of city spaces, it was not subordinated to a specific political goal. By contrast, the administration's programmes for urban renewal were politically motivated; though they entailed the modernization of city infrastructures and the promotion of a more participatory urban culture, thus resulting in an amelioration of many *madrileños*' living conditions, the ultimate purpose was to create a new, modern, democratic image for Madrid that would help consolidate democratic change nationwide, reaffirm the Socialist Party's hold on power at the local and national levels, and eventually ease Spain's integration into the European Economic Community. As Stapell notes, once these goals had been achieved in the late 1980s, the Socialist Party's emphasis shifted from urban renewal through cultural innovation at the local level to assimilation into and identification with the wider European economic and socio-political contexts (2010: 180).[35]

In terms of scope, Madrid's municipal administration's capacity for intervention in efforts at urban transformation was, of course, far larger than that of *La Luna*. *La Luna* sought to change Madrid by altering its readers' views of the city, and by encouraging them to take an active part in city life. Though this strategy was in part conditioned by the magazine's very nature (as an independent publication with, at least initially, relatively modest economic means and little influence, it is difficult to see how it could have been effective at other levels), the fact that those working on *La Luna* refused to articulate a general urban renewal programme in the manner of, for instance, the Situationists, also points to their implicit understanding that any real transformation of city life had to take place from the bottom up. As Javier Olivares has explained,

> Cada una [de estas revistas: *La Luna de Madrid* (1983–1988), *Madrid me mata* (1984–1985) y *Madriz* (1984–1987)] a su manera, se inventaron una ciudad que todavía no era europea ni moderna pero que anhelaba serlo. Y mientras el mundo volvía los ojos hacia ella, Madrid se improvisaba cada día en el kiosco de prensa. (Cadahía 2007: 43–44)
>
> [Each of them [the magazines *La Luna de Madrid* (1983–1988), *Madrid me mata* (1984–1985) and *Madriz* (1984–1987)] in their own way invented a city that was not yet European or modern, but that longed to be those things. And while the world turned its eyes towards it, Madrid was being improvised daily at the newspaper stand.] (Cadahía 2007: 43–44)

The last phrase of this excerpt, 'Madrid se improvisaba cada día en el kiosco de prensa', is particularly revealing. The choice of the verb 'improvise' suggests that the city was not merely being reimagined or reinvented; it implies a degree of agency, albeit of a spontaneous and temporary nature. However, the act of improvisation is not seen as taking place at the level of the magazines themselves, which, as Olivares notes, merely 'invented' a new city, but at the level of the kiosk or newsagent, that is, at the point where the interaction between the publications and its readers took place. In other words, *La Luna* offered reimaginations of what Madrid could be, but these new visions of the city could only be actualized by the magazine's readers.

The programme of urban renewal implemented by Madrid's municipal authorities, on the other hand, was characterized by top-down interventions from the local authorities in different realms of city life, such as the restoration of monuments and historical buildings, the improvement of transport facilities and means of access to the city centre, and the organization and sponsorship of cultural events. Though these interventions substantially improved many *madrileños*' quality of life, succeeded in establishing a new image for the city, and helped popularize *la movida*, they also had other, less positive, effects. As Manuel Castells's (1983) study on Madrid's Citizen Movement illustrates, Madrid's administration failed to engage the grassroots neighbourhood associations that had been instrumental in achieving urban renewal and political change during the 1970s, and which, by the early 1980s, according to Castells, had come to be seen by the main political parties as 'a potential challenge to their overwhelming electoral superiority' and as 'a platform manipulated by communists and radicals' (1983: 273). Along similar lines, Stapell's otherwise positive analysis of Tierno's administration's 'remaking' of Madrid nevertheless concedes that 'the promotion of active participation and peaceful coexistence through cultural activity came at a political price' (2010: 197). Both Castells and Stapell agree that the municipal project for urban change, because of its top-down approach and its favouring of the cultural over the political, ultimately contributed to neutralize the political activity and capabilities of grassroots groups which had played an active and decisive role during the 1970s. In cultural terms, the administration's support for creative initiatives also led to some (possibly unintended) negative outcomes. On the one hand, municipal sponsorship of certain concerts and publications made it more difficult for those wishing to remain independent to compete. Several *movida* participants have remarked that municipal subsidies contributed to inflate artists' salaries artificially, particularly in the case of musicians

(Compitello and Larson 1997). Along similar lines, Javier Domingo describes the launch of the municipally sponsored comics magazine *Madriz* in 1984 as an act of unfair competition, inasmuch as this title, thanks to public financial backing, could afford to sell at a fraction of its production cost (Domingo 1989). More generally, the administration's support for and promotion of *la movida*, though beneficial for the movement in the short term, for it provided the funding for and increased the visibility of a range of events and initiatives (concerts, festivals, debates, exhibitions, publications, and more) that would have otherwise been either unviable or gone largely unnoticed, also allowed local authorities to appropriate, take credit for and manipulate what had essentially begun as a spontaneous urban movement — a process of co-option which ultimately led to *la movida*'s discredit and demise.

The top-down approach of Tierno Galván's project for urban change in Madrid, with its implicit belief in its ability single-handedly and rationally to mould a new identity for the city, confirms Susan Larson's description of the administration's programme as a fundamentally modernist project (2003), characterized, as Hamilton Stapell has remarked, by an 'unquestioned faith' in 'reason, progress, and a utopic destiny' (2010: 39–40). In contrast, underlying *La Luna*'s attempts to reinvent Madrid was an understanding that the process of reimagining and reclaiming the city was an ongoing one, without possible closure. This awareness of the impossibility of ever finalizing such a process stems, in part, from the recognition that urban space simultaneously shapes and is shaped by its inhabitants, and that this process, by virtue of its dialectical nature, and because it is also conditioned by a range of other forces (economic, social and political), is constantly evolving. Further, as shown in the section *La Jungla de Madrid*, those working on the magazine acknowledged that not all the forces involved in the process of shaping the city can be understood in rational terms; violent, irrational, and repressed pulsations are also at play within urban space. The recognition of permanent fluctuations within the process of urban redefinition, and of the existence of irrational forces at play within it, led those working on *La Luna* to consider the remaking of Madrid a process that could not be entirely controlled by any one agent, but that might, at best, be influenced in a certain direction. Hence, rather than promulgate a comprehensive programme of radical urban change, those working on *La Luna* tried to affect their urban reality by local, small-scale interventions — through the production of a new urban imaginary, and by encouraging its readers to become active participants in city life. *La Luna*'s approach to urban transformation, with its implicit understanding of urban reality as uncontrollable flux, its acknowledgement of the limitations to any one form of intervention in the city, and its attempts to effect change through limited and localized intervention, echoes postmodernism's questioning of the flaws and limitations of the modernist project's faith in the potential of human reason and technological progress to bring about universally and unequivocally positive transformations.

Both *La Luna*'s urban reimaginings and the urban renewal programme implemented by Madrid's local authorities constituted attempts at constructing a new identity for the city, and, by extension, for its inhabitants. But while Madrid's administration saw this process of identity reformulation as a finite process, and one whose eventual outcome could be entirely and rationally determined and controlled by the city's municipal authorities, those working on *La Luna* acknowledged the open-ended, dynamic and unpredictable nature of such processes of identity de- and reconstruction. In essence, then, one of the fundamental differences between *La Luna*'s attempts to reinvent the city and the official programme for the transformation of Madrid, which provides a wider context of urban change within and against which we can situate the magazine's project, is the notion of identity at the core of each of these initiatives. If the concept of identity underlying the administration's programme for change considered identity a stable entity, albeit one that could be shaped and manipulated by those in power (a view that situates their project within modernist thought parameters), *La Luna*, as will be discussed in more detail in the following chapter, conceived of identity as an open-ended, dynamic, fluid and fluctuating process, subject to and conditioned by a diverse range of interdependent factors.

Notes to Chapter 2

1. This section is signed with the pseudonym 'Mieldeluna', thus obscuring the identity of its author or authors. However, in his contribution to the catalogue of the 2007 exhibition *La Luna de Madrid y otras revistas de vanguardia de los años 80*, Vicente Patón affirms that he was involved in the making of at least some of the 'Recortables' (Cadahía 2007: 36–37); and Patón confirmed to me in email correspondence (October 2014) that he had used Mieldeluna as a pseudonym, and that this section was produced by him in collaboration with Rodrigo Muñoz Ballester.
2. Vicente Patón is listed as 'Jefe de Sección (Grafismo)' [Section Head (Graphic Design)] in the index page of *La Luna*'s first two issues, and from issue three as 'Jefe de Sección (Grafismo y Arquitectura)' [Section Head (Graphic Design and Architecture]. From issue 21, following the editorial schism that led to the departure of the first editor Borja Casani, he no longer featured as a permanent member of the editorial team, although he contributed an article to issue 23 (66). He is the author or co-author (with Manuel Blanco) of the main feature of this section in issues 1–5, 7–19 and 23.
3. Although the architecture section focuses primarily on everyday elements of the urban landscape (blocks of flats and offices, urban regeneration schemes) rather than on the city's landmarks, the importance of the latter is explicitly acknowledged in Manuel Blanco's impassioned defence of Madrid's Plaza Cibeles in issue 17 (72).
4. The concept of postmodernism was featured prominently in *La Luna*'s pages from the magazine's first issue, which included a long editorial by Borja Casani and José Tono Martínez entitled 'Madrid 1984: ¿la posmodernidad? (1: 6–8). The final chapter of this book traces the magazine's engagement and evolving relationship with postmodern ideas and practices.
5. Michel Foucault, for instance, argues that in a society, it is the ensemble of 'different bodies of learning, philosophical ideas, everyday opinions, but also institutions, commercial practices, police activities, mores [...] what makes possible at a given moment the appearance of a theory, an opinion, a practice' (Drolet 2004: 67).
6. The existence of a connection between built environment and personal development is expressed in particularly explicit terms by Manuel Blanco in his critique of Madrid's school buildings: schools, he claims, are 'un lugar donde un niño puede descubrir lo que quiere ser de mayor. Y eso no se aprende tan sólo en los libros sino también del espacio que lo rodea' [a place in which a child can discover what he might want to be when he grows up. And that is something which is not only achieved through books, but also through the surrounding space] (issue 18: 84).
7. Constant never completed New Babylon, a vast multimedia ensemble which consisted of drawings, models, paintings and text, and which was featured in an exhibition of the same title at The Hague's Gemeentemuseum in 1974.

8. Catherine de Zegher suggests that New Babylon was never finished because Constant eventually 'foresaw the destructive part of his proposed environment [...]. As liberating as the first demonstration of a new city may have seemed in opposition to functionalist architecture, so repressive the high-tech labyrinthine "construction of atmosphere" may have become in the end' (Zegher and Wigley 2011: 11).
9. An article based on my analysis of Rodrigo Muñoz Ballester's *Manuel* was published under the title 'Sex and the City: Urban Eroticism in Rodrigo Muñoz Ballester's *Manuel* series' in *Hispanic Research Journal* vol. 14 no. 5, October 2013, 394–408.
10. Although since its publication in *La Luna*, *Manuel* has become a cult comic, republished in an extended version under the title *Manuel no está solo* by Sins Entido in 2005, its author is not known primarily as a comic author, but as a multi-disciplinary visual artist, whose later work includes a series of murals for some of Metro Madrid's newer stations, such as Aeropuerto Barajas, Colombia and Nuevos Ministerios.
11. To my knowledge, the only in-depth critical analyses of *Manuel* to date are Paul Julian Smith's 2006 essay '*La movida* relocated' and Michael Preston Harrison's 2009 doctoral dissertation, 'Comics as Text and Comics as Culture. Queer Spain through the Lens of a Marginalized Medium', at University of California, Irvine, which devotes one of its chapters to an analysis of Rodrigo Muñoz Ballester's comic. While Harrison's work considers the spatial dimension of *Manuel*, his analysis is primarily concerned with the development of queer identities in post-Franco Spain.
12. This law, which branded homosexuals as socially dangerous elements and made provisions for their prosecution and 'rehabilitation' through their internment in special centres, was passed in 1970 and parts of it remained in force until 1995. However, those paragraphs of the law concerned with homosexual practices were repealed in 1979. For more information, see Javier Ugarte's 2008 study *Una discriminación universal: la homosexualidad bajo el franquismo y la transición* (Barcelona: Egales Editorial).
13. The comic artists Nuevo and Plasti are credited in the instalment published in issue 3 as 'artistas invitados', although it is not made clear which of them authored which frame. There are two frames within issue 3 (one on page 40, one on page 41) that are executed in a clearly different style from the rest of the segment. A comparison of this frame and other work by the artist suggests that Nuevo authored the frame on page 40. Plasti must therefore have authored the frame on page 41.
14. This sequence is preceded by a segment in which the protagonist adopts a remarkable resemblance to the Dick Bogarde of Visconti's 1971 film adaptation of *Death in Venice*, so the character's visual collapse in this frame could be read as a metaphorical disintegration that results from his obsessive pursuit of Manuel.
15. Pablo Peinado refers to these visual citations in more detail in his introduction to the 2005 book edition of the series (8–9).
16. *La Luna*'s first editor, Borja Casani, explained that, during the process of setting up the magazine, the editorial team chose 'un lema pragmático y humilde: "Hay otros mundos pero están en éste" [a pragmatic and humble motto: "There are other worlds, but they are in this one"] (Cadahía 2007: 21). This motto appeared in the first issue of *La Luna* as a heading to the editorial piece entitled 'Madrid 1984: ¿la posmodernidad?' (1: 6–8).
17. In the same text in which Casani refers to the motto of the magazine, he states that 'Nunca he sabido quién dijo esa frase, sólo sé que muchas veces me ha servido de acicate y de consuelo' [I never knew who coined the sentence, but it often offered me encouragement and consolation] (Cadahía 2007: 21), which suggests he was not aware of the Surrealist origin of the phrase.
18. While Walker attributes the phrase to Éluard (and the translation given above is his), its origin and exact wording remain contested. Variants of the quotation include 'Un autre monde est possible mais il est dans celui-ci' [Another world is possible but it is in this one] and other authors, including the Mexican Octavio Paz, appear to have articulated their own variations without explicitly citing or acknowledging an awareness of Éluard's line. Hence the tentative phrasing.
19. This section was published intermittently in *La Luna*. It appeared in issues 1–7; issue 9/10; issues 16–20; and issues 34/35–41.

20. Examples of incorporation of *fait divers*, or of items inspired by this news category, in Surrealist reviews include an unsigned piece entitled 'Un faux médecin', published in the first number of the second period of *Littérature* (March 1922); press reports of suicides regularly included in *La Révolution surréaliste*; or the text by Paul Éluard and Benjamin Péret appeared in issue 5 of *Le Surréalisme au Service de la Révolution* (May 1933) in response to the Papin affair, the crime of two sisters who battered their employers to death, which attracted extensive press coverage in France at the time. A further article by Jacques Lacan in response to this crime, entitled 'Motifs du crime paranoïaque: le crime des sœurs Papin', was published in the third issue of the Surrealist review *Minotaure* (December 1933).
21. This episode may be seen as reminiscent of Dalí's painting 'Cannibalism in Autumn' (1936–1937). Although Dalí's painting is likely to have been inspired by the violence of the Spanish Civil War, its depiction of two decomposing figures (one seemingly male and one apparently female) feeding off each other, and the reference to autumn in the title, with its symbolic connotations of old age and decay, suggest that the painting, like Madrid's story, could also be read as a reflection on the corrosive nature of the unconditionally permanent cohabitation legally and socially enforced through marriage.
22. Juan Madrid's characterisation of violence as not only a response or challenge to the system, but also a mechanism for its perpetuation may have also been influenced by his own experience of growing up under Francoism, a repressive dictatorship that used violent means to suppress opposition.
23. My hypothesis that *La Luna* was not read in a linear fashion is also reinforced by the way in which the magazine's contents page was set up. Rather than a simple list of items sorted in order of appearance (i.e. linearly), *La Luna*'s contents page offered two separate and complimentary indexes: a general index which included items not encompassed within the magazine's topical sections (e.g. columns by regular contributors, opinion pieces, interviews, comics); and a section index listing the magazine's sections (music, art, fashion, architecture, cinema, sport, literature, etc.). Because the contents of both indexes are interspersed within the magazine's pages, even the contents page defies linearity, with noticeable jumps (in terms of the page number) between the items listed.
24. Juan Madrid, Eduardo Haro Ibars and Fernando Savater were all actively involved in clandestine anti-Francoist militancy activities during the late 1960s and 1970s. However, unlike other members of their generation, who went on to occupy positions of political power and/or economic influence with the advent of democracy, all three remained staunchly independent and, in the cases of Ibars and Madrid, profoundly critical of the neo-liberal, capitalist model of democracy adopted by Spain.
25. This exclusion of items from the contents page is frequent, and there are examples in virtually every number of *La Luna*. In issue 2, for instance, the following items do not appear in the contents page: an unsigned sketch (2: 29); an illustration by Fernando Vicente (2: 30); an illustration by Ceesepe (2: 47); a photomontage by Pablo Pérez-Mínguez (2: 48); and the 'encuesta' or inquiry 'Mi primera experiencia sexual' (2: 51).
26. In issue 2, for example, the section 'A la recherche du champs [sic] perdu' is wrongly listed as appearing on page 13, when it is in fact published on page 26; and in issue 14 the section 'Tengo una debilidad' is listed as appearing on page 6, when it is in fact published on pages 4–5. In issue 3, a content listed as 'Ocurrió en Madrid' in the contents page changes its title to 'Madrid me mata' (3: 66), while in issue 2 Fernando Savater's article is listed as 'Intimidad del teórico', when in fact its title on the relevant page is 'Placeres inconfesables del renunciamiento' (2: 31).
27. At its peak, *La Luna* sold around 30,000 copies, an unprecedented figure for an arts title, as second editor José Tono Martínez has argued (Cadahía 2007: 13). However, the immense influence the magazine wielded, reflected, for instance in the fact that its founding members were soon offered the opportunity to contribute to mainstream media, as the first editor Borja Casani has recounted (Gallero 1991: 9), was not commensurate with its readership.
28. The resignifying ability of urban spatial practices finds a paradigmatic example in the adoption in the early 1980s of the term *movida* as the label used to refer to Madrid's countercultural circles. As Paloma Chamorro -presenter of the TV programme *La Edad de Oro* (1983–1985) and a key *movida* figure- recalls, in the 1970s the word *movida* was used as slang to describe a spontaneous

expedition to Madrid's Rastro area in search of hashish by two friends who happened to chance upon each other in the street, at a concert, or at an exhibition (Chamorro in Gallero 1991: 179). A term originally coined to refer to a very specific type of urban spatial practice engaged in by a minority thus eventually came to designate an entire (counter)cultural movement.

29. Sheringham's study traces the emergence and development of the tradition of the everyday in French culture, starting with Surrealism and the critical approaches of Blanchot and Lefebvre, and also analysing the contributions of Situationism, Roland Barthes, Michel de Certeau and Georges Perec to the subject. In the final two chapters, the author considers the proliferation of the everyday in French discourse from 1980 to the present day, looking at the work of authors and artists such as Jean Echenoz and Sophie Calle.
30. Despite his stated intention of focusing only on discourses and practices of the everyday in France, Sheringham also discusses the contributions of Heidegger, Lukács, Adorno and Benjamin to the field, noting their influence upon French theorists and artists. Sheringham's ultimate inability to restrict his study to one country and one language is perhaps symptomatic of the everyday's ubiquity (its simultaneously being everywhere and nowhere); and of its porosity, which makes any strict setting of boundaries (whether linguistic, national or disciplinary) virtually impossible.
31. Juan Antonio Andrade Blanco suggests that the consensus politics of Spain's transitional process led to the moderation of the policies and rhetoric of the two main anti-Francoist parties, the Partido Comunista de España (PCE) and the Partido Socialista Obrero Español (PSOE), arguing that '[e]l fracaso de la ruptura democrática llevó a la izquierda a negociar con el gobierno posfranquista el ritmo y la intensidad de los cambios, pero también con su propia integración en el futuro sistema. La dinámica reformista [de la Transición] funcionó en este sentido como un filtro ideológico. El PCE, por ejemplo, sufrió una importante coacción ideológica para obtener la legalización, en virtud de la cual tuvo que neutralizar su identidad republicana' [the failure of the democratic break model led the left to negotiate with the post-Francoist government the rhythm and degree of change, and its own integration in the future system. The reformist dynamics [of the transitional process] worked, in that sense, as an ideological filter. The PCE, for instance, suffered from considerable ideological pressure in order to achieve its legalisation, and to that end it had to neutralise its Republican identity] (Andrade Blanco 2012: 422).
32. Barcelona underwent a similar, arguably more comprehensive process of urban renewal from the late 1970s and onto the 1990s. Scholars such as Antonio Sánchez (2007), Joan Ramón Resina (2008) and Mari Paz Balibrea (2001) have written extensively on Barcelona's transformation from modern industrial centre to postmodern international tourism and leisure destination. While Sánchez sees Barcelona's transformation as a positive example of the progressive potential of postmodern pragmatism, Balibrea and Resina are critical of what they regard as the commodification and branding of public urban spaces. To my knowledge, there has not yet been a comparative study of urban regeneration processes in Madrid and Barcelona, although a comparative analysis of the Plan General de Ordenación Urbana de Madrid (1985) and its contemporary *Reconstrucció de Barcelona* (1985) could be a productive starting point for such a project.
33. Carnival celebrations were banned during Franco's dictatorship, but were reinstated in Madrid by Tierno Galván's administration in 1980.
34. For more details of the politics of consensus during Spain's transition to democracy, see Carme Molinero's 2006 edited volume *La Transición, treinta años después* (Barcelona: Ediciones Península).
35. 1986 marked Spain's integration into the European Economic Community and confirmed the Socialist Party's absolute majority in Parliament at the general election held on 22 June of that year.

CHAPTER 3

❖

La Luna de Madrid's Destabilization of Identity: Gender, Nationality, and the Individual

As was shown in the previous chapter, *La Luna* configured its own editorial space in an analogous manner to that of the (post)modern city, with participation, movement and the pursuit of pleasure as not only recurring themes, but also structuring principles and practices that helped navigate and make sense of the magazine's widely diverse output, often chaotic layouts and highly eclectic visual style. *La Luna*'s preoccupation with the city is, in fact, closely related to its understanding of identity as open-ended process, as flux: individuals, like urban spaces, are seen as distinctly defined, and yet constantly changing, always in the process of becoming. Further, city and individual shape each other; citizens can and do contribute to shape their city — if not directly affecting its material constitution, then at least having an effect on how public space is perceived and used. Reciprocally, as Fincher and Jacobs remind us, 'people's relationships with places help construct their identities' (Fincher and Jacobs 1998: 20). Urban space and identity within *La Luna* will be therefore considered as two separate thematic and conceptual poles, although the links between space and identity formation are made manifest by the recurring, often subtle, allusions to space and place which will be examined in this chapter.

La Luna's parody of traditional notions of gender and of national symbols and clichés testifies to efforts to deconstruct old identity paradigms. This challenge to established models of gender, sexuality and nationhood does not constitute an attempt to construct and present a new identity; rather, the magazine's undermining of widely accepted identity categories is coupled with a refusal to formulate any clear alternatives. *La Luna*'s destabilization of identity thus goes beyond the rejection of a series of dated gender and national stereotypes and their replacement with a new set of identity models, and extends to a broader questioning of the very notion of identity (or rather, identities in the plural), as stable, unchanging, monolithic essences. The treatment of identity in *La Luna* suggests an understanding of identity as a fluid, performative and open-ended process of de- and reconstruction. Further, the explorations of identity that take place within the magazine's pages often entail a simultaneous questioning of the mechanisms and limits of (self-)representation.

This view of identity as elusive and polymorphous flux implicit in *La Luna*'s pages and the parallel inquiry into modes of (self-)representation can be related to the postmodern theories emerging during the 1970s and 1980s. *La Luna*'s engagement with postmodernism, discussed in detail in the fourth chapter of this book, suggests that, even if not directly aware of the polemic around identity taking place within Western critical discourse at the time, those working for the magazine were at least familiar with some of the theories and ideas that led to the emergence of those debates. It is also worth noting that several *movida* cultural products have been retrospectively described as queer *avant la lettre*.[1]

The understanding of identity as process also affects the way in which *La Luna* articulates its own editorial identity, or rather the ways in which it resists such an articulation — opting, instead, deliberately to position itself at the juncture of established categories, such as glossy/fanzine, underground/mainstream and global/local. The final part of this chapter considers the strategies the magazine uses in order to resist a clear and closed definition, and how its notion of identity affects its constitution and trajectory.

Destabilizing identity in *La Luna*

From the very first issue of *La Luna*, the magazine's preoccupation with identity and identity categories becomes obvious. This inaugural number launches three of the regular series (*Autorretratos*, *Patty Diphusa* and *Luz de Boudoïr*, the latter renamed *Somos unas señoras* in issues 11, 12 and 14) which constitute the focus of this analysis of how identity is destabilized in *La Luna*'s pages. These three series question different presuppositions and categories that determine our understanding of identity: the individual as the immutable anchor for identity in the case of *Autorretratos*; gender identity and sexual orientation (and the correspondences that can be established between those two categories) in the case of *Patty Diphusa*; and female and feminine identities in *Luz de Boudoir/Somos unas señoras*. Although the subject of identity is also explored in individual art works and articles throughout the magazine's existence,[2] the chosen sections are particularly significant since, by virtue of their serialized nature, they illustrate the tensions, contradictions and ambiguities that underlie the magazine's approach to individual, gender and sexual identities. While there is no one section or series within *La Luna* that specifically addresses the question of national identity (or identities in the plural), there is a wealth of elements (drawings, photos, articles) throughout the magazine that bear witness to an enduring fascination with symbols associated with traditional Spanishness: bullfighting, Catholic religious imagery, Spanish popular musical genres such as flamenco and *copla*, and traditional folkloric dress items such as the *mantilla* and the fan. The magazine's approach to the notion of Spanishness fluctuates between a humorous, self-conscious caricaturing of the notion of national 'otherness' with respect to the rest of the Western world instigated over decades by the Francoist propaganda apparatus,[3] and a reclaiming of some of the elements, such as flamenco and bullfighting, upon which the image of Spain as exotic and other was built.

Identity, more specifically individual personal identity, is the subject or thematic core of issue 5 of the magazine. This edition features different approximations to the concept of "yo" ("I") in a compactly laid-out, double-page spread. The unusual density of text in these pages is perhaps intended to reflect the conceptual density of the subject discussed. José Luis Brea links the emergence of 'un individualismo feroz' (5: 6) to the postmodern loss of faith in the great meta-narratives and values of the past, and regards this new individualism as an opportunity to generate what he terms 'nuevos modelos de legitimación pública' (5: 6), open to difference and dissent as they will no longer rely on one-dimensional modernist reason. Javier Sádaba points to the unknowability of the "I" by the individual, who can never gain the necessary distance to have a full view of his or her identity. Further, Sádaba contends that multiple "I"s coexist within each of us, a multiplicity which we can either chose to suppress or ignore (at the price of becoming 'imbeciles'), or which we can acknowledge — a step that involves accepting that identity as a singular, unified and coherent entity is a fiction that exists only in our imaginations. Sádaba favours the second approach, though he warns that it risks leading us to the verge of madness (5: 7). Eduardo Subirats considers the historical-contextual dimension of processes of 'individualization' and 'de-individualization', indicating how modernity can be seen to have had a 'de-individualizing' effect, as scientific-technological advances and the freer flow of individuals, ideas and capital eroded the historical-geographical grounding of personal identity. But paradoxically, he argues, the 'mass society' that resulted from those processes of modernization relies, for its survival, upon a heightened degree of individualization, in the sense of diversity and personal inventiveness and mobility. Finally, in a highly personal account entitled 'Carne de presidio', Eleuterio Sánchez, better known by his nickname of 'El Lute', a quasi-folkloric figure within Spain since the 1960s, reflects with bafflement upon his own trajectory from imprisoned, reoffending criminal and social outcast to popular hero by virtue of his repeated jailbreaks and his outspoken denunciation of social injustice (5: 6).[4]

The incorporation of the piece by Sánchez creates an interesting contrast to the other three pieces, penned by three young intellectuals[5] and of a markedly theoretical and academic tone. Sánchez's transformation from criminal to folk hero highlights the multiplicity and plasticity of identity, its changeable and unstable nature. But his testimony also reminds us of the role of others in shaping and reshaping how we are perceived and how, in turn, we perceive ourselves. In his case, this external influence is made more obvious and magnified by his status as a public media figure. His contribution can thus be read as an illustration of some of the themes approached in the other pieces from a theoretical perspective, and also serves as counterpoint and balance to the other articles. Further, this juxtaposition of critical writing by emerging thinkers and of personal testimony by a charismatic popular figure is characteristic of *La Luna*'s inclusive and eclectic approach to intellectual debate. Another noticeable feature of this topical spread is that there is no unifying thesis or view underlying the pieces published; rather, they approach the subject of identity from different angles and stress different aspects: individualism's liberating potential in Brea's case, the multiplicity of the "I" in Sádaba's, and the historical conditions that contribute to 'individualization' in Subirats'. The articles complement each other, but they do not offer any closure or resolution. Instead, their aim appears to be to underline the relevance and complexity of the topic. There is some tentative position taking (a tacit and cautious optimism regarding the creative and intellectual possibilities the exploration of identities can open up, and a belief that the present and immediate future will prove conducive to such experiments), but the authors' tone is far from programmatic. This non-dogmatic approach is coherent with the views expressed with regard to identity, for, if individuals' self-knowledge is always incomplete and constrained by external factors, as is argued here, then it follows that every utterance is of necessity equally limited in its validity and applicability. Though consistent with the theories formulated in the texts, this implicit admission of the contingency of any belief or opinion can, as we shall see later in this chapter, prove problematic, as it leads to a relativism that limits the scope for collective agency. In other words, if a belief can no longer be regarded as holding universal truth value, but is seen as the view of a particular individual who may not (or cannot be expected to) hold that same opinion beyond a specific spatio-temporal context, beyond a particular moment in time, then political agency, understood as a collective pursuit of a set of agreed goals, risks becoming compromised.

Individual identity and self-representation

The photographic self-portraits of the *Autorretratos* section published in the first 12 issues of *La Luna*, characterized, with a few exceptions (1: 23, 3: 23 and 6: 23), by their playfulness and theatricality, are a further example of the magazine's focus on the exploration of personal identity (or rather identities, in the plural). In issue 2, the portrayed subject and author of the image, Juan Ramón Yuste, uses photographic manipulation in order to depict himself simultaneously in the process of posing for and of taking the picture (2: 23; Figure 3.1). Within a conventional domestic setting, the portrayed subject appears doubled. To the left of the image, his posing self can be seen sitting on a sofa, looking ahead so that his gaze meets that of the viewer, whilst his photographing self is depicted to the right of the image, on the other end of the sofa, while taking the picture of the other figure. The unfolding of the portrait's subject into portrayed and portraying figure can be read as an attempt to capture the creative process, a physical impossibility since we, as viewers, can never witness that process, but only its result, the finished work. Even when an image self-reflexively comments upon its coming into being, as is the case here, this commentary cannot step beyond the realm of representation, it cannot be dissociated from the work itself. This impossibility to transcend representation, to allow readers/viewers to see beyond the frame of the image, in fact underlines the illusory immediacy and naturalness of all representation, including that of a mimetic type, unmasking it as construct. By depicting himself simultaneously posing for and taking the picture, Yuste does not create the illusion that we, as viewers, are witnessing the 'making-of' the portrait, but rather, the presence of camera and photographer in the image subtly and indirectly allude to the necessary, if invisible, presence of a second camera which enables us to see the two figures simultaneously. And it is

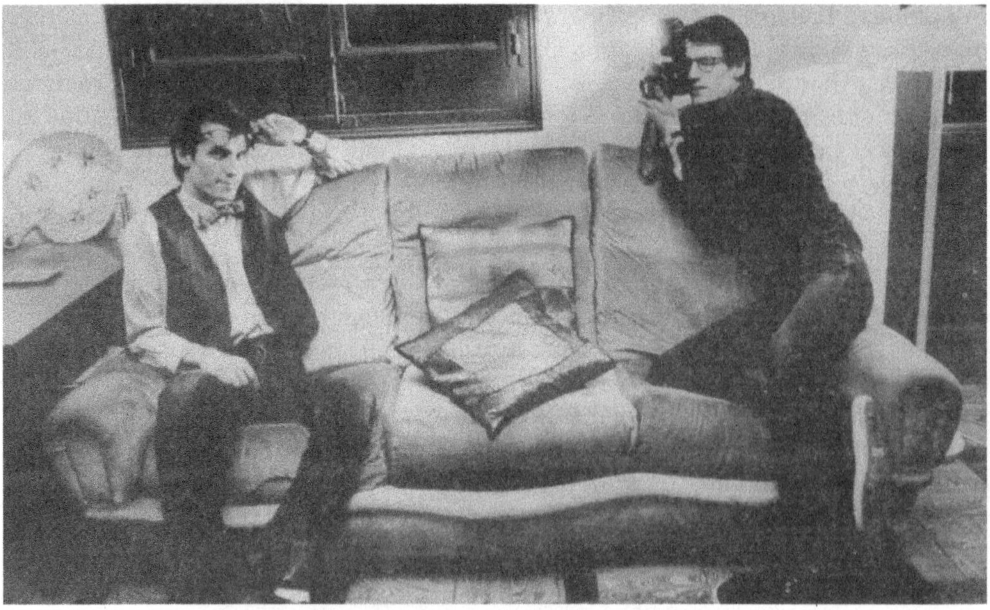

Fig. 3.1. Self-portrait by Juan Ramón Yuste
© Juan Ramón Yuste

this allusion to a realm beyond the image that reinforces its borders, that reminds us, as viewers, that the photograph does not merely capture 'life as it is', or, in this case, the individual as he is, but that there is a concealed degree of construction and fabrication behind even the most seemingly mimetic or objective representation. This point is reinforced in the text that accompanies the self-portrait, as Yuste muses about a friend's surprise at his photographic image, which to him, 'demasiado acostumbrado a la imagen invertida que de nosotros devuelven los espejos' [too accustomed to the inverted image of us offered by mirrors] (2: 23), appeared false, as it showed him 'the wrong way around' ('al revés').

The unfolding of Yuste within the image into portrayed and portraying individual can also be interpreted as an allusion to the splitting of the self into subject (an active conscience making sense of the world and of itself) and object (an entity as perceived by others). While the tradition of self-portraiture bears witness to individuals' ability to perceive themselves as objects, as artists have through the ages used themselves as their object of representation, Yuste's photograph addresses the impossibility of the individual seeing itself as perceiving subject while s/he considers itself as object. The photographer in the image becomes, by virtue of his inclusion in the picture, a further object of representation, and the actual representing subject, whose vantage point we as viewers share, remains invisible, unrepresentable, beyond the frame of the photograph. This limit of representation, and, specifically, of self-representation, made manifest in this image is linked to the limit of our knowledge with regard to identity: the perceiving subject who depicts itself as portrayed object cannot represent itself as perceiving subject because s/he cannot see or know itself as such. Thus, the vanishing point of the photograph, which coincides with the position which we viewers occupy, refers also to the blind spot of identity, to that which remains unknowable to the individual about itself.

Yuste's use of doubling is reminiscent of a strategy widely used by the Surrealists. In her essay 'The Photographic Conditions of Surrealism', Rosalind Krauss argues that doubling is the most important strategy used by the Surrealists in photography, since '[t]hrough duplication, it [doubling] opens the original to the effect of difference, of deferral, of one-thing-after-another, or within another: of multiples burgeoning within the same' (Krauss 1981: 25). Further, Krauss suggests that the strategy of doubling is particularly effective in photography because of the special, even privileged, status of photography with regard to reality: because photography is assumed to be an objective, neutral medium; a 'deposit of the real itself' (1981: 26), doubling in photography succeeds in communicating what Krauss describes as the quintessentially surreal experience of 'reality as representation' (1981: 28). The text that accompanies Yuste's self-portrait, written by the author of the image, evidences a desire to underline this special relationship of photography with the real. In it, Yuste describes the coming into being of the photograph as the result of a mysterious and unexplained occurrence that escapes his understanding. His words do not invalidate my analysis of his picture; on the contrary: the photograph's implicit critique of the reliability of representation, or rather of our tacit acceptance of representation as reality, depends on Yuste's claim that his work is a faithful, mimetic depiction of a real instant. The ambiguities and oscillations between the reality and its representation, between the individual as representing subject and as object of representation, which confer this image its complexity and power of fascination, would be immediately dispelled were he to acknowledge and explain the technical means used to produce the doubling effect in the image. Yuste's tongue-in-cheek closing remarks stating that he has written to Professor Jung[6] and The Police (the 1980s rock band) requesting that they detail their theory of synchronicity, which, he suggests, may provide some clues to help solve the mystery of his doubling within the image, are characteristic of *La Luna*'s (and, more broadly, the *movida*'s) irreverent mix of high and popular cultural elements,[7] and further suggest that the text should not be read as an analysis that clarifies the many possible meanings of the image, but rather, as a device that deliberately and playfully complicates and equivocates them.

While Yuste's portrait makes use of a device commonly deployed by the Surrealists in order, like them, to question the demarcation between reality and representation, the visual effect of doubling in his self-portrait is noticeably different from that of surrealist works. In images such as Hans Bellmer's *La Poupée* (1934) or a photograph by Man Ray published in the first issue of *La Révolution Surréaliste* (1924),[8] the doubling is effected over a fragment of the (female) body — legs in Bellmer's case, breasts in Man Ray's. Leaving aside the fetishist implications of their focus on specific female body parts, the effect of doubling in these examples is unsettling, uncanny: the disembodied and proliferating body parts have a quasi-monstrous quality. Proliferation has a threatening quality to it, not least because it appears to compromise bodily integrity. By contrast, Yuste's use of doubling has a playful effect: readers or viewers do not feel shocked or repulsed, but curious; it is intriguing, rather than shocking. These differences are symptomatic of a wider shift from modernism to postmodernism. The Surrealists celebrated and exploited many of the possibilities opened up by modernity, as evidenced by their engagement with the then nascent technique of psychoanalysis or their use of relatively new media such as cinematography. But their response to modernity was guarded in some respects: the danger and fear of madness and dissolution is frequently addressed explicitly, or implicitly alluded to, in much Surrealist writing and painting.[9] In comparison, Yuste's depiction of reality as representation (or, indeed, as simulacrum) is entirely ludic and celebratory, free from the anxieties underlying many Surrealist works. The Surrealists' anxiety is symptomatic of their implicit belief in the existence of a stable, integral core to human beings, often identified with the subconscious, the unity and stability of which is seen as threatened by external forces. While Yuste does not necessarily eschew notions such as conscious and subconscious, internal and external, or self and other, he complicates them by questioning the nature, stability and permeability of the boundaries that shape such dichotomies. But this blurring of boundaries, which also entails a general and generalized loss of certitude, as the accuracy and relevance of classificatory and epistemological categories is thrown into question, does not seem traumatic, perhaps because in the postmodern context within which Yuste is working, the multiplicity, instability and flux associated with the experience of modernity are no longer perceived as threats, but as creative opportunities. Surrealism's convulsively (and, one senses, somewhat reluctantly) de-centred subject is thus replaced here by a playful, joyfully multi-centred postmodern subject.

In issue 5 we find a different, though similarly playful, game of visual planes and illusions. Antonio Suárez's self-portrait shows the photographer reflected in a round wall mirror (5: 25). The use of mirrors in self-portraiture is common, with artists often painting or photographing themselves as they appear in a mirror. However, whereas the mirror is normally obliterated from the portrait, and used only as an aid that allows the artist to either see or capture his/her reflection,[10] in this case the mirror is turned into the central motif of the photograph. Not only do we see the mirror, but also the wall surrounding it, so that we as viewers are immediately made aware of the coexistence of two visual planes or levels: that framed by the borders of the image, within which we see the wall containing the mirror, and that framed by the mirror itself, in which the rest of the room and the photographer are reflected. The photographer appears wearing reflective sunglasses, the reflection of which creates an additional visual level or surface, thus establishing a complex, multiple-level *mise en abyme* — the mirror reflecting the photographer whose glasses, in turn, reflect the mirror, which contains his reflection. The oversized glasses not only introduce a new reflective surface into the image, but also significantly conceal the portrayed individual's face, thus rendering him a virtually anonymous character. This partial concealment of the portrayed object and the simultaneous playful proliferation of reflective surfaces can be read as a typically postmodern commentary on the fallacy of the existence of depth or meaning beneath any sign or surface, as the relatively opaque surfaces depicted here are shown to be reflecting their own reflections *ad infinitum*. However, the text that accompanies the image throws such a reading into question: 'A veces, los autorretratos cuentan mucho sobre uno mismo, la mayoría de esas veces, se rebelan contra ti, mostrando lo que tú no deseas que se sepa' [Sometimes, self-portraits say a lot about one, and more often than not they rebel against one, revealing that which you do not want others to know] (5: 25). The claim that self-portraits can reveal something which the author cannot choose or control seems to suggest that the play with surfaces we see here may in fact be a tactic to prevent or limit the exposure of what the author wishes to conceal ('lo que tú no deseas que se sepa'), rather than a postmodern negation of stable meaning. This ambivalence between what might appear a postmodern rejection of meaning, and its affirmation through a holding on to authorial subjectivity and agency, may seem contradictory. However, I would argue, with Linda Hutcheon, that postmodernism itself is 'a contradictory phenomenon that uses and abuses, installs and then subverts, the very concepts it challenges' (Hutcheon 1993: 243–44), and that, as such, it is characterized precisely by the type of oscillation between a negation and an affirmation of depth and meaning manifest in this self-portrait and its inscription.

Reflection and self-reflection are also key features of Javier Campano's self-portrait in issue 12. The image is taken in an outdoor, urban setting, with Campano's reflection as he takes the picture becoming visible on the side-mirror of what appears to be a kiosk (12: 31). His face is entirely obscured by the camera and his hands holding it up, but we can see the rest of his body, though the distance from which the image is taken does not allow us, as viewers, to appreciate much detail. Like Suárez in issue 5, the portrayed figure becomes here a non-identifiable, quasi-anonymous being, barely more distinct than the passers-by that appear in the background. The effect generated by the reflection is alluded to in the caption that accompanies the image: 'Yo-no-soy, a-él-se-le-ve-y-no-a-mí. No-es-más-que-la-luz' [I-am-not-him, you-can-see-him-and-not-me. It-is-just-the-light] (12: 31). These words once again insist on the distance and dissociation between self and reflection, portraying subject and portrayed object, reality and representation, alerting us, as viewers, to the illusory nature of what we see in the image. The caption, like the doubling into two figures in Yuste's photograph discussed above, is a mechanism that prevents us from unequivocally and unproblematically identifying the portrayed figure with the author of the image, introducing an area of slippage between the depicted individual and the author which suggests that the author is always already absent from the image, beyond representation. The distance alluded to here is none other than the distance between self-representation (which is what is ultimately at stake in the self-portraits), and identity. While self-representation (the way the individual perceives him/herself as object and presents him/herself to others) is revealed as always mediated, and thus unreliable, identity, understood here as the subjective agency that partly determines self-representation, and which allows for the type of self-reflexive commentary the discussed portraits display, can only be referred to as absence, as something that can perhaps be inferred or alluded to, but that cannot be known or rendered visible. This impossibility of knowing is not, however, bemoaned; on the contrary, these portraits appear to celebrate it, since it allows artists to abandon any pretence of realism or 'authenticity' in favour of more experimental and playful approaches.

Even those self-portraits which are not characterized by the presence of self-reflexive, self-referential elements display a heightened degree of performativity or theatricality. In issue 4, for example, Alberto García Alix's photograph shows him holding two knives, one of them placed over his eyes, which we cannot see. From the left margin of the picture, we see a female arm emerging, threateningly holding another knife over Alix (4: 23). In issue 7, Jesús Peraita appears submerged in a bath, but his hands are placed over his face so that we, as viewers, are left unable to determine the identity of the portrayed individual. We assume it is Peraita since it is he who signs the self-portrait, but we cannot establish it from the image itself (7: 25). In issue 11, Javier Vallhonrat can be seen suspended upside down in the company of two dogs (11: 37). In these instances, the questioning of the limits of representation and the allusions to the disjunction between self-representation and identity are less explicit, but can nevertheless be inferred from the deliberate obscuring of the portrayed individuals' faces, the most obvious and readable element for visual identification. Additionally, these images challenge the traditional generic conventions of self-portraiture because the objects of the portrait are not always recognisable or identifiable, and because in some cases the portrayed individual no longer appears as the central figure of the work, but becomes a mere element placed in a wider, often incongruous situation or setting.

The underlining of the staged and constructed nature of the self-portraits, either through self-reflexive means or through the use of unusual perspectives and settings, points to an awareness of the constructed and mediated nature of all representation, and of self-representation in particular. Such awareness throws into question the very stability and nature of individual identity itself. If the way in which an individual perceives itself and presents itself to others is subject to not entirely transparent processes of mediation, symbolization, and reproduction, which can be affected by external circumstances and altered by the individual itself, the very existence of an essential, unchanging kernel of identity becomes questionable. But while the theatrical nature of the self-portraits dissolves the illusion of immediacy and authenticity associated with traditional portraiture, unmasking the mimetic fidelity between portrait and original as illusory, inasmuch as all forms of representation are shown to be mediated and thus unreliable, and because the 'original' of the portrait is itself revealed as always already a construct or a representation, these works do not entirely renounce representation or the quest for self-expression. Indeed, the authors' careful staging and use of self-reflexive techniques suggest a desire to underline their agency in creating the image we see. This subjective agency cannot, as was seen in the case of Yuste's self-portrait, be depicted within the portrait itself; it cannot enter the realm of representation, but it can be alluded to in the images, or inferred from them as the premise that makes possible their coming into being. There is thus a paradox at the centre of these works, for though they make manifest the temporary, contingent and limited nature of all forms of representation, including, and particularly, self-representation, our central means of knowledge with regards to identity, they simultaneously reaffirm and celebrate the role of individual subjective agency in the shaping of the self-portraits. While the portraits question the ways in which individuals know, present and represent themselves to themselves and to others, they nevertheless hold on to the belief that there remains something that can be expressed and communicated, namely the awareness that what can be known and represented is always limited, provisional and contingent. And this awareness proves liberating, both for the works, which are no longer bound by imperatives of tradition, transparency and universality, and for individuals, whose consciousness of the conditionings and constraints that shape and limit their perceptions and self-knowledge in fact spurs a vigorous and playful exploration of their own identities and creative capabilities.

Gender and sexuality: identities vs. practices

This new understanding of identity and (self)representation as mediated, constructed and performative also affects the way in which collective identity categories are perceived and treated within *La Luna.* The theme of gender and gender roles, for example, comes particularly to the fore within the regular section 'Luz de Boudoir' (1–9/10), later renamed 'Somos unas señoras' (11, 12 and 14; discontinued from issue 15). This section normally occupies two pages and features some of the staples of conventional women's magazines: beauty remedies, make-up advice, recipes, personal testimonies or chronicles, as well as profile pieces on inspiring female figures past and present. At first sight, the contents and tone of the section echo and apparently reinforce a traditional notion of femininity[11] associated with qualities such as domesticity, delicacy and docility. However, a closer look reveals the parodic purpose of many of the pieces contained within 'Boudoir'. For example, 'Confidencias de Frivolina' (Frivolina's Secrets), a column that appears regularly within the section, offers beauty advice in overly formal and frequently euphemistic language, and the home-made remedies it proposes involve such obscure ingredients as 'tintura de benjuí' [benzoin dye] and 'bálsamo de la meca' [balm of Gilead] (issue 12: 34), which readers would have been unable to procure. The questionable practical applicability of the remedies offered and the deliberately dated language used thus suggest that the column is primarily intended to mock, rather than replicate, the beauty tips on offer in conventional women's publications.

The parodic intent of the section is further underlined by its visual configuration, which features black-and-white images of 1920s flappers (1: 32–33), 1940s housewives (5: 42–43) and 1950s and 1960s models and pin-ups (3: 32–33), as well as comic-inspired pop drawings of women (4: 34–35). These illustrations do not feature women in contemporary, everyday settings; instead, they portray female "types": the care-free flapper, the dedicated housewife, the athletic young girl, the vamp, the mini-skirted, big-haired pop heroine. This visual 'bricolage of features pilfered from fantasies of the bygone' is, according to Andrew Ross, the discourse through which camp speaks (Ross 1989: 159). Indeed, this choice of imagery can be read as a commentary on the imposture, the performance involved in enacting femininity, as well as an illustration of the ways in which such performances change over time, a notion of femininity that echoes Susan Sontag's definition of camp's understanding of 'Being-as-Playing-a-Role' (Sontag 1982: 109). The effect of the images displayed oscillates, in true camp style, between irony and nostalgia — an oscillation that is also reflected in the section's contents, which alternate moves to conform to or exploit clichés relating to femininity with instances in which the same notions are mocked and challenged.

The female figures featured within the section, either in profile pieces or in interviews, exemplify this ambiguous attitude to established conceptions of femininity. Generally, the profiles portray women who defied the gender conventions of their day, such as the seventeenth-century French libertine and intellectual Ninon de Lenclos (1: 33), the nineteenth-century Irish dancer and courtesan Lola Gilbert, better known by her stage name of Lola Montez (2: 32), or the German punk icon Nina Hagen (7: 53). But we also find among them women whose challenge to the gender norms of their day is either much more subtle (for example, the respected Spanish academic and author Carmen Bravo-Villasante, interviewed in issue 9/10, whose academic achievements and standing made her an exceptional figure within the Spain of the 1940s and 1950s, but whose life and views remained attached to relatively conventional bourgeois values) or entirely absent, as in the case of the piece on Lesley Aday in issue 12 (35), who is featured only on the basis that she is the wife of the rock musician Meatloaf. The title of this particular piece, 'El reposo del guerrero', refers to the well-known cliché of the female who assumes the role of carer and emotional support for her 'warrior' or 'man of action' male partner, incarnating his realm of calm and respite. Though the title could be read ironically, the article itself does not suggest that such a reading is intended. Instead, the rhetorical questions that close the article ('Dicen que el rock and roll es machista, pero, ¿es machista la vida familiar? y ¿qué puede hacer el rock and roll contra una esposa feliz?'; They say rock and roll is sexist, but, is family life sexist? And, what can rock and roll do against a happy wife?, 12: 35) turn the feminist questioning of gender roles on its head. These questions suggest a need to re-evaluate what constitutes sexism or male chauvinism ('machismo') in order to accommodate individual women's choices when these follow traditional gender patterns, for example, as is the case here, opting to devote oneself to 'family life' instead of establishing a career of one's own, yet nevertheless result in the happiness and fulfilment of the woman concerned. However, rather than a reinforcement of traditional gender and family values, I would argue that what is at stake here is a defence of personal choice and freedom over any prescriptive model of what women should be or how they ought to behave, regardless of whether any such normative view is formulated by those who seek to perpetuate traditional gender roles, or by those who seek to challenge them.

Despite this emphasis on individual choice over any feminist political imperative, feminism is not rejected or regarded as outdated within this section. In fact, issue 5 contains the first of a series of openly feminist articles. In a piece entitled 'Poneos las pilas' (5: 42–43), Marta Moriarty contends that, despite the numerous advances for women's rights achieved during the twentieth century, there still remain serious obstacles ahead for women. For Moriarty, the main danger for her contemporaries is that they risk being coerced, by what she describes as the latent male subliminal domination apparatus, into one of two categories: the 'mujer-objeto' [objectified woman] (43), who assumes a traditional, passive role and is merely the object of male desires and fantasies, or the working female who, in her quest to emulate the successful men around her, suppresses her interest in and enjoyment of certain fine pleasures that have traditionally been associated with femininity, such as cookery, cosmetics or storytelling. The key message of the article is that, while women should claim their equal share of power (in economic, political, social and sexual terms) from men, a claim which, it is argued, men have throughout the ages sought to repress, they also have 'la obligación de repudiar la mimesis de lo que no merece ser imitado' [the duty to reject the mimesis of that which does not deserve imitation] (5: 43). In other words, gender equality should not come at the price of suppressing difference, in this case female difference with respect to the dominant male/masculine norm, but as a result of its acceptance and recognition. This affirmation of difference and of the right to difference is relevant inasmuch as it allows the section to situate its feminist discourse in an ambiguous realm that, on the one hand, acknowledges the achievements and subscribes to some of the underlying assumptions of the preceding feminist movement, but, on the other hand, points to a need to re-evaluate some of its principles and strategies. While the affirmation, implicit within the article, of the existence of an essential difference between men and women appears to reinforce the strict male-female gender binary upon which much feminist discourse of the 1960s and 1970s, retrospectively labelled 'second-wave feminism', was constructed,[12] the rejection of any clear-cut definition of what characterizes such differences suggests an understanding of the gender binary not as a fixed, immutable and universally valid opposition, but rather as a continuum or spectrum of difference resulting from an evolving network of interconnected factors, social, historical and political as well as biological. This understanding of gender difference as complex and changing arguably anticipates the shift from second wave feminism's focus on a fixed and unproblematic gender binary, to third wave feminism's emphasis on broader notions of otherness, which can no longer be defined in terms of a clear-cut male-female opposition, but which needs to be considered alongside other forms of difference, such as sexual orientation, ethnicity, race, class and disability, among others, which intersect with and contribute to determine individuals' gender(ed) identity. This awareness of a need to revise and renew feminist discourse, implicit throughout Moriarty's article, is made explicit when she proclaims the advent of 'un feminismo alternativo y militante, poderoso y brillante' (5: 43). Although the guiding principles and goals of this new feminism are not defined here, its labelling as alternative points to a desire to distinguish it from more established and better-known forms of feminist discourse. In particular, this new feminism rejects the false dichotomy between a traditional-passive and an enlightened or liberated model of woman, a difference constructed, according to the author, by the still dominant 'subconsciente colectivo masculino' (5: 43), but also accepted as true and valid by many women, including some feminists. More broadly, this form of feminism rejects any normative or prescriptive model of being, acting or behaving for women (or men, for that matter), advocating instead individuals' rights to chose the terms in which they self-define and self-identify, even when such terms are shaped by patriarchal discourse. Indeed, it is precisely this inextricability from dominant patriarchal discourse (or, as Moriarty puts it, from the collective male subconscious) which this new form of feminism seeks to expose. This consciousness of the impossibility of establishing a feminist (or any other) position that is entirely independent from, outside of or beyond patriarchal discourse, does not, however, lead to an abdication of the feminist struggle. In fact, the closing lines of Moriarty's article call on readers to get in touch and get involved in a series of unspecified initiatives. Rather, this awareness of the inescapability from patriarchal discourse expands feminism's mission beyond the deceptively straightforward task of combating sexist discrimination and prejudice, to consider also the ways in which feminism itself (its language, the assumptions it operates on, the strategies it mobilizes) is informed by, and hence potentially complicit with, the very patriarchal mechanisms it seeks to undermine.

Isabel Escudero's article in issue 6 (50), entitled '¿Lo femenino? No gracias', insists on this idea that even the most seemingly liberated and liberating discourses on femininity can, in fact, be potentially repressive. The piece begins by decrying the 'creciente ola mitificadora' [increasing mystifying wave] (6: 50) surrounding women and femininity. For Escudero, the current wave of discourses glorifying women's power, in particular their sexual prowess, is dangerous not only because it constitutes a collection of 'solemnes pedanterías' (6: 50), but, more importantly, because it opens the door to manipulation and exploitation. In the same way that women's supposed selflessness and heightened capacity to endure suffering was invoked in the past to justify the hardships they faced, this new form of superficial praise, Escudero argues, is in fact a cunning trap which seeks to seduce women into fulfilling what she sees as, ultimately, a male fantasy — that of the highly sexualized woman, a glamorous and profitable prototype dreamt up by men and put to the service of the male-dominated fashion and media industries. The ideal of femininity may have changed over time, shifting from the sweet, devoted housewife of the 1940s and 1950s to the sexually liberated, economically independent career woman of the 1980s, but for Escudero, it seems, the latter model of woman is no less constraining than the former, inasmuch as both ideals have been shaped by the dominant patriarchal discourse and have been manipulated to its advantage. In fact, this latest imposition is seen as potentially more dangerous to women, since it is much more subtle, and thus more difficult to resist, than previous incarnations — as evidenced, according to Escudero, by the fact that most feminists have unquestioningly embraced this new model of femininity.

The question that arises at this point is whether Escudero proposes any alternative to what she clearly regards as a suspect wave of discourses on femininity circulating within Spanish intellectual, feminist and academic circles at the time. While she does not formulate an alternative model of femininity, we can infer her stance from her call to men (and women) to abstain from attempts to define women, to abandon efforts to uncover the female "Mystery", essence or difference. Underlying her appeal is the belief that any attempt to uncover or define gender and sexual difference inevitably entails a degree of falsification, as all definitions are always constructed from within the dominant male order, and thus constitute moves towards integration within it. Aside from the danger of falsification, Escudero also argues that something might be lost through these efforts to define and integrate female otherness — namely the secret, untapped potential of that which refuses to let itself be known by, and thus resists integration within, the dominant order: 'No nos deslumbréis más descubriendo nuestras íntimas potencialidades, pues bien pudiera ser que ellas sigan todavía realmente activas porque no sabían de sí mismas, ocultas y vivas en la noche de los tiempos' [Do not dazzle us further by uncovering our intimate potentialities, as it may well be that they actually remain truly active because they were unknown to themselves, concealed and alive in the night of times] (6: 50). Escudero's words do not contest the existence of female difference, referred to in this instance as 'nuestras íntimas potencialidades', but she questions its knowability ('no sabían de sí mismas, ocultas y vivas en la noche de los tiempos'). This view of sexual difference as unknowable even to itself echoes Luce Irigaray's theorization of Woman, according to which Woman is outside and beyond representation in Western culture. And like Irigaray, Escudero regards this unknowability of female difference as opportunity, inasmuch as it is this very invisibility or indefinability that has allowed difference to resist attempts at integration within the established order, avoiding the 'reduction of the other in the Same', as Irigaray puts it (1977: 74). But the question arises: if Woman's difference cannot be known, is it not thus condemned to remain invisible, passive and silent? Is there any way in which women can undermine patriarchal discourse without becoming integrated or complicit with it? Irigaray suggests a way out of this bind through mimesis:

> To play with mimesis is thus, for a woman, to try to recover the place of her exploitation by discourse, without allowing herself to be simply reduced to it. It means to resubmit herself [...] to ideas about herself, that are elaborated in/by masculine logic, but so as to make "visible", by an effect of playful repetition, what was supposed to remain invisible: the cover-up of a possible operation of the feminine in language. (Irigaray 1977: 76)

Irigaray's proposal of mimesis understood as playful, and, as she writes elsewhere, excessive emulation (1977: 78), is reminiscent of Sontag's theorization of camp, which sees artifice and exaggeration as its essence (1982: 105). But while Sontag is sceptical about camp's subversive potential, branding it 'disengaged, depoliticized — or at least apolitical' (1982: 107), Irigaray seems hopeful that it might be possible to '*undo* the effects of phallocentric discourse simply by *overdoing* them' (Moi 1985: 140). This hope finds echo in Butler's formulation of the subversive potential of drag queens' hyperbolized femininity, which she sees as offering 'possibilities of doing gender [which] repeat and displace through hyperbole, dissonance, internal confusion, and proliferation the very constructs by which they are mobilized' (1990: 31). Irigaray's and Butler's approach to deconstructing patriarchal discourse operates obliquely; rather than a direct challenge to or rejection of its premises and categories (any such frontal challenge is viewed with suspicion since it would inevitably be forced to shape itself in the language and within the parameters imposed by patriarchal discourse itself) they attempt to undermine discourse through imitation, hyperbole and excess, in an attempt to uncover discourse as discourse, that is, as a historically mediated, ideological construct shaped by, and simultaneously shaping, power relations. This approach coincides with the strategies of mimicry and parody in the *Luz de Boudoir/Somos unas señoras* section, and though there is no analogous theorization to explain these strategies, nor any suggestion that those working on *La Luna* were familiar with the work of either Irigaray and Butler (given the publication and translation dates of the works of both scholars, it is unlikely), the adoption of such oblique strategies probably stems from a similar awareness of the pitfalls and limitations of second-wave feminism, whose fight for equal rights, though instrumental in improving women's lives, in some cases entailed a renunciation to or repudiation of difference, itself arguably becoming a dogmatic and constraining discourse.

However, this strategy of exaggerated emulation to parodic effect has its dangers. Firstly, parody can be elitist, since it relies for effect on readers having a similar set of cultural references and a similar sensibility to that of the section's authors. In other words, the implicit wink, or metaphorical quotation marks, with which the author frames his or her work can be lost to a non-initiated reader, who may just take the section's contents at face value. Secondly, these attempts to challenge the dominant discourses on gender through discursive means (mimicry, hyperbole, parody) often fail to acknowledge and address more specific and immediate issues and forms of discrimination faced by women, and resulting from those hegemonic discourses. In other words, the focus on discourse appears to detract from women's everyday, practical problems, such as economic disadvantage, access to education and the job market, availability of contraception, and the threat of physical violence, in short, the causes around which second-wave feminism rallied. An article entitled 'Problemas' and published in issue 11 illustrates the fact that the approach to feminism showcased in this section largely rests on the assumption that most, if not all, of the issues enumerated above have been, or are about to be, overcome, an assumption that is, however, revealed as illusory. The unsigned article deals with the topic of domestic violence, details a series of programmes set up to help women victims, and calls on readers to become involved. The piece is remarkable because of its exceptionality: it is the only article within the section to deal with a specific problem faced by women. Its tone is particularly revealing: the author expresses shock and surprise at the prevalence and extent of domestic abuse, as she writes 'hace unos días todos nos hacíamos cruces con la noticia: Se abre una casa refugio para mujeres maltratadas y se llena al segundo. ¡Dios mío, qué barbaridad, cómo puede ser esto!' [some days ago we were in shock at the news: a refuge for abused women opens and is immediately filled up. My god, how appalling, how can this be!] (11: 49). The author's shock seems to be founded upon the gulf that separates the author, whose identity is not disclosed, but who we can assume to be a professional, middle-class, educated woman, from the victims of domestic abuse, portrayed here as dependent, uneducated, lonely and afraid:

> Da como apuro comentar que hay muchas señoras que no tienen independencia económica ni moral, que viven sin formación intelectual para salir de casa, acoquinadas por la soledad y el miedo físico, el miedo físico que nosotros tuvimos que buscar en "La fura des Baus", porque nos sonaba a exaltación infantil casi desconocida. (11: 49)

[It seems kind of embarrassing to remark that there are many ladies who have no economic or moral independence, who live with no education to enable them to leave the home, paralysed by loneliness and physical fear, a physical fear that we had to seek out in [the theatre group] "La fura des Baus", as we thought of it as a barely known childish exaltation.] (11: 49)

The distance between both groups, the 'muchas señoras' who suffer violence, and the 'nosotros' in which the author includes herself, using, interestingly, the masculine plural form, is rendered particularly vividly by the reference to physical fear, which for the victims of violence is a daily, draining experience, to which the author can only relate in terms of the sought-after thrill resulting from an experimental theatre experience. Herein lies a key weakness of *Luz de Boudoir/ Somos unas señoras*: its authors, a group of young, professional, educated, middle-class, progressive women take their own experience as a benchmark by which to judge the situation of women in Spain. And when their situation is shown not to be reflective of reality, as in this article, the reaction is not only of acute surprise, but also of embarrassment ('Da como apuro comentar...'), as the issue of domestic violence is presented as a shameful anachronism, rather than as symptomatic of a wider gender(ed) problem.

While *La Luna*'s feminine section's camp frivolity may be more justified than one contemporary reviewer of the magazine gave it credit for,[13] given that its parodic approach can be seen as an attempt to challenge the male monopoly on discourse, a strategy that reflects a wider shift within feminist discourse from the second wave's emphasis on equality to the third wave's reaffirmation of difference, this strategy is nevertheless hampered by the authors' failure or unwillingness to relate their deconstructive efforts to the all too real everyday problems and forms of discrimination faced by women. Further, the section's parody of feminine gender stereotypes is in some instances undermined by a simultaneous vindication of female sexual difference that is itself often reliant upon and articulated through a mobilization of gender(ed) clichés, as seen, for instance, in Marta Moriarty's description of art and small simple pleasures ('los finos placeres culinarios, el encanto de las lociones perfumadas', 5: 43) as quintessentially female preoccupations. Such tensions and contradictions illustrate the inextricable relationship between socially constructed gender (femininity) and biologically determined sex (femaleness), which is further compounded by the fact that both terms are conflated into one in the Spanish original (*femenino*). While the section does not explicitly address or acknowledge this inextricability of sex and gender, its discourse can be located in the area of slippage between both terms, and both its inconsistencies and its potential for play derive from this ambiguous positioning.

The playful de- and reconstruction of female identity that takes place within the *Luz de Boudoir/Somos unas señoras* section is taken further in Pedro Almodóvar's Patty Diphusa page. This section, published intermittently in the first 20 issues of *La Luna*, chronicles the adventures of Patty, an endearing optimist and megalomaniac who presents herself to readers as a 'sex-simbol [sic] internacional, o estrella internacional del porno' (1: 13). Although Patty insistently describes herself as female, her gender is brought into question by the fact that the character, which first appeared in Almodóvar's 1982 film *Laberinto de Pasiones*, was originally played by a male actor, Fabio/Fanny McNamara, in drag, and photos of McNamara as Patty are used to illustrate the section (issue 4: 11). Additionally, Patty admits to a tendency to use male toilets (18: 86); her sexual partners include a male homosexual (3: 13) and a female-to-male transvestite (19: 86); and she herself is taken to be a transvestite by the mother of one of her lovers (15: 78). Reflecting this gender indeterminacy, Patty's first question for Almodóvar in the interview she conducts with him in issue 20 in order to get to know herself better is whether she is a man, a woman, or a transvestite. Almodóvar assures Patty she is a woman, but he later introduces an element of doubt and ambiguity, as he adds that Patty is ultimately 'una fantasía de los lectores. Eres lo que a los lectores les gustaría ser' [a fantasy of the readers. You are what readers would like to be] (20: 94). Patty's queerness derives not only from her uncertain gender, reflected in Almodóvar's use of the gender neutral pronoun 'lo', but also from the dissonance between her self-proclaimed identity as a heterosexual female, and the nature and variety of her sexual practices and partners, an incongruity that suggests that the relationship between gender, sexual orientation and desire is far more complex and equivocal than what the established, unproblematic identity binaries male/female, heterosexual/homosexual and gay/lesbian would have us believe.

Two Almodóvar scholars have read Patty Diphusa as a female alter ego of Almodóvar. Marsha Kinder has described the Patty Diphusa series as Almodóvar's 'parodic memoirs' (Kinder 1987: 36), and Robert Richmond Ellis has argued that Almodóvar 'weaves his own autobiographical persona' through Patty (Richmond Ellis 1997: 106). Patty's camp sensibility, with its combination of sentimentality and eschatology, certainly echoes Almodóvar's, and her intense party lifestyle and cinematic ambitions mirror her author's experiences in 1980s Madrid, including his encounter with Andy Warhol, which is reproduced in Patty's debut appearance (1: 13). Given these overlaps, Patty may be viewed as a figure analogous to Duchamp's female alter ego, Rrose Sélavy, or to Warhol's 'Altered Ego' portraits in partial drag. Both Duchamp and Warhol adopt female personas whose gender is problematized through the inclusion of elements coded as male. In Duchamp's case, his cross-dressing as Rrose in conventionally bourgeois female attire, photographically documented by Man Ray, is undermined by his deliberately unshaven stubble. In Warhol's 'Altered Ego' portraits, shot by the photographer Christopher Makos and intended as a homage to Duchamp's Rrose Sélavy, Warhol appears as a convincing, attractive female from the neck up, coiffed and heavily made-up, but the rest of his body, dressed in shirt, tie and jeans, appears as male, creating a gender dissonance between face and body. Similarly, the portraits of Fabio McNamara as Patty do not attempt to make him 'pass' as female; though he is dressed in female clothes, which range from scant, dominatrix-type attires (1: 13) to kitschy, glamorous-bucolic outfits (4: 11), there are always visible signals that point to his male gender: his chest is exposed (2: 13), or he is photographed sporting remarkable sideburns (3: 13). And Patty's textual persona is, as already mentioned, undercut by an analogous gender ambiguity, as some of the episodes she recounts in the series cast doubt on her femaleness. The fact that Duchamp, Warhol and Almodóvar do not assume unequivocally female identities, opting instead to create feminized, but ambiguous, alter egos results in something more complex than a mere reversal of the gender binary. What all three artists are engaged in is not simply an attempt to reimagine and refashion themselves as women; rather, their gender queering throws into question the stability and impregnability of gender boundaries. The fact that such a questioning is undertaken through the adoption of alter egos adds another dimension to these creatures: they do not only challenge the gender binary, but further erode any clear demarcation between subject and object. Rrose, Warhol's altered ego and Patty are simultaneously passive objects of our gaze, and, by virtue of their contiguity with their creators, subjects engaged in their own self-representation. Writing about Duchamp and Warhol, Amelia Jones suggests that by 'presenting the male artists as a feminized object of art historical desire, they expose the assumption of masculinity built into the art historical model (or, for that matter, the modern western conception of subjectivity) and deny its "neutrality"' (Jones 1995: 22).

While I agree with Jones's assertion that Duchamp's and Warhol's alter egos reveal, de- and reconstruct the gender(ed) dimension of representation, her analysis is centred on male artists' self-fashioning, that is, their use of clothing as a vehicle for subjectivity, and is primarily preoccupied with its potential to 'unfix gender, class, and ethnic distinctions' (Jones 1995: 30). This focus on the subversive possibilities of Duchamp's and Warhol's gender-bending self-fashioning fails to acknowledge a wider problematization of representation and self-representation. By exposing 'the assumption of masculinity built into the art historical model' and 'the modern western conception of subjectivity', Duchamp, Warhol, and, inasmuch as he mobilizes an analogous strategy, Almodóvar, do not only uncover a gender bias to representation, but also, implicitly, throw into question the reliability of representation itself: its neutrality denied, it can no longer be assumed to have universal value or truth. In other words, Patty, like her predecessors, not only queries gender categories, but, by revealing a gender(ed) dimension to representation, she also questions the ways in which the gender binary is articulated through representation, while simultaneously influencing the dynamics of representation itself.

This problematization of representation extends to language. The names of all three of these creatures are word games: Rrose Sélavy is a phonetic rendering of the French 'Eros, c'est la vie' [Eros is life], although it could also be read as 'Arroser la vie' [to sprinkle water on life]. Warhol's Altered Ego is semantically ambiguous, as it simultaneously refers to the term 'alter ego', and to the idea of transforming one's ego. Patty Diphusa's name, in turn, is a pun on the Spanish term 'patidifusa' (colloquial for 'astounded'), but simultaneously evokes a notion of diffuseness. Additionally, both Rrose Sélavy and Patty make liberal use of puns: in Rrose's case, these take the form of nonsensical aphorisms, while in the case of Almodóvar's character, it is her friends Addy Posa, Ana Conda and Mary Von Etica who bear pun names. While these puns serve a primarily playful and comedic purpose, they also underline the plasticity of language, a plasticity which, in this instance, can be seen as analogous to the gender fluidity these creatures exhibit. Further, such language games contribute to remind readers that, as Patty tells one of her lovers, language is but a convention (6: 13).

Patty's liberal use of puns is also reminiscent of the Dadaists' language games. Given the chronological and geographical distance that separate Patty from Dada, the association may seem far-fetched. However, a piece by Almodóvar published in issue 11 of *La Luna*, 'El nacimiento del Dada' (11: 86), reveals not only his familiarity with the movement, but also his ability for using and mimicking some of its strategies. In true Dada spirit, the text makes no reference to the Dada movement itself; the term 'Dada' is used only in the title and in the last sentence of the piece, in which we are told that '[e]l Dada acababa de nacer' [Dada had just been born], but what or who this Dada is remains unsaid.[14] Instead we are presented with an absurdist tale of bourgeois discontent, punctuated by language play, nonsense and heteroglossia. The story's starting point is ANONADADO — a word synonymous with 'patidifuso/a', but which is described, in this context, as 'un grupo formado por dos parejas progres y una chica sola, intrépida y brutalmente espontánea' [a group formed by two liberal couples and a lone, intrepid and brutally spontaneous girl] (11: 86). From this description, it seems clear that 'A', the single girl, can be regarded as a new incarnation of Patty. The other members of the group are a couple formed by No and Na, and a second consisting of Da and Do. The entire story is articulated around the linguistic permutations and puns that can be constructed from these syllables. For instance, when 'A' leaves the group, the remaining members become 'Nonadado', and, because of their inability to swim (No-nadado), they are forced to move to a desert. The dialogues between Na and Da are inevitably vacuous, and those between No and Do echo the content and tone of the Francoist news and propaganda films by the same name, the No-Do's. The piece's nonsensical plot turns, structured around a series of language puns, and its chaotic mix of different linguistic registers -the informal narration style is punctuated by the reproduction of popular sayings and by the propagandistic tone of the No-Do that characterizes some of the dialogue- are pure Dada, even if the movement is not mentioned explicitly in the text. Given the knowledge of and admiration for Dada that this piece demonstrates, it does not seem unreasonable to conclude that the puns that appear in the Patty Diphusa column, as well as some of her more deliberately outrageous statements, may have also been inspired, at least in part, by the Dadaist love of provocation and wordplay.

The awareness of language, representation and gender as conventions, as socially sanctioned constructs, underlying the Patty Diphusa column does not, however, entail their repudiation. Rather, for Almodóvar, as for Duchamp and Warhol before him, language and gender become useful vehicles that can be simultaneously utilized and exposed. But this position is not without its dangers. As both Linda Hutcheon and Leo Bersani remind us, in very different contexts, strategies of parodic reappropriation such as Patty's camp posturing partly subvert and partly reaffirm the very objects of their parody.[15] In the case of the Patty Diphusa series, the problem of reactionary reaffirmation comes to the fore in the rape scene recounted in the second instalment of the chronicles:

> No di un grito porque no soy tan ñoña, pero mentalmente me formulé las típicas preguntas de "dónde estoy", "qué hago aquí" etc. [...] Que a una la violen dos sicópatas es normal, pero que después me dejaran tirada en la Casa de Campo,

> de madrugada y con una pinta como de película mejicana de vampiros, no lo soporto. [...] Realmente aquello me molestó, comprendí que hay situaciones en que a las mujeres no les queda más remedio que hacerse feministas. (2: 13)
>
> [I did not shout because I am not that prudish, but mentally I formulated the usual questions of "where am I", "what am I doing here", etc. [...] It is normal to be raped by two psychopaths, but then to be left lying around Casa de Campo, in the early hours, and looking like something out of a Mexican vampire film, I cannot stand. [...] I was truly annoyed and I understood that in certain situations women have no choice but to become feminists.] (2: 13)

Robert Richmond Ellis argues that 'by inverting the normal/abnormal binary' in this passage (when she states that being raped by two psychopaths is normal), Patty 'aims to minimize the violence done to her', reappropriating hegemonic norms 'in an effort to introduce a wedge between oppressor and oppressed' (1997: 109–10). Richmond Ellis claims that, by focusing 'on the surface plane of her body, responding not to the violation of her being but her appearance [...] flattening her identity to that of a screen image from a low-budget, "low-culture" film' (1997: 109), Patty is able to distance herself from the experience, and thus her frivolous account should not be too readily condemned, but rather seen as a strategy of resistance or as a coping mechanism. But, despite his best interpretative efforts, Richmond Ellis cannot ignore the highly problematic nature of this representation of rape, which, he concedes, partly re-idealizes the very norms it sets out to subvert. Indeed, Patty's claim that she did not scream because she is not prudish appears to imply that the acceptance of sexual violence and abuse is part and parcel of women's sexual liberation. Her subsequent disparaging reference to feminism, which is portrayed here as, at times, a necessary evil, reinforces the reactionary view that regards the movement as dull and irrelevant.

It is clear that this rape scene is (re)constructed with a deliberate intent to shock readers by portraying sexual violence as a matter of mere inconvenience. Such an exploitation of rape through its trivialization for purposes of titillation and provocation is not new: there is an obvious Surrealist precedent in Benjamin Péret's definition of rape as 'l'amour de la vitesse' [the love of speed][16] — a definition that in fact finds echo in the final lines of this text, in which Patty tells readers 'soy una mujer de vida vertiginosa' (2: 13). Patty's allusion to speed within this instalment might be a simple coincidence, but given Almodóvar's very broad frame of cultural references, which, as I have argued, includes the historical avant-gardes, it is not inconceivable that Patty's words are in fact intended as a nod to Péret's characterization of rape. Additionally, the reference to speed, widely considered the defining trait of (post)modernity, helps situate both Patty and the rape experience within a specific spatio-temporal configuration: that of the (post)modern city. This association of violence with urban space is further underlined by the representation of rape in terms of displacement; what Patty appears to resent most in this episode is not the sexual violence done to her, but the fact that she is left stranded in Casa de Campo, a large stretch of parkland on the city's edge. This emphasis on location (or rather, dislocation) is relevant for it suggests that Casa de Campo not only provides a setting for the crime perpetrated against Patty, but that her involuntary transposition to this heterotopic site (simultaneously part of the city, and oblivious to what takes place within it) constitutes an act of violence commensurate with the rape itself. Location and crime thus become conflated, and hence the sexual attack Patty is subjected to could be interpreted as metonymic of the violence inherent to the (post)modern city, a theme that is also central to Juan Madrid's *Jungla,* as we saw in the preceding chapter. But as Patty's eventual escape from Casa de Campo, during which she meets and becomes infatuated with a delicate, mysterious man, illustrates, urban space is as much a space for freedom, opportunity and pleasure as it is a site of violence and danger.

The autobiographical dimension of the series noted earlier becomes most explicit in Patty's (provisional) farewell in issue 9–10, in which as Almodóvar writes in the introduction to the 1991 book edition of the series, Patty, 'fiel reflejo de mis sentimientos' (1991: 10), vents her anger at her own success and expresses her weariness at a situation which she has unwittingly contributed to create:

> Detesto crear modas, si lo llego a saber no escribo ni una línea. LA LUNA se ha convertido en mi sombra, pero multiplicada. Todo son fiestas, todo es sexo, todo es alegría e inconsciencia. Pues no. Los juegos dejan de serlo cuando se convierten en una manifestación cultural. Antes una fiesta era un lugar donde a una le robaban las joyas o el novio, lo cual creaba una tensión, una historia digna de ser vivida. Ahora una fiesta es un plató donde tus antiguas amigas convertidas en momias se pasan la velada posando para fotógrafos amaters [sic] que después escogen las peores fotos y las publican. (9–10: 23)
>
> [I detest creating trends, if I'd known I would not have written a single line. LA LUNA has become my shadow, but multiplied. It is all parties, sex, joy and thoughtlessness. Well no. Games stop being games once they become a cultural manifestation. Before, a party was a place where one might get one's jewellery or one's boyfriend stolen, which created some tension, a story worthy of being experienced. Now, a party is a TV set in which all your old friends, now mummified, spend the evening posing for amateur photographers who then chose the worst photos and publish them.] (9–10: 23)

Given Almodóvar's status as the poster-boy of *la movida* at the time these lines were first published, it is virtually impossible to discern where Patty's tirade ends and where Almodóvar's lament begins. Interestingly, Patty's/Almodóvar's despair results not only from a success-induced self-consciousness that kills the original spontaneity and possibility inherent to the *movida* experience; it also originates from the realization of the constraints resulting from their popularity and the ways in which their identities are perceived: 'Si eres una chica graciosa esperan que lo seas siempre' [If you are a funny girl, they expect you always to be funny] (9–10: 23). In the face of such pressure, Patty opts for silence: 'No tengo nada que decir y no quiero decir nada' [I have nothing to say and I don't want to say anything] (9–10: 23). Although Patty does eventually return to *La Luna*'s pages,[17] her resolve to disappear rather than to assume a crystallized, stable identity bears witness to her resistance to what Richmond Ellis describes as 'the grounding of identity' (1997: 153). Such a resistance involves not only a challenge to the gender binary and the resulting ascription of sexual identities, but also a wider questioning of practices of self-representation, as well as of discursive and creative processes. The Patty Diphusa chronicles begin as a quest for self-expression ('me convencí inmediatamente de que lo mejor y más interesante [sobre lo que escribir] era YO MISMA'; I immediately convinced myself that the best and most interesting thing [to write about] was MYSELF, 1: 13), but Patty quickly realizes that 'cuando una escribe muchas veces te salen cosas ligeramente falsas, eso que los críticos llaman "una creación"' [when one writes, often things come out slightly false, what critics call "a creation"] (2: 13). The series thus illustrates the tension between self-expression through creative-discursive practices, and the inevitable reduction, falsification and appropriation that such practices entail and enable. Patty Diphusa's resistance to definition is articulated through camp, through her joyful frivolity, ingenuity and shamelessness. The danger of her parodic approach, however, is not only that it risks reinforcing the very values and attitudes it parodies, but also that it becomes predictable; as the series advances, the very qualities which were supposed to illustrate her volubility and lack of depth become her essence, a defined and defining mode of being that is potentially constraining. In that sense, the fate of Patty mirrors that of the *movida* itself: its success and popularity lead to a crystallization process that inevitably blunts its ludic appeal and subversive potential.

There are thus multiple dimensions to the Patty Diphusa series: firstly, Patty can be read as Almodóvar's female alter ego, an incarnation that allows her author not only to engage in an exercise of gender queering, but also to carry out an exploration of the mechanisms and limits of self-expression, and, more generally, of representation. The Patty Diphusa chronicles also need to be considered in their spatio-temporal specificity: Patty is not only Almodóvar's female alter ego, she is also his *movida* persona. Patty's spatio-temporal anchoring in early 1980s Madrid may seem at odds with the notion of identity flux embraced by those working in *La Luna,* including Almodóvar himself — after all, if we claim identity to be fluid and dynamic, its attachment to a specific place and time becomes problematic. However, such an attachment in fact underlines the contingency and provisionality of any one assumed identity, of any one incarnation, as Patty's eventual demise, which coincides chronologically with the demise of *la movida,* and is marked not so much by her disappearance from *La Luna*'s pages as by her ascension to mainstream 'respectability' via the publication of her chronicles in book format in 1991, makes clear. Once Patty becomes a *movida* icon, she ceases to be useful as a creative vehicle for Almodóvar, and is thus left behind.

The playful and parodic approach to gender and sexual identity categories showcased in the *Luz de Boudoir/Somos unas señoras* and *Patty Diphusa* sections bears witness to the radical experimental intent of those working on *La Luna*, to their desire to not take anything for granted: their refusal to define what or how anything or anyone should be runs parallel to a questioning of the very reliability of representation and language as means of (self-)expression. Such a position is not without its pitfalls: parody can be excluding, as it relies on readers understanding the intended joke; it risks being taken at face value; and it can contribute to reinforce, rather than subvert, the values it mocks. Further, the refusal to take anything too seriously can lead to a trivialization of important problems, as in Patty's account of rape, and to a failure or inability to address specific issues, such as the discrimination and violence which often derive from, or at least are related to, the gender roles queried in these sections. Finally, parody relies on ambivalence (it plays out and can be read in contradictory ways) and surprise or shock: the outrageous is presented as normal, while the everyday is seen as exceptional. Both of these modes or qualities, ambivalence and shock, are only effective in the short term: over time, audiences come to expect the unexpected and to 'essentialize' the ambiguous, that is, to give it a name and define it. And yet, despite all these contradictions and limitations, the sections discussed demonstrate the creative potential of parodic strategies, allowing its authors to explore fresh approaches to the themes of gender, sexuality and (self-) representation. Additionally, despite the fact that the sections discussed avoid any form of explicit or conventional political engagement (in *Luz de Boudoir*, there is only one instance in which public policy is discussed, in the context of measures taken against domestic violence, and in Patty's case, her volubility prevents any lasting political, or other, engagement) they do have a political dimension. In the socio-historical context from which they emerged, within a newly democratic Spain that was only just beginning to shake off a long tradition of machismo and homophobia,[18] these tentative attempts to query the ways in which gender, sexuality and identity are produced and reproduced were both pioneering and courageous. If nothing else, they contributed to dismantle old gender clichés, encouraged much-needed public debate, and opened up to creative experimentation and critical engagement identity categories and representational practices that until then had been unquestioningly, and often unthinkingly, accepted.

Beyond national identity: local and supra-national identities

La Luna's attitude and approach to traditional notions of Spanishness is somewhat ambiguous. While the image of Spain as different and exotic with respect to its European neighbours (a vision frequently used by the Francoist propaganda apparatus to justify its legitimacy) is often mocked, with elements associated with Spanish folklore such as bullfighting and Catholic imagery regularly parodied, there is a simultaneous desire to preserve and protect some of those very elements. For instance, though bullfighting imagery is regularly used to parodic and comedic effect, the magazine's pages also testify to a genuine interest in the art of bullfighting. These moves to preserve difference partly respond to a desire to challenge what is perceived as Anglo-Saxon cultural dominance, and to resist assimilation to its modes and models of expression. A further strategy used in and through *La Luna* to counter such cultural hegemony is the formulation of alternative alliances at both the local level of the city, as discussed in the previous chapter; and at a supra-national level, through, for instance, the creation of a 'horizontal axis' to link Lisbon, Madrid, Barcelona, Rome and Athens (15: 7), or through the establishment of cultural dialogue with the then emergent Latino culture within the US (44: 32–36). *La Luna*'s attempts to preserve local specificity, however, do not entail a rejection of English-speaking culture; indeed, British and North American writers, artists, and especially bands and musicians are regularly featured within its pages; and the referents for the magazine are, as discussed in the Introduction of this book, two American publications. Rather than a nationalistic-chauvinistic attempt to re-establish Spanish, Hispanic, or Mediterranean, cultural pre-eminence, *La Luna*'s parallel engagement with elements linked to traditional Spanish popular culture and with global cultural trends originating abroad (Pop, punk, glam rock, postmodernism) should be interpreted as an attempt to make sense of contemporary cultural manifestations through an open and reciprocal dialogue that allows for and respects cultural difference. The magazine's coverage of global cultural phenomena further reflects Spain's new openness towards international culture.

The elements associated with traditional Spanish culture featured in *La Luna* can be roughly grouped into three categories: those involving religious imagery, those concerned with bullfighting, and those dealing with popular music genres such as flamenco and *copla*. The pieces involving religious imagery have an unequivocally parodic purpose: for instance, in the second issue of *La Luna* we find an ironic, contemporary version of Murillo's painting of the Immaculate Conception (2: 48). The result of a collaboration between the conceptual artist Paz Muro and the photographer Pablo Pérez-Mínguez, the image depicts Muro as the Virgin, gazing up, with her hands on her chest, floating in the sky and surrounded by angels. While the composition clearly emulates that of the painting by Murillo, its effect is entirely different: the black-and-white photography of Muro, with its obviously mocked-up sky background and plastic angels, does not evoke the original's sense of beauty, purity and grace; its transposition of the iconographic image of the virgin to a (post)modern, largely secular context, by what Walter Benjamin would term mechanically reproducible means (photography), has an undoubtedly kitsch effect. The *Santoral de Estío* [Summer Saints' Days Calendar] published in issue 9/10 (62) operates in a similar fashion: it borrows from traditional religious iconography, but the images deployed are emptied of religious meaning by the introduction of prosaic everyday elements (a thermometer, a comb, a tap, a pistol, a corset, some brooms and a screw) which allude to and ironically resignify the tradition of requesting the aid of a specific saint for a specific type of problem. In both of these instances, there is no engagement with the original religious dimension of the imagery, which is used purely for its kitsch potential.

La Luna's treatment of bullfighting is more nuanced. The magazine features a bullfighting page in several of its issues,[19] which includes reviews of bullfights and bullfighting literature that testify to its authors' in-depth knowledge of and genuine interest in the tradition and aesthetic dimension of bullfighting. But the kitsch and camp potential of bullfighting imagery is also explored and exploited within *La Luna*. The most salient example of this can be found in the cover of issue 12 of the magazine, a drawing by Fernando Vicente depicting a close-up of a bullfighter's buttocks (Figure 3.2). The gender of this quintessentially male, virile figure remains undetermined in this instance, as only a section of the back of the bullfighter is shown. This highly suggestive image lends itself to multiple readings: on the one hand, the macho figure of the matador is here 'camped up' and turned into a pin-up — a transformation that might suggest an inversion of the dynamics of the gaze, which posits the object of the gaze as a passive and female object of male desire.[20] But because the figure's gender can only be assumed, rather than unequivocally known, to be male, the picture complicates, rather than reverses,

Fig. 3.2. Cover of La Luna by Fernando Vicente © Fernando Vicente

this dynamic. On another level, this image, though unconventional in style, can be seen as a reminder and remainder of the erotic dimension of bullfighting. But while the eroticization of the bullfighter undertaken in the drawing is steeped in a long-established tradition that sees the bullfight as an aesthetic (and therefore also erotic) pursuit, the means used to render explicit this erotic dimension of the fiesta are highly unconventional. The drawing can thus be read both as a challenge to traditional bullfighting, inasmuch as its fresh, pop-influenced style and its 'camping' of the figure of the matador constitute a departure from tradition; and as an attempt to give bullfighting new currency, to make it relevant to a new generation through its emphatic eroticization of the figure of the bullfighter.

The comic strip *Toreras*, published in issue 4 of the magazine (48), further exemplifies this tension between parodic resignification and a desire to preserve, albeit in updated form, the tradition of the bullfight. The strip places different famous women associated with *la movida*, such as the TV presenter Paloma Chamorro and the musician Olvido Gara, alias Alaska, in reimagined bullrings that feature pop-influenced symmetrical backgrounds. The frames are accompanied by an excerpt of the lyrics of the *pasodoble* 'El niño de las monjas',[21] by José Soriano, a text with clear Lorquian echoes:

> Era una tarde de feria, tarde de feria, de toro y de sol.../La niña cayó en la arena, el toro la corneó.../Era su herida de muerte.../Por eso no se pudo salvar.../Y estando ya en la agonía con emoción se oye clamar.../Ya no seré torera, torera no seré.../Que muero como Granero y Valerito y el Gran José.../Pobres monjitas buenas que llorareis por mí, rezad por la pobre niña que recogisteis allí. (4: 48)
>
> [It was a festive afternoon, festive, of sunshine and bulls.../The girl fell to the sand, and the bull gored her.../It was a deadly wound.../So she could not be saved.../And in her agony we hear her cry out.../I shall no longer be a bullfighter, a bullfighter I shall not be.../I die like Granero and Valerito and the Great José.../Poor, kind nuns who shall cry for me, pray for the poor girl you took in.] (4: 48)

The juxtaposition of these female *movida* icons with bullfighting imagery and with this lyrical text has a striking effect. As readers, our attention might be drawn, in the first instance, to the association of these female figures — all strong, independent, successful women — to the traditionally macho art of the bullfight. Their labelling as 'toreras' can be read in different ways, not least because the term 'torero'/'torera' does not only mean bullfighter, but can also be used as an adjective that denotes bravery, grace and confidence. The characterization of these women as 'toreras' could thus be read as merely an endorsement, a commentary on their strength and courage. But the fact that such an endorsement is articulated through the mobilization of tradition should not be overlooked: by situating these women in the context of the bullfight and the *pasodoble*, the comic strip anchors these modern (or even postmodern) women within a specifically Spanish (and, one might add, macho) cultural tradition. The effect of this anchoring can be read in contradictory ways: it could be seen as a move to re-essentialize the women, to remind us of, and underline, their 'Spanishness'. However, such a reading ignores the fact that the women featured are made to occupy a traditionally male position, that of the bullfighter. By virtue of this gender reversal, the essentialist and essentializing dimension of tradition, if tradition is understood as fixed, permanent and static, is undermined, and the relationship of the individual to his/her cultural tradition(s) is revealed as reciprocal. In other words, these women are no more the product of tradition than they are its producers. Their adoption of the role of bullfighter does not only allude to their courage and strength, attributes associated with the (usually male) *matador*, and situate them within a specific cultural tradition; it also brings to the fore, and turns on its head, some of the gender(ed) prejudices and assumptions underlying that tradition, thus contributing to its resignification. This resignification takes place primarily through the identification of different women with the figure of the bullfighter, but also through the reimagining of the bullfighting arena as a pop-inflected space, not always distinguishable from a club or disco setting. This resignification or recontextualization of tradition may seem at odds with the aforementioned desire to protect tradition, inasmuch as it entails its transformation. But for those working on *La Luna*, tradition and transformation do not constitute mutually excluding opposites; transformation is in fact understood to be crucial if tradition is to retain its currency and live on.

This view of tradition as an evolving construct that can be resignified and transformed over time comes to the fore in *La Luna*'s treatment of traditional Spanish popular music genres such as flamenco and *copla*. Although these forms of music are not given anywhere near as much space as more mainstream genres such as pop and rock,[22] the very fact that they feature at all in a publication directed to a young audience is nevertheless significant. The treatment these genres receive is far from homogenous. Flamenco is treated with reverence: in a piece by José Ramón Ripoll entitled 'Rarezas del flamenco' (5: 20), for instance, the genre is celebrated for the fierce individuality of its interpreters and for its melancholic rawness, attributes which, according to its author, are betrayed or lost by attempts to commercialize the genre and by efforts to theorize it. Similarly, an article by Pedro Atienza on the flamenco clan 'Los Sordera', published in issue 24, underlines flamenco's otherworldly nature:

> porque como canta de nuevo y se le sube la media voz a la garganta parece tomado por un fantasma que le transporta a un mundo de sonidos purísimos, dolientes unas veces, alegres y vivaces otras. Sonidos de un mundo que no se conduce por las leyes de la gravitación universal. [...] "Sonidos negros" dictados por ese fantasma del cante gitano al que alude él mismo. (24: 25)
>
> [because as he sings again, and his half-voice rises to his throat, he seems possessed by a ghost that transports him to a world of the purest sounds, sometimes hurting, sometimes joyful and vivid. Sounds of a world that is not governed by the laws of universal gravitation. [...] "Black sounds" dictated by that ghost of gypsy *cante* to which he himself alludes.] (24: 25)

This insistence on purity and otherness is striking, given the proclivity to parody and the profound scepticism towards transcendentalism found elsewhere in the magazine. The characterization, in the quotation above, of flamenco as phantasmatic, and therefore beyond rational comprehension or articulation, echoes

Isabel Escudero's postulation of an indefinable female difference in issue 6 of *La Luna*, discussed earlier in this chapter. In both instances, the impulse to protect what is perceived as other runs parallel to the affirmation of a difference that eludes definition. This refusal to clearly delineate the contours of difference can, as suggested earlier, be seen as an attempt to preserve it from assimilation and commodification. In the case of flamenco, the risk of commodification is addressed directly by Ripoll through his condemnation of 'los desafortunados intentos de las multinacionales discográficas' (5: 20) to market a homogenized and sanitized version of the genre. But such vindications of flamenco's radical difference (radical not only by virtue of its distance from dominant cultural forms, but also in the etymological sense of originary) also risk essentializing flamenco, particularly when they are expressed in the quasi-mystical tone of the quotation above. By arguing that flamenco 'no se conduce por las leyes de la gravitación universal', Atienza presumably intends to underline the uniqueness of that musical genre, but his words also suggest a problematic view of flamenco as free and detached from both the socio-historical reality within which it emerged, and other cultural forms contiguous and contemporary to that genre. This essentialist insistence on flamenco as radically other not only obscures the genre's development over time and its links to other cultural manifestations, it also risks rendering it inaccessible and irrelevant to all but a handful of experts and initiated fans.

Copla or *canción española* is also celebrated within *La Luna*'s pages, but the genre is not treated in the same reverent manner as flamenco. While flamenco is endorsed for its purity and otherness, *copla* is admired for its melodramatic quality, which lends itself to camp rearticulations. The feature on *copla* legend Miguel de Molina published in issue 15 (40–41), for example, focuses on his unique performance style: his adoption of a repertoire of songs originally written for female singers and his onstage cross-dressing, as well as on his off-stage persona as a (for the period) defiantly 'out' homosexual. The singer's past success is set in stark contrast with his bleak present as an aged, lonely and reclusive exile in Buenos Aires, and the article may thus be read as an attempt to rescue Molina from oblivion and restore him to his rightful place within the canon of *canción española*. But there is more to the article: despite the emphasis on Molina's originality, the article also suggests that he could be considered part of a tradition of cross-dressing male singers of previous centuries, such as Pablo de la Serna and Cristóbal Serrano (15: 40). This reference to Molina's predecessors is significant not only because it frames the singer's undoubtedly innovative style within an already existing (if little known) tradition, but also because it implicitly suggests that Molina himself may be seen as a precursor to (and perhaps an inspiration for) contemporary performers, such as Martirio, featured in the cover of issue 34 of the magazine, or the cross-dressing parodic duo formed by Pedro Almodóvar and Fabio McNamara, whose style, though more directly influenced by American drag queens such as Divine and by 1970s glam rock, nonetheless shared some of the histrionics of Molina's, albeit in such an exaggerated, camp and irreverent fashion as to make it entirely devoid of the pathos which characterized Molina's performances. This implied connection of Molina to a genealogy of performers is by no means one of linear continuity;

rather, by devoting a lengthy double-page feature to this legendary figure, *La Luna* is, I would suggest, both acknowledging the value of his art and style, and exposing their potential and making them available as elements or building blocks for contemporary Barthesian bricolages.

This hybridizing approach to tradition comes to the fore in the feature 'La canción española: el auténtico glam', published in issue 39 *of La Luna* (20–21). The very title of the piece suggests a link between the Spanish popular music of the first half of the twentieth century and the genre of glam rock. Of course, there is no direct connection between these genres; what Sardi, the article's author, postulates is rather that the glamour and dramatic posturing of glam can also be found, albeit in a less ironic and self-conscious form, in the music and performances of *canción española* stars such as Conchita Piquer, Estrellita Castro, Manolo Caracol or Juanita Reina, and that contemporary Spanish musicians ought to learn and draw inspiration from its expressive richness, instead of merely copying what is done abroad, particularly in the UK and the US. The piece is remarkable not only because it attempts to reclaim the tradition of *canción española* for a younger audience, but also because its association of the genre with a contemporary global phenomenon such as glam rock reinscribes it within a contemporary and international context. Jo Labanyi observes that

> It is because of its stress on spectacle that 1940s Spanish culture lends itself so well to postmodernist pastiche. But the appeal of 1940s kitsch is also that its reproduction in a modern internationalist context deconstructs the essentialist concept of national identity that such cultural images were originally designed to promote. (Labanyi 1995: 406)

It is precisely in what Labanyi terms the 'stress on spectacle' of 1940s Spanish culture (and, in this specific context, *copla*) that Sardi finds an affinity with glam rock; but, as Labanyi notes, reinscriptions such as the one undertaken in Sardi's article, though seemingly motivated by a desire to preserve tradition, simultaneously transform it, neutralising its essentialist and essentializing properties. Additionally, presenting *canción española* as a sort of Spanish predecessor to glam rock affects the way in which the potential new audience for the genre approach and make sense of it. Implicit in this recontextualizing approach is thus a non-essentialist view of cultural tradition as something that changes and evolves over time, and, further, as something which not only shapes individuals' identities and their understandings of the world, but which individuals also, dialectically, contribute to reinvent and rearticulate.

This non-essentialist view of cultural tradition is made explicit in issue 25 of *La Luna*, in which its second editor, José Tono Martínez, refers to *la movida* as follows: 'Todo lo sucedido en los últimos cinco años ha sido realizado a base de pasión, a base de inventarnos los mitos que empedraran las calles de unas ciudades entusiastas pero pobres' [The events of the past five years have been the result of passion, of our inventing myths to pave the streets of enthusiastic but poor cities] (25: 6). Tono Martínez's linking of *la movida* to myth-making not only reveals an awareness of the connection between myths and cultural traditions; with myth arguably the cornerstone of cultural tradition, *la movida* needed to create its own myths in order to establish itself as a cultural movement. His reference to the invention of myths further suggests that myths (and, by extension, cultural traditions) are not static and permanent, but rather that they can be reshaped, indeed, made anew (invented). It is further worth noting that myths, and more specifically the newly-invented myths of *la movida*, are not invoked here in relation to metaphysical problems, or treated as vehicles for transcendental truths. Instead, the stated purpose of these new myths is a more humble one: to pave city streets, in other words to furnish the spatio-temporal realities of those who create and share them. This association of myth and city suggests that the spatial or geographical dimension of identity, the individual's sense of belonging to a place, which conditions his/her sense of self and his/her world view, needs to be considered at a local, rather than at a national level. This primacy of the local over the national can be interpreted as a reaction against the attempts by the Francoist propaganda apparatus to create a homogenous Spanish identity by repressing cultural difference and by conflating a plurality of regional identities into one single mould of Spanishness. But this emphasis on the local is also indicative of a desire to effect change from the bottom up, improving citizens' daily lives by enriching their everyday. Further, the city's loosely defined, porous boundaries -both internally, in terms of the nature and uses of specific spaces, and externally, in terms of its continually expanding and contracting contours- fit more closely with *La Luna*'s understanding of identity as fluctuating, dynamic construct than the clearly delineated and generally stable borders of the nation-state (or of the post-Franco Comunidades Autónomas).

This emphasis on the local can also be linked to the postmodern valorization of (local) difference within an increasingly globalized -and therefore, arguably, homogenous and homogenizing- world. *La Luna*'s attitude to globalization, much like its views on postmodernism, is somewhat ambivalent: on the one hand, the risk of homogenization is acknowledged, with Tonò Martínez, for instance, warning that Spain's integration within the European Economic Community, now the European Union, could bring about 'el fin de una forma de ver el mundo' (15: 8) unless peripheral Mediterranean countries such as Spain, Italy and Greece work together to affirm and preserve their difference. On the other hand, globalization is seen as an opportunity, since it facilitates inter-cultural dialogue, as exemplified by the popularization of *la movida* beyond Spain's borders, noted by Tono Martínez in his editorial of issue 25 (6); and it also allows for the emergence of new transnational identities and alliances.

La Luna's call for the creation of a Mediterranean axis and its interest in the emergence of *chicano* and *latino* identities within the US can be regarded as moves to counter what is perceived as the cultural hegemony of the UK and the US, which is alluded to explicitly on several occasions.[23] Underlying these efforts is an awareness of the strategic and political usefulness of these new identity categories. But in order to justify such identity-based alliances, those working on *La Luna* do not always succeed in avoiding the spectre of essentialism. Particularly in discussions regarding the logic and necessity of a Mediterranean axis, we witness the emergence of a vague, essentialized notion of a 'South' that is defined in opposition to an equally essentialized and universalized North that encompasses Northern Europe and

North America. Luis Racionero's article 'El sur mental' (17: 5–6) is a paradigmatic example of this tendency to essentialism. In this piece, he opposes a 'norte frío, guerrero y puritano [que] se volcó hacia la máquina y el trabajo' [cold, warring and puritan North [which] gave itself over to machines and work] (17: 5) to a voluptuous, indolent South (17: 6). This South is defined not merely as a geographical space, but also as a mythical one. However, in this instance myth is not dismantled, destabilized or parodied; instead, Racionero appears to revel in it, and, seduced by its suggestive force, fails to acknowledge its historically constructed nature and constraining and conditioning effects for the present and the future. While the desire to affirm and protect difference in the face of assimilation is understandable — Spain's imminent entry into the European Common Market is alluded to within the article[24] — it does not justify Racionero's essentialism, which ignores the politically loaded ways in which difference is articulated and obscures the diversity and nuances that exist within what he labels as 'el Sur'. Paradoxically, his view of a distinct and cohesive South, though motivated by a desire to protect difference, in fact entails an erasure of the plurality of landscapes, identities, lifestyles, values and beliefs that make up what he labels as 'the South'.

La Luna's approach to national or place-based identity (or rather identities, in the plural) is thus not consistent, but marked by ambivalence and contradiction. On the one hand, the magazine's parodic use of Catholic and bullfighting imagery suggests a desire to challenge and dismantle dated national identity clichés associated with Francoist nationalist discourse. But such parodic reformulations go hand in hand with a serious engagement with subjects such as bullfighting and traditional popular music genres, and can thus also be read as attempts to reappropriate cultural forms that were seen as tainted by their association with Francoism. The magazine's co-founder Carlos de Laiglesia remarked in that respect that '[n]o estábamos dispuestos a ceder al franquismo los toros y el flamenco, y no dejamos que nos los robaran' [we were determined not to hand over bullfighting and flamenco to Francoism, and we didn't allow it to steal them from us] (Cadahía 2007: 23). Further, *La Luna*'s reclaiming of traditionally Spanish cultural forms such as bullfighting, *copla* and flamenco, both through their inclusion within the magazine's pages and through their association with contemporary and/or foreign phenomena such as pop and glam rock, is indicative of a desire to draw new audiences to these forms, and to affirm and preserve their specificity within what is perceived as an increasingly globalized and homogenous cultural landscape. While the magazine's ironic approach and recontextualizing efforts may have succeeded in engaging a younger generation with a rich cultural legacy that seemed headed for oblivion as a result of its association with and appropriation by Francoism,[25] its attempts to forge supra-national alliances to counter 'Northern' (that is, Northern European and North American) cultural hegemony are marred by a recourse to essentialist and essentializing language and imagery that contradicts the notion of identity as process and flux underlying most of the magazine's output on the subject, and that threatens the very diversity and heterogeneity it intends to preserve.

Within *La Luna*, we find a series of tensions and contradictions in its approach to identity. While the 'I' of individual identity is presented as multiple and unstable, there is a simultaneous, if implicit, affirmation of the subject as the generator or originator of the work of art; while gender clichés are destabilized through parody, there is also a parallel vindication of gender(ed) difference which in some cases relies on, or contributes to reinforce, some of those very stereotypes; and while the magazine's treatment of cultural forms and practices associated with a traditional notion of Spanishness underlines their camp and kitsch potential, thus undermining their essentialist charge, its attempts at articulating alternative supra-national identities (such as Southern European/Mediterranean/Hispanic/Latino) fall back on essentialist rhetoric. These fluctuations between parody and reaffirmation, deconstructive and essentialist moves may seem inconsistent at times, but in fact they fit the notion of identity as open-ended, dynamic and occasionally contradictory process that informs the magazine. Despite occasional lapses into essentialist rhetoric or essentialist arguments, *La Luna*'s success at exposing and exploiting the creative potential of identity paradigms remains unquestionable. At their most radical, the explorations of identity featured within the magazine query not only the constructed and performative nature of identity, but also the visual and linguistic mechanisms of (self-)representation through which identity is articulated. As the final part of this chapter will illustrate, this awareness of a complex and reciprocal relationship between identity and (self-)representation informs *La Luna*'s tentative, uneasy articulation of its own editorial identity.

La Luna's editorial identity: resisting definition

The implicit view of identity as flux, as a dynamic, provisional construct in a process of constant de- and reconstruction that underpins much of *La Luna*'s output on identity also affects the magazine's own constitution. During its first period (1983–1985) at least, *La Luna* successfully resisted a clear-cut definition, positioning itself at the junction of established categories such as fanzine/glossy, mainstream/underground, local/global, highbrow/lowbrow, and modernist or avant-garde/postmodernist. This rejection of and resistance to conventional classificatory labels should be seen as an attempt by the magazine to open up an editorial space for itself that sought to negotiate the gap between these categories, blurring their boundaries in the process.

La Luna is visual eclecticism and the heterogeneity of its contents are key to its ability to elude a closed and clear-cut definition, and the wealth of references and influences makes it virtually impossible to link the magazine to one single movement, style or current. To an extent, it could be argued that eclecticism and heterogeneity in fact became *La Luna*'s defining traits, a style of its very own; indeed, such an assertion applies to the later issues of the magazine, particularly from 1986 onwards, in which contents are presented in a striking but streamlined and thus fairly predictable manner. However, during its initial period under the editorship of Borja Casani, the magazine's often messy combination of disparate elements does not appear as a calculated move to project a particular image (that of an avant-garde or countercultural arts magazine), but rather as a reflection of the very diverse range of interests and influences of the publication team, as well as of its extensive list of collaborators and contributors; and perhaps, too, as a an echo of the city's bustle, as suggested in the previous chapter. The inaccuracies that can be found in these early issues (errors in its table of contents;[26] lapses in the regularity of publication;[27] or mistakes in dating)[28] testify to the magazine's attempts to capture the cultural effervescence of Madrid with absolute contemporaneity (cf. Smith 2006: 57), as well as being symptomatic of its producers' scant editorial experience (cf. Cadahía 2007: 16; Gallero 1991: 28). In contrast, the later issues of the magazine (from 1986 onwards) look far more polished and professional; their eclecticism a self-conscious style strategy.

Irreverence is another key strategy that allows *La Luna* to remain something of a puzzle; its passion for the city and for creative and existential experimentation punctuated by wry comments that suggest that one should not take anything too seriously, least of all oneself. Madrid, for instance, is described in the first issue of the magazine as 'la ciudad enana más alta del mundo' [the tallest dwarf city in the world] (1: 7), a characterization that helps balance and put into perspective the piece's overwhelmingly positive and hopeful view of the city. The magazine's irreverence enables it to create some distance between itself and the object of its mockery, thus avoiding any kind of pathos or transcendentalism. One of the most frequent objects of derision is the magazine itself: Patty Diphusa refers to *La Luna* as 'la revista más pretenciosa de todos los tiempos' [the most pretentious magazine of all times] within her column (14: 86); and in issue 13, Jorge Berlanga mocks the magazine's postmodern eclecticism in 'Cómo escribir un artículo para *La Luna*', in which he advises prospective writers to resort to some scissors 'para preparar un pastiche apañadito que satisfaga las apetencias ecléticas del cotarro contemporáneo' [in order to prepare a handy pastiche that satisfies the eclectic appetites of the contemporary bustle] (13: 10), borrowing from and combining mayor Tierno's speeches, the philosophical ramblings of Javier Sádaba, Duchampian puns and *greguerías* by Gómez de la Serna, among other materials. *La Luna*'s irreverence is also evident in its deliberate choice of provocative slogans, such as 'Contra la juventud' (issue 11). The magazine's denunciation of youth here is understandable, as youth is defined as 'el último mito de la modernidad gregaria' (11: 6), that is, as the last remaining obligatory identity category imposed on individuals; but it is also deeply ironic, considering that the majority of *La Luna*'s readers, as well as most of its contributors,[29] were (or considered themselves) young, and given the pivotal role the magazine played in shaping the youth culture of its day.

La Luna's complex relationship and approach to apparently opposed notions such as local and global further exemplifies the ways in which the magazine defies conforming to a stable or clearly delineated editorial identity. While the publication's focus on the local, on what was happening in the streets of Madrid, is made explicit from the title itself (*La Luna de Madrid*) and, further, becomes manifest in the emphasis given to the work of local artists, the listing of events taking place in the city, and the space and attention devoted to Madrid (from its architectural make-up to the different encounters and experiences that the city makes possible), the titles upon which the magazine modelled itself were two American publications, *Interview* and *Village Voice*. In a sense, it could be argued that by using two American titles as templates for *La Luna*, Casani and his team applied a foreign perspective or form to what was taking place at the local level in Madrid. But *La Luna*'s appropriation of American editorial models and its patent interest in 'foreign' movements such as Pop Art, punk, glam rock and postmodernism should not be considered merely as a symptom of the globalization and progressive Americanization of youth and popular culture, a phenomenon which, as we have seen, in fact concerned the magazine's editorial team, but rather as a reaction against the policies of cultural censorship and isolationism imposed by the Francoist regime over the preceding four decades, which, according to Borja Casani, had left the country a cultural wasteland (15: 7). The fact that those working on *La Luna* used synchronic foreign models, rather than referring to Spanish models of the past for inspiration, is symptomatic of the inter-cultural transferences and dialogues made possible by globalization processes. That globalization granted Casani and his collaborators easier access to, and a better understanding of, what was taking place beyond Spain's borders does not, however, mean that they simply copied or extrapolated from foreign models; rather, the magazine's appropriation of ideas, styles and strategies originating abroad resulted in a highly idiosyncratic cultural product, its originality residing precisely in the hybridizing approach used, which combined the foreign or global with everyday elements firmly anchored within a specific spatio-temporal reality, that of 1980s Spain. Those working on *La Luna*, like most of their contemporaries, could not (and perhaps more importantly, did not want to) resist or deny the appeal of punk, glam rock and other 'foreign' phenomena, but they did recognize the importance of creating their own versions of, or approximations to, those styles. In so doing, they arguably succeeded in creating a style of their own.

There is a further twist to the amalgamation, within *La Luna*, of the global and the local. In the first instance, the magazine's focus on the local and the everyday might appear as a strategy to resist the globalization and/or Americanization of culture decried in several instances within the magazine's pages, as a move to protect and affirm local specificity in an increasingly homogenous world. However, critics such as Fouce (2002) and Urrero (2003) have argued that *la movida*'s embrace of traditional Spanish popular forms and everyday elements is influenced or mediated by Pop Art's fascination with 'low' or popular culture. Thus *La Luna*'s engagement with Spanish popular culture and Madrid's everyday constitutes, on one level, a response to the tendency towards cultural standardization resulting from globalization processes; but simultaneously, and somewhat paradoxically, it is also the result of those very processes, inasmuch as the use of elements of Spanish popular culture is likely to have been inspired, at least in part, by an originally Anglo-American movement such as Pop Art.

The intricate interplay between global and local, foreign and autochthonous, that takes place in *La Luna*'s pages leads to a blurring of the boundaries of such categories, as it becomes problematic (if not impossible) to dissociate one from the other. The permeability of such descriptive and classificatory categories is further underlined through strategies of juxtaposition, with the work of local artists, musicians and thinkers granted as much, if not more, space as that of internationally renowned foreign figures, and presented alongside it; and transposition, with traditionally

Spanish genres such as *canción española* or bullfighting playfully recontextualized in globalized (post)modern contexts (cf. 4: 48 and 39: 20–21). While some critics have attacked such practices of appropriation and hybridization as empty neo-avant-gardist gestures (Subirats 2002: 75), the tension and play between local and global artistic styles and cultural references led to the production of highly original, semantically and semiotically rich works, even if (and sometimes because) their complexity is ostensibly denied by their self-proclaimed frivolity. As we shall see in the following chapter, the contradictions that make *La Luna* such a rich and diverse cultural product arise, at least in part, from the magazine's parallel (and often tangled) engagement with modern and postmodern tropes and practices.

Notes to Chapter 3

1. Paul Julian Smith, for instance, argues that 'Almodóvar anticipates that critique of identity and essence that was later to become so familiar in academic feminist, minority, and queer theory' (Smith 1994: 3).
2. For instance, Edgardo Oviedo's article 'El síndrome del bigote o quien lleva los pantalones' (25: 22–24) considers the role of the feminist liberation movement in changing traditional gender roles.
3. This notion of Spain as 'other' was encapsulated in the phrase 'Spain is different', which was popularized during the 1960s as a slogan to attract foreign tourists. Although the coinage of the slogan has been frequently attributed to Manuel Fraga, Minister of Information and Tourism between 1962 and 1969, the first known instance of the phrase being used for tourism promotion purposes dates back to 1929, when it was used as part of the logo of a series of tourist posters issued by the Patronato de Turismo. In 1948, a variation of the slogan, 'Spain is beautiful and different', was launched, but failed to catch on (Afinoguénova and Martí-Olivella 2008). Additionally, historians such as Juan Pablo Fusi have argued that the notion of Spain as exotic and different from the rest of Europe predated even the Romantic period, and can in fact be traced as far back as the seventeenth century (Fusi 2000).
4. Eleuterio Sánchez (b. 1942), 'El Lute', was initially convicted and imprisoned for stealing two hens. In 1965, he was arrested again and convicted for the murder of a jewellery store security guard. He was sentenced to death, but this was later commuted to 30 years' imprisonment. While in gaol, 'El Lute' protested his innocence, taught himself to read, wrote the autobiographical books *Camina o revienta* (1977) and *Mañana seré libre* (1980), later turned into two films by Vicente Aranda, and began a law degree, which he completed after his release. He escaped from prison twice, in 1966 and 1971, but was finally pardoned and released in 1981.
5. José Luis Brea (1957–2010) would go on to become Professor of Aesthetics and Contemporary Art at Madrid's Carlos III University, an independent arts curator and editor, and author of *Las auras frías* (1990), *La era posmedia* (2002), *El tercer umbral. Estatuto de las prácticas artísticas en la era del capitalismo cultural* (2003), and *Imagen-materia, film, e-image* (2010). Javier Sádaba (1940) is Professor of Philosophy at Universidad Autónoma de Madrid and has published extensively on Wittgenstein and the relationship between religion and philosophy, among other subjects. Eduardo Subirats (1947) is Professor of Spanish Intellectual History at New York University and the author of *La ilustración insuficiente* (1981), *El alma y la muerte* (1983), *América o la memoria histórica* (1994), *El continente vacío* (1994), and *Linterna mágica* (1997), among other titles.
6. Carl Gustav Jung died in 1961, while the second issue of *La Luna*, in which the analysed image and accompanying text appeared, was published in December 1983.
7. In this instance, Yuste is referring to Jung's theory of synchronicity, explored in his 1952 *Synchronicity: An Acausal Connecting Principle*, and to The Police's fifth studio album, released in 1983 and entitled *Synchronicity*.
8. Both these works are reproduced within Krauss's essay and used to illustrate her theory about the use and effect of doubling in Surrealist photography.

9. It is also worth noting that many Surrealists had first-hand experience of World War I, and that both their guardedness with respect to modernity and their use of imagery involving dismembered limbs and body fragmentation can be read as a response to the carnage of war. *Movida* artists, though born and raised during the Francoist dictatorship, did not directly experience anything comparable to the explicit and large-scale violence and destruction of the Great War.
10. Indeed, this appears to be the case in Jaime Gorospe's self-portrait, published in issue 6 (23), in which we can infer the use of a mirror from the fact that Gorospe appears holding a camera, even though no mirror can be seen in the photograph itself.
11. It is worth noting that in Spanish the terms 'female' and 'feminine' are conflated into one word ('femenino'). My choice of either 'female' or 'feminine' in this discussion is largely determined by the contextual factors that point to the word as either referring to socially sanctioned gender (feminine) or to biological sex (female). However, I am aware that their conflation into one term in the Spanish original creates an area of indeterminacy or slippage between both terms, and that my choice of either term in English is thus also an interpretative gesture.
12. I am thinking, for instance, of Betty Friedan's 1963 *The Feminine Mystique*, which, though considered groundbreaking at the time of its publication, and regarded by many as a foundational text of the feminist movement, has also been criticized for its universalising of women's experiences, amalgamating them into a distinctly white, middle class, heterosexual, suburban type which ignores and excludes women who do not fit into those categories (cf. bell hooks 2000).
13. In an otherwise fairly positive review of the magazine published in *La Vanguardia* in January 1984, Ana Basualdo referred to the Luz de Boudoir section as follows"'Otro detalle decepcionante: los chicos de "La Luna" son tan modernos, tan posmodernos que vuelven a la tradición "camp": una sección femenina (!) con potingues y consejos cuya "frivolidad" no alcanza a justificar.' (*La Vanguardia*, 31/01/1984).
14. One of Dada's most salient features is its resistance to definition, exemplified in Dada statements such as 'Dada has 391 different attitudes and colours' (Tristan Tzara: 'Dada is a Virgin Germ', first published in issue 7 of *Dadaphone* no. 7 (Paris, March 1920), translated by Ian Monk and reprinted in Ades 2006: 66) and 'As for Dada it means nothing, nothing, nothing.' (Francis Picabia: 'DADA Manifesto', originally published in issue 12 *391* (Paris, March 1920), translated by Michelle Owoo and reprinted in Ades 2006: 125).
15. In her theorisation of postmodernism, Hutcheon claims that parody is a quintessentially postmodern form because 'it paradoxically both incorporates and challenges what it parodies' (1988: 11). Echoing this statement, Bersani argues, in a discussion of Butler's *Bodies that Matter*, that the reappropriation of hegemonic forms proposed by Butler 'partly subverts [such norms] and partly re-idealizes them' (1995: 51).
16. Péret offered this definition in response to André Breton's question, 'Qu'est-ce que le viol?' [What is rape?], as part of a quick question-answer game published under the title 'Le Dialogue en 1928' in Surrealist magazine *La Révolution Surréaliste*, no. 11 (March 1928), pp. 7–8.
17. Patty's farewell appears in issue 9–10 of *La Luna*, as the sixth instalment of the 12-part series; despite her resolve to quit, Patty returns for a further seven instalments. However, the farewell piece is published as the last instalment in the book edition of the series, even though Almodóvar claims in the introduction to the volume that the pieces have not been edited in any way. This discrepancy is interesting since it points to a wish to grant the book edition a degree of linearity or coherence *a posteriori* not present in the original, which is at odds with Patty's unreliability, capriciousness and unpredictability.
18. Legal equality between men and women was granted only in 1978, through the promulgation of a new constitution; and homosexuality was not decriminalized until 1979.
19. The writer and journalist José Luis Moreno Ruiz wrote most of these pieces, for instance in issue 6 (54), 7 (54) and 11 (61). Further, issue 9/10 (81) includes a review by Francisco Guio of the bullfights of San Isidro, and issue 22 features an interview with the legendary bullfighter Antoñete (37–41).
20. In her seminal 1975 article 'Visual Pleasure and Narrative Cinema', Laura Mulvey postulates a theory of the gaze according to which narrative cinema constructs the viewing subject as male and the object of its gaze as female.

21. The text published in *La Luna* and cited here reproduces verbatim a fragment from Soriano's *pasodoble*, but it changes the gender of the protagonist of the song, who is a boy in the original, but a girl in the version that appears in the magazine.
22. In the 48 issues of *La Luna*, I have only found four pieces of significant length dealing with traditional Spanish popular musical genres: 'Rarezas del Flamenco', by José Ramón Ripoll (5: 20); 'Miguel de Molina. De las luces a las sombras', by Javier Rioyo and Manolo Ferreras (15: 40–41); 'Cante Jondo. Viaje por la casa de los "Sordera"', by Pedro Atienza (24: 25) and 'La canción española: el auténtico glam', by Sardi (39: 20–21).
23. In issue 15, Tono Martínez suggests the creation of a horizontal Mediterranean axis to counter the pre-eminence of 'los nórdicos', a loose terms that appears to encompass North America and Northern Europe (15: 8). In issue 17, Luis Racionero refers to 'la indiscriminada presión hacia el "American Way of Life"' experienced by Spain and other Mediterranean countries (17: 6). And in the aforementioned piece on *canción española* published in issue 39 (20–21), its author decries the tendency of contemporary Spanish musicians to copy what is done in the UK and the US.
24. Spain joined the European Common Market, or European Economic Community (the predecessor of today's European Union) in 1986, months after the publication of this article.
25. My analysis of several examples of parody and recontextualization of tradition within *La Luna* illustrates the textual and visual effectiveness of these approaches; however, the extent to which these efforts succeeded in capturing the public's imagination is difficult to determine, as it requires an in-depth reception study, and, more importantly, because the magazine did not appear within a cultural vacuum, but operated alongside a wealth of other cultural products. While it would be tempting to credit *La Luna* with, for example, the resurgence of flamenco that took place in Spain throughout the 1980s and 1990s, it would be wrong to postulate an unproblematic cause-effect relationship between the magazine's endorsement of the genre and its revival. *La Luna* contributed to inform and shape the Spanish cultural landscape of the 1980s, but it also reflected it, and the extent to which its role was proactive or reactive remains open to debate.
26. In the second issue of *La Luna*, the contents page lists Javier Utray's 'A la recherche du champs perdu' as appearing in page 13, when it in fact appears on page 26.
27. Throughout its five-year existence, *La Luna* published one extended summer issue for the months of July and August, reflecting the slowdown of activity in Madrid (and generally across Spain) during those months, and presumably also to allow for editorial staff and contributors to take leave. But in 1984 and 1985 the magazine ostensibly extended its summer break onto September, failing to produce an issue for that month and only reappearing in kiosks in October. Hence, while there are 11 issues of the magazine published in 1986 and 1987, only ten appeared in 1984 and 1985.
28. Issue 18, for instance, is dated 'Abril 1985', when in fact it appeared in May 1985.
29. Most of the members of *La Luna's* first editorial team were in their 20s at the time of the magazine's launch. Editor Borja Casani, born in 1952, was among the older members of the team.

CHAPTER 4

❖

Modernity and Postmodernity in and of *La Luna de Madrid*

The previous chapters of this book, which analyse *La Luna*'s urban reimaginings and its destabilization of fixed identity categories, have already suggested a relationship between the magazine and what may be described as characteristically postmodern preoccupations. The focus on the city is not only characteristic of postmodernism: the urban exerted a strong power of fascination over modernist and avant-garde writers and artists, too. There is, however, a shift in emphasis: while modern(ist) subjects perceive urban space as a setting that is distinct from their own subjectivity, and can hence be described as a visual tableau seen and enjoyed from a privileged, external vantage point, in postmodern cultural practice there is an awareness of the all-encompassing nature and generative power of space, and hence the boundary between self and space becomes problematic. Similarly, while identity is as much of a concern for artists and thinkers of the modern period as it is for their postmodern counterparts, the former's anxiety with regard to the instability and fragmentation of the self, and their quest for a 'human totality', are replaced in the postmodern era by a more positive view of the possibilities of a multiple, fluid and dynamic self.

If the previous chapters implicitly anticipated the relationship between *La Luna* and postmodernism by considering the oscillations within the magazine between modern(ist) and postmodern(ist) attitudes and approaches to urban space and identity, this chapter explicitly engages with postmodernism as subject matter (that is, as a theme that features within the magazine), as style (insofar as it influences the magazine's visual and editorial configuration), and as historical period (taking into account the socio-historical context in which the magazine appeared). This compartmentalization is intended for purposes of conceptual and structural clarity, and finds echo in a range of binaries (style/thought; art/politics; individual/collective) used throughout the chapter to explore the tensions at work in *La Luna* and to help make sense of its trajectory. But these categorical divisions are not always clear-cut; indeed, *La Luna* frequently undertakes a postmodern questioning of precisely such neat categorizations, thus contributing to blur classificatory boundaries.

It has become commonplace to link *la movida* to postmodernism: Eduardo Subirats, for instance, sees in the hedonism of the Spanish movement an attitude that is wholly 'en consonancia con el posmodernismo trasnacional' [in agreement with transnational postmodernism] (2002: 75), while for Juan Luis Cebrián *la movida* 'es el primer anuncio de lo que sería luego el movimiento posmoderno' [is the first sign of what would later become the postmodern movement] (Gallero 1991: 313). However, neither of these critics explores the relationship between the localized, (sub)cultural Madrid movement and the global postmodern phenomenon in any detail. While I do not deny that there are postmodern echoes and affinities in *la movida*, labelling the localized, spontaneous (sub)cultural Madrid movement as postmodern is potentially problematic: firstly, because simply establishing a relationship of analogy or correspondence between these two phenomena does not tell us much about either of them (to say that *la movida* was a postmodern manifestation is meaningless unless we clarify what we understand by 'postmodern', and trace the specific aspects of *la movida* that fit in with our definition); and also because the characterization of the Spanish movement as postmodern posits both *la movida* and postmodernism as stable, monolithic entities, rather than as processes whose nature and meanings remain contested to this day. Additionally, the unproblematic identification of *la movida* with postmodernism by critics such as Eduardo Subirats or José Carlos Mainer relies on a view of both phenomena as departures from or breaks with the modern Enlightenment project of intellectual and political emancipation.

My exploration of the evolving and often contradictory relationship of the *movida* cultural object *La Luna* to postmodernism seeks to trace the postmodern ideas and practices the magazine engages with, in an attempt to delineate its own understanding of the term — an understanding that, as we shall see, is often bound together with modern concepts and values. This view of modernism and post-modernism as contiguous (and, to an extent, overlapping), rather than as opposing movements whereby the latter constitutes a radical and clear break with the former, is expressed by intellectuals contributing to *La Luna*, such as the art historian Juan Antonio Ramírez, who writes:

> cuanto más modernos somos, más postmodernos parecemos; cuanto menos postmodernos más premodernos o, sencillamente, menos modernos. Post-moderno no significa, pues, algo contrario, opuesto o posterior a la modernidad. Tal vez (last but not least) es sólo su último disfraz. (24: 22)[1]
>
> [the more modern we are, the more postmodern we appear; the less postmodern, the more premodern, or simply, less modern, we seem. Postmodern does not, thus, mean something opposed to or following modernity. Maybe (last but not least) it is just its latest disguise.] (24: 22)

Ramírez's words echo the views of two theorists of the postmodern: Jean-François Lyotard, for instance, considers that '[a] work can become modern only if it is first postmodern. Postmodernism thus understood is not modernism at its end but in the nascent state, and this state is constant' (1984: 79); while for Linda Hutcheon 'the modern is ineluctably embedded in the postmodern' (1988: 38). Interestingly, Ramírez's statement postdates Lyotard's but predates Hutcheon's, a temporal framing that suggests that, despite a degree of self-consciousness with regard to Spain's perceived cultural lagging behind expressed elsewhere in *La Luna*, Spanish academics and intellectuals of this period were not just repeating or reflecting upon what was being said about postmodernism beyond Spain, but rather aimed to be part of a global conversation on the subject.

Postmodernism is a highly contentious term that still polarizes scholars. There is a broad consensus on what its defining features are: 'ephemerality, fragmentation, discontinuity, and the chaotic' (Harvey 1989: 44); 'concern for pluralism' and 'a critique of monolithic culture' (Jencks 2011: 33); 'an ideal of emancipation based on oscillation, plurality and, ultimately, on the erosion of the very "principle of reality"' (Vattimo 1992: 7). These definitions emphasize plurality and fragmentation as core characteristics of postmodernism, and as traits that undermine or challenge what Lyotard terms 'legitimising metanarratives' (1984), that is, the discourses that support and structure any form of authority, whether political or intellectual. Although there is agreement on the characteristics that define postmodern works and approaches, critical opinions on the causes, implications and effects of postmodernity (understood as the historical period that follows modernity) and postmodernism (the cultural paradigm of postmodernity) vary significantly, from those who condemn postmodernism's alleged abandonment of the Enlightenment emancipation project (Habermas 1993, Subirats 2002) or its departure from a Marxism-informed model for social change (Jameson 1991, Harvey 1989), to those who greet the new period with a guarded optimism (Lyotard 1984), and those who underline and celebrate its ludic and liberating aspects (Hutcheon 1988, Hassan 1987, Vattimo 1992). These critics differ not only in their prognosis of the postmodern condition, but also in other aspects, including the degree of continuity or discontinuity between the modern and the postmodern periods, the role of the mass media in inaugurating and shaping postmodernity, and the very definition and status of art and culture within a context in which the division between 'high' and 'low' cultural forms, or between art and entertainment, appears increasingly porous.[2] This chapter does not intend to resolve or arbitrate these discrepancies; rather, this sketch of the multiplicity of critical responses to postmodernism seeks to illustrate the polyphony that surrounds any attempt at a definition of, or a coming to terms with, the postmodern — a polyphony which is itself typically postmodern. The aim of this chapter is not to articulate a critique of postmodern theory, but to trace those elements in and of *La Luna* that may be considered postmodern in the broadest possible sense of the term, as well as to identify the influence of postmodern thinkers over the magazine. By drawing out the connections between *La Luna* and postmodernism, this analysis will localize a concept that, while insisting on the importance of local specificities (regional, ethnic, as well as sexual and gender difference, for instance) and localized action (small scale grassroots initiatives that replace the utopian political projects of the past) has all too often been applied indiscriminately to works, individuals and manifestations with little regard for their specific socio-historical context.

Modernity and postmodernity in *La Luna de Madrid*

One key challenge to any consideration of *La Luna*'s engagement with modernity/postmodernity and modernism/postmodernism resides in finding a balance between attempts to make sense of the magazine's responses to these themes, and the need to do justice to their complexity. Conversely, the polyphony of views expressed in the magazine's pages, which evolve and change over the publication's five-year existence, should not compromise the critical duty of analysing, making connections and identifying patterns among the textual evidence. In order to balance these two imperatives, in what follows I undertake a close textual analysis that seeks to reflect the heterogeneity and (often deliberate) ambiguity of *La Luna*'s contents, while also proposing a chronology to map the evolution of the magazine's views and attitudes towards postmodernism; and identifying a series of conceptual binaries (individual/collective; arts/politics; style/thought; modern/postmodern) that help explain the tensions and contradictions at work in the magazine.

Postmodern Madrid: the first issue of La Luna

La Luna's engagement with postmodernism is most explicitly articulated in its editorials, in the form of opinion pieces, round-table debates, and manifesto-like proclamations that offer shifting and sometimes contradictory views on a range of (post)modern topics. The publication's first editorial, signed by the editor Borja Casani and José Tono Martínez and entitled 'Madrid 1984: ¿la posmodernidad?', already points to the magazine's awareness of the then emergent concept of postmodernity, and can be seen as an attempt to apply the new paradigm to their experiences in Madrid in order to make better sense of it. The tone of the editorial is decidedly optimistic; something has changed, readers are told, and, for the first time, Madrid can make its 'primera irrupción seria en el terreno de las llamadas vanguardias' [first substantial incursion into the terrain of the so-called avant-gardes] (1: 6). The simultaneous association of Madrid with postmodernity (in the title of the piece) and the avant-garde (in its body) may seem odd, even paradoxical, given that the advent of postmodernism is generally seen as precluding the emergence of an avant-garde. Zygmunt Bauman, for instance, argues that '[t]he phrase "postmodern avant-garde" is a contradiction in terms' (1997: 100), since 'the concept of the avant-garde conveys the idea of an essentially orderly space and time, of an essential co-ordination of two orders' (1997: 95), a condition that is not (and cannot be) given in a postmodern context.

However, the authors of the editorial are quick to point out that this new Madrilenian avant-garde is not a conventional one; that is, it is not made up of a select group of individuals trying to impose a new conception of art and culture on the masses, but rather, it is happening from the bottom up, spreading first through the city streets and only later being identified and reflected upon in cultural, artistic, and academic fora. Given this description of Madrid's avant-garde as a spontaneous and disorganized street phenomenon, its characterization as postmodern seems less odd. The phrasing used to refer to the city's new state is revealing: Madrid, we are told, 'se ha puesto en vanguardia' [has put itself in the vanguard] — an interesting turn of phrase in Spanish that plays on the common idiom 'ponerse en guardia' (to be or become on guard). This wording not only reflects the transient nature of Madrid's present vanguard status, but also, implicitly, alludes to its spatial (or positional) dimension, suggesting that the city has adopted an avant-garde position or pose. Moreover, we are led to associate 'vanguardia' (avant-garde) and 'guardia' (guard) through the replacement of the latter by the former in an established idiomatic expression, made all the more striking by the phonetic and semantic closeness of both terms. By reworking 'vanguardia' from its current, purely cultural and artistic usage into a phrase that reinvests the term with martial connotations, we are not only being reminded of the military origins of *vanguardia* (or avant-garde); the expression also links being or becoming avant-garde to a general state of alertness and readiness.

The initial positive valorization of Madrid as a city 'on avant-garde' is, however, juxtaposed with a description, later in the text, of Madrid as 'ruina'. These two apparently contradictory images are brought together as follows: '¡Ruina! Esa es la palabra mágica que debería alegrar nuestros corazones. Esa es la situación límite a partir de la cual cualquier esfuerzo de la imaginación se convierte en una obligación social' [Ruin! That is the magic word that ought to bring joy to our hearts. It is the extreme situation in which any effort of the imagination becomes a social obligation] (1: 7). Ruin is perceived positively here, as it makes the use of imagination mandatory, a 'social obligation'. It is Madrid's state of ruin, we are told later on, that has led (unemployed) architects to become painters, or idle electricians to form rock bands. The challenge now, according to the authors, is to allow this already existing ferment of creativity to mature, and to create the necessary channels and structures to allow a new generation of artists to make a living out of their art. For Casani and Tono Martínez, creating a mythology of Madrid is central to enabling such a consolidation. The authors remark how other cities around the world (Paris, New York, London) established themselves as cultural centres not only on the basis of their actual living conditions or the talent pool within their artistic milieus, but by creating and projecting a certain image that contributed to attract artists and visitors from around the world. In the case of Madrid, it is suggested that such a mythology could be built upon the fact that the inhabitants of the Spanish capital 'nos hemos mamado así, de sopetón, más novedades que un neoyorkino en toda su existencia' [have absorbed, quickly and suddenly, more novelties than a New Yorker in his whole existence] (1: 7). According to the authors, the rapid social and political change in Spain from the early 1970s onwards has had the effect of compressing into barely ten years cultural and political movements that developed elsewhere over several decades. Such spatio-temporal compression — a defining trait of postmodernity, according to Harvey (1989: vii) — has resulted in '[u]na imagen falsa y lúdica del mundo. Una agradable mitificación de lo moderno. Una superficialidad a prueba de bomba y un liberalismo bastante sincero' [a false and ludic image of the world. A pleasant mystification of the modern. A bombproof superficiality and quite a sincere liberalism] (1: 7). This diagnosis, while acknowledging the illusory nature of the new Madrilenian worldview and underlining its superficiality, is not overtly critical, but rather is seen as a necessary stage in the progression towards a true modernism: 'La modernización se ha producido ya. ¿Ahora qué pasa? La posmodernidad o lo que venga, se llame como se llame, vendría a ser el modernismo auténtico: la profundización y la síntesis de todo lo recibido en apenas dos lustros' [Modernization has already taken place. What happens now? Postmodernity, or whatever follows, regardless of its name, ought to be the authentic modernism: a deepening and synthesis of all the influences received in barely a decade] (1: 7).

This brief excerpt exemplifies the oscillations and entanglements between concepts such as modernization, modernity, modernism, postmodernity and postmodernism often found in *La Luna*. The description of postmodernity in this passage as a consequence of modernization arguably renders the new period indistinct from modernity, which is generally understood as, among other things, a reaction to and a result of scientific and technological advances originating in the Enlightenment period. This indifferentiation between modern/ism/ity and postmodern/ism/ity is further underlined by the assertion that the time to come will lead to 'el modernismo auténtico'. This allusion to an authentic modernism is interesting, for it implicitly points to the insufficiency or inauthenticity of historical modernism. Although this point is not developed further by the authors, the implicit critique of historical modernism can be read on two levels. On the one hand, the term 'modernismo' within a Hispanic context is frequently used in a much more narrow sense than the English 'modernism'. Hispanic 'modernismo' refers to a late nineteenth-century literary school influenced by French Parnassianism and Symbolism, rather than to the multiplicity of responses to modernity denoted by its English counterpart. With this contextual and semantic difference in mind, it is not difficult to see why the authors of the text may find historic Hispanic 'modernismo' insufficient, and their call for an authentic 'modernismo' could be understood as a call for modernism in the broader, Anglo-Saxon sense of the word. Such an interpretation is supported by their definition of this authentic modernism in terms of a systematization ('profundización', 'síntesis') of the novelties to which the authors (and Madrilenians in general) have been exposed in recent years — a project that appears unviable within a postmodern context characterized by information overload and the collapse of systems of meaning. This notion of 'authentic modernism' as a localized version of Western modernism, by this time widely considered dead and buried in most Western countries, points to an awareness on the part of the authors of Spain's cultural backwardness with respect to its neighbours and to an urgent need to 'catch up', a view made explicit elsewhere in the magazine.[3]

There is, however, a second possible interpretation in terms of how this new 'modernismo auténtico' constitutes a departure from historic modernism, namely, its mass and popular nature and appeal. This new modernism is described throughout the article as originating in the city's streets and finding its expression in new ways of speaking, dressing and interacting with others, and in popular or 'low' cultural forms (particularly pop music, comics and fanzines) rather than in more established creative disciplines such as literature and architecture. These two interpretations are, however, not incompatible: indeed, Borja Casani argued elsewhere that Spain, by virtue of its uneven and unfinished modernization was uniquely placed to liberate itself from some of the assumptions and exigencies of modernity, and hence more readily embrace the new postmodern era (cf. Gallero 1991: 29–30), a view echoed by Gianni Vattimo in his prologue to the 1990 Spanish edition of *The Transparent Society*, in which he celebrates Madrid and Spain as new postmodern centres and suggests that it is precisely the country's distance and distinctiveness from the Webberian, Anglo-Saxon, Protestant work ethic characteristic of modernity which might explain its affinity with postmodernity (Vattimo 1990: 67–70).[4] Once again,

Spain's situation of cultural and economic ruin is perceived positively, as granting the opportunity, space and freedom to build something new.

The editorial closes with a juxtaposition of the concepts of modernism and postmodernism: 'El modernismo ha sido la iniciación creativa, el posmodernismo es simplemente ganar dinero con ello' [Modernism was the creative initiation, postmodernism merely means we can make money out of it] (1: 7). This statement can be interpreted in different ways. Susan Larson, for instance, wonders whether these are the words of a generation that is beginning to lose its innocence and creative power, or whether it constitutes the recognition of the unavoidable destiny (co-option by the market) of every avant-garde movement (Larson 2003: 315–16). However, this apparently cynical affirmation is followed by remarks that echo the celebratory, hopeful tone of the article as a whole: 'Y además: reírse de un presente dudoso, embriagarnos pero guardando el tipo, sin que nos tomen el pelo. Y desde luego todo lo que se os ocurra' [And also: laughing at an uncertain present, becoming intoxicated while maintaining our form, and not being taken for a ride. And, of course, anything else you may come up with] (1: 7). Unlike Larson, then, I would suggest that the characterization of postmodernism as a means of making money through creative endeavour is neither cynical, nor resigned or mournful. The authors are simply stating their consciousness of art's dependence on the market, or, in other words, of the need of artists to make a living out of their art in order to be able to carry on with their creative activity. This awareness of art's dependency on or submission to market forces was already present in the work of some modern(ist) thinkers such as Theodor Adorno (1991), but while for the German critic art's exposure to modern capitalism threatened its autonomy and thus its very *raison d'être*, the signatories of this editorial show no such signs of alarm, but rather appear to find the acknowledgement of this relationship liberating, inasmuch as it absolves artists and cultural practitioners from any transcendental imperative or utopian social goal. Indeed, the closing sentence of the piece ('Y desde luego todo lo que se os ocurra') reads as an open invitation to readers to contribute to shape the new period, and thus highlights the democratizing potential of such a non-auratic conception of artistic and cultural practice.

The optimism that accompanies this recognition of art's dependence on industrial processes and market forces can be better understood when considered in conjunction with contextual, socio-historical factors. Given that censorship had operated in Spain until 1977,[5] the identification of economic factors as the key determinants of artistic and cultural production is indicative of the liberalization these sectors have undergone. The fact that individuals engaged in artistic and cultural production in Spain at this time concern themselves primarily with whether their activity is economically viable or not suggests that they operate in an environment within which their freedom of expression is not curtailed by censorship or by the threat of legal or political reprisals. Within the context of *la movida*, this newfound creative freedom after four decades of censorship is perceived as a profoundly individual experience, as Borja Casani notes:

> [*La movida*] Era como la adolescencia de la individualidad, de todo el proceso de individualización [...]. El proceso de ruptura con las teorías absolutas, con

> las verdades ciegas, salvadoras, no produce tanto una decepción como una obligación de definirte a ti mismo. Si no soy un número dentro de la masa, ¿quién soy? Eso, inicialmente, es siempre un juego atractivo y adolescente. Te exige conocimiento, búsqueda, riesgo, algo que en una primera época siempre resulta brillante y emocionante. (Casani in Gallero 1991: 42)

> [*La movida*] was like the adolescence of individuality, of the whole process of individuation [...]. The process of breaking with absolute theories, with blind, saving truths, which leads not so much to disappointment as to an obligation to define oneself. If I am not a mere number within the mass, who am I? That, initially, is an attractive and adolescent game. It demands a quest for knowledge, risk taking, something which, initially, is always brilliant and exciting. (Casani in Gallero 1991: 42)

Interestingly, Casani does not refer to the end of the dictatorship as the key factor in making possible the individualization process of *la movida*, although it undoubtedly constituted a necessary pre-condition for the emergence and free circulation and distribution of a publication such as *La Luna*. For Casani, the imperative to define oneself as individual is rather related to the crumbling of totalizing systems inaugurated by postmodernism, a phenomenon which, in the Spanish context, coincides with the demise of Francoism and arguably therefore lends the individualization process a particularly urgent and explosive character. The quest for self-definition outlined by Casani in the quote above was, however, a collective experience, as evidenced by the fact that it came to be known as a movement (*la movida*), as well as by the proliferation of collaborative projects during these years, of which *La Luna* is but one example.[6] The tension between individual expression and collective experience; between the urge to define oneself as an individual and the tendency to do so, in part at least, through creative collaborations that contributed to the forging of a group identity (as *movida* participants) spans not only *La Luna*, but *la movida* as a whole, as the painters Sigfrido Martín-Begué and Guillermo Pérez-Villalta have noted.[7]

Postmodernism is invoked in this editorial not so much as a concept that describes or explains what is happening in Madrid, though the characterization of the urban (sub)cultural phenomenon that would come to be known as *la movida* as a spontaneous, disorganized and grassroots or popular avant-garde helps understand why it rapidly became identified with postmodernism, but rather as a new context within which it may be possible for a peripheral (in postmodern terminology) city such as Madrid to become a new cultural centre. But despite this generally positive valorization of postmodernism, the views expressed in this editorial are not without tensions and contradictions. In the call for Madrilenians to maximize the cultural revival the capital is experiencing through myth making, for instance, can be read a typically postmodern rejection of the notion of a transcendental or absolute truth. Madrid, the authors appear to suggest, can and will become the city we want it to be, if our urban reimaginings are ambitious and persuasive enough. However, alongside this acknowledgement of the power of mystification is a call to deepen and systematize the experiences made possible by the anarchic Madrilenian avant-garde, to impose order upon disorder, to theorize the chaos of *la movida*. This need to make sense of (rather than simply enjoy) what is taking place in Madrid appears as a somewhat incongruously modern(ist) throwback within a text that purportedly celebrates postmodernity. However, it is precisely such oscillations between positions which are generally thought of as modern(ist) and postmodern(ist) positions which, in my view, characterizes postmodernism. The text's foremost postmodern trait is not its deployment of certain topoi (spontaneity, creativity, mystification, the market) or its occasionally irreverent tone, but rather, its blurring of established dichotomies, such as modern/postmodern, myth/truth and autonomous (high) art/ commercial (low) art. A reading of this editorial as a postmodern text thus relies not merely, or even primarily, upon its ostensible interest in and sympathy for postmodernity, but upon the unresolved tension it exemplifies between a desire to celebrate the spontaneous nature of the creative moment Madrid is experiencing, and the urge to theorize and systematize it.

Chaos and carnival

Such oscillations between apparently contradictory stances can also be detected in the second issue of the magazine, dedicated to the topic of chaos and disorder. Rather than a single editorial, in this issue we find different approaches to the subject: a short story, a brief essay, two opinion pieces and the translation of a poetic fragment by the nineteenth-century poet Gerard Manley Hopkins make for an appropriately chaotic mix.[8] Eduardo Haro Ibars signs the story 'Caos y desorden' (2: 6), a dystopian tale (albeit with a happy ending) that features some of the cult science-fiction author Michael Moorcock's characters (superhero Jerry Cornelius, as well as deities Arioch and Xiombarg). The text is a prime example of postmodern writing. Generically speaking, it falls within a category traditionally associated with 'low' culture (that of science fiction); the references we find within it are broad and disparate (ranging from a Biblical Hebrew expression to Nordic mythology to physics to the 1981 failed coup attempt led by Antonio Tejero), and its repertoire of registers is similarly eclectic. The pseudo-scientific dystopian discourse with which the tale opens is soon undermined by irreverent humour, as the narrator's Chivas whisky is transformed into the cheaper Spanish brand Dyc by the effects of entropy. Later in the text, there is a disconcerting aside in which the narrator refers, in passing and using slang that may not have been intelligible to all readers, to a drug overdose experience that is of no consequence to the plot, and not mentioned again — hence suggesting that this insertion is merely intended to disrupt the narrative flow, as well as, perhaps, to undermine the narrator's credibility. The story postulates Law as leading to destruction (a point loosely illustrated in the text by recourse to the Second Law of Thermodynamics), and chaos, in contrast, constituting perpetual creation, the origin of all things. The characters, whose very existence is threatened in the opening of the story by ever-increasing levels of entropy, are finally saved by this realization, as their embrace of chaos and carnival overcomes the Second Law of Thermodynamics. Ibars's text should read as a literary, and, as such, an artistic-aesthetic, approximation to the theme of postmodern chaos, a topic which features as the main theme of his story, and also affects its structure, its language, and its not entirely coherent or necessarily believable dénouement.

The vindication of chaos in Ibars's story is toned down in Javier Sádaba's short essay 'La descaotización del caos', published within the same double-page spread (2: 7), which approaches the theme from a theoretical-metaphysical perspective. Although Sádaba's opening statement, in which he notes the status of chaos as generative principle within Hesiod's *Theogony*, echoes Ibars's notion of chaos as creation, the philosopher goes on to establish a distinction between 'good' chaos (described as internal to individuals, and as an element that nurtures reason) and 'bad' chaos (a result of the "return of the repressed" internal chaos, which has been engulfed and devoured by reason). For the author, postmodernity is characterized by the proliferation of the latter form of chaos, that is, the blind, sterile and poisonous chaos at the heart of 'el aburrimiento colectivo' [collective boredom], 'el ocio programado' [planned leisure] and 'las conversaciones que comienzan con un final ya sabido' [conversations that begin with an already known ending] (2: 7). Sádaba does not offer a solution to what is described as a postmodern bind, but rather, appears to suggest the rediscovery (or recovery) of our capacity for awe, in other words, of our 'internal' chaos, may offer a way out.[9] This piece thus offers a more complex and nuanced conception of chaos than Ibars's unconditional embrace of disorder, suggesting that there is more to the postmodern vindication of chaos than juvenile rebelliousness or a thoughtless pursuit of hedonistic pleasures. The acceptance and exploration of 'internal' chaos may indeed result in an increased ability to negotiate the challenges posed by postmodernity, but such a project entails more than a simple disavowal of reason and order, which, for Sádaba, stand in a symbiotic relationship to chaos.

This complication of any simple opposition of chaos-order or chaos-reason is taken up again in José Tono Martínez's piece 'Stultifera navis forever' (2: 8), in which the author considers the vital-experiential dimension of chaos, contending that '[e]n un contexto de caos se amenaza con el propio caos' [in a context of chaos, the threat to use is chaos itself]. For Tono Martínez, the acute feeling of chaos characteristic of the postmodern period is the result of the increasingly complex (and chaotic) network of power interests and bureaucratic bodies that shapes our daily lives, which, paradoxically, uses the threat of chaos to justify its existence. Chaos is hence not placed in clear opposition to order and reason, but is rather seen as both its by-product and its legitimizing mechanism. This entanglement of chaos and order does not, however, entail a rejection of chaos; quite the opposite. For the author, it is only by accepting contradiction, by losing our fear of chaos, that we may break free from the constraints imposed upon us: 'Sólo la imaginación, la audacia para crear caos, para explotar las contradicciones, puede hacer que nos lo montemos quedándonos algo fuera' [Only our imagination, our audaciousness in creating chaos and in exploiting contradictions, may allow us to thrive while remaining partially outside]. This appeal to imagination, chaos and contradiction as liberating principles echoes both the attempt of the historical avant-gardes, particularly Dada and Surrealism, to transform life through a creative practice based on spontaneity and the exploration of subconscious and libidinal pulsations, and some of the slogans of the 1968 movement.[10] However, while the earlier movements sought revolutionary political change, the aim here is much more modest, as Tono

Martínez notes that in the current context, '[n]adie plantea una salida revolucionaria vieja escuela. Nadie cree en ninguna revolución' [no-one suggests an old-school revolutionary way out. No-one believes in any revolution]. Indeed, the phrasing of his appeal ('quedándonos algo fuera') implicitly suggests that imagination may, at best, help us achieve an increased, but inevitably only partial, level of freedom from the structures and strictures that govern our lives. This recognition of the impossibility of revolution or of a radical break with and from the current order is not mournful, but rather viewed as inviting a challenge — namely, a role inversion (the author proposes, for instance, that the unemployed ought to have money without working and the elderly should abandon themselves to hedonistic excess) that may contribute to undermine order from within. Of course, one can contend that Tono Martínez's words are but naïve proclamations, inasmuch as it is difficult to see how, for example, imagination alone might improve the living conditions of the unemployed. And yet the enthusiasm of the article is not only genuine, but contagious, and there is something almost heroic in its call on readers to propose and engage in individual, small-scale acts of defiance. In the face of the impossibility of large-scale revolution, a condition acknowledged in the text, and which can be seen as stemming from the experience of the failures of the 1968 movement globally, and the shortcomings of the consensus politics of the transition to democracy within Spain, which forced left-wing parties (and the Communist Party in particular) to abandon many of their pledges,[11] non-conformism appears as the only interstice through which to express resistance to the system, or to claim some degree of independence from it.

These three pieces approach the topic of chaos from different perspectives and offer different views on its meanings and value. For Eduardo Haro Ibars, who undertakes a fictional, creative approximation to the theme, chaos constitutes an unequivocally positive force for its liberating and generative qualities. For Sádaba, who approaches the subject from a philosophical angle, chaos constitutes a paradox, and though he acknowledges its potential, he remains cautious as to its effects. Tono Martínez concerns himself with the vital or experiential dimension of chaos, and, while he is optimistic about its usefulness, his positive outlook is nevertheless qualified by an awareness of its limitations. These different diagnoses of chaos, which are at least in part determined by their authors' differing approaches, are significant because, as this chapter will illustrate, they reflect similar fluctuations regarding the qualities ascribed to postmodernism, which vary depending on whether what is under consideration is its creative-aesthetic possibilities; its theoretical underpinnings, and thus its ethical and political implications and consequences; or its liberating potential at the level of individual personal experience.

'Luna y postmodernidad', written by Llorenç Barber in response to the editorial of the first issue of the magazine, also appears in this second issue. Barber warns about some of the pitfalls inherent in *La Luna*'s celebration of postmodernism: the fact that it could obscure the coexistence of modern (or late-modern) and postmodern stances and attitudes; the danger that the magazine's embrace of postmodernism may be read as anti-modern (and therefore, as reactionary and conservative); and the risk that, given the equivocal nature of postmodernity, there may be a temptation to appeal to the market, money or success as the new criteria through which to judge the value of artworks and cultural products. Despite these warnings, the article nonetheless praises *La Luna*'s ascription to the movement, which it sees as symptomatic of the magazine's focus on multiplicity, eccentricity, the fragment and the local. Thus, in a typically postmodern gesture, given its apparently contradictory nature, Barber simultaneously endorses and rectifies *La Luna*'s alignment with postmodernism.

These first two issues of *La Luna* advance some of the features that characterize the magazine's engagement with postmodernism during the first phase of the magazine (1983 to mid-1985): far from clear, unequivocal support for the new cultural paradigm, what we find here is a series of approximations to some of the discussions inaugurated by the global debate on postmodernism, such as how to make sense of the rapid change that is taking place on an international scale, but that is being felt with particular acuteness, for clear historical reasons (the end of four decades of Francoism and the transition to democracy), within Spain and especially in Madrid (issue 1), or how to navigate an uncertain and ever-shifting social and cultural landscape (issue 2). It is the publication's engagement with such issues, as well as the proliferation within its pages of often-conflicting approaches and responses generated by these questions, that justifies its consideration as a postmodern cultural product. The magazine's preoccupation with these topics is articulated around a series of tensions between modernity and postmodernity, between individual experience and collective initiative, and between the artistic-aesthetic and the political — binary divisions which are, however, undermined and problematized throughout, as those working on *La Luna* strive to find ways in which to make art out of lived experience, and to make a living out of their art.

A (very postmodern) fluctuating relationship with postmodernism

A prime example of *La Luna*'s oscillating relationship with postmodernity and postmodernism can be found in the fourth issue of the magazine, in an editorial by José Tono Martínez which disowns the term: 'Murió el tiempo de la palabreja; la posmodernidad está dejando paso a la **hiperrealidad**' [The odd word is dead: postmodernity is giving way to **hyperreality**] (4: 7) [emphasis in the original]. This apparent disavowal is complicated by the mobilization, within the same text, of tropes commonly associated with postmodernism: carnival, sensual pleasures, and the vindication of a postmodern, Nietzschean 'razón vital' over and above the modern, Kantian 'razón transcendental' (cf. 4: 6–7). In yet another twist, 'hiperrealidad' is described here as 'un método de trabajo, una actitud consecuente con la que buscarnos para ir más allá' [a work method, a consistent attitude with which to search ourselves to go further] (4: 7) — a definition that, in its arguably modern(ist) insistence on method, coherence and transcendence, contrasts with the editorial's simultaneous call to indulge in the coming 'primavera más espídica y anfetamínica del siglo' [most speed-influenced and amphetamine-addicted spring of the century] (4: 6). In this article, however, reason and desire, work and pleasure, method and chaos are not treated as opposing principles, but as forces that can be combined or reconciled within a scenario in which individuals have the freedom to build their future according to criteria of their own choosing, and in which 'más que en ningún otro momento el nivel de posibilidades se acerca al nivel de invención de nuestro propio destino' [more than at any other point, the level of possibilities approaches the level of invention of our own destiny] (4: 7). The article thus shares the optimism of the magazine's first editorial with respect to the possibilities offered by the creative moment Madrid is experiencing, and yet here Tono Martínez choses to distance himself from the concept (or 'palabreja', in his rather more pejorative choice of word) of postmodernity and the postmodern mobilized by himself and Casani in relation to Madrid's cultural resurgence only three months earlier. Although Tono Martínez later suggests that the label we apply to what is taking place in Madrid (be this 'posmodernidad', 'hiperrealidad', or something else) is ultimately irrelevant, as long as its creative potential is adequately harnessed, the proclamation within this text of postmodernism's demise can only be read as an attempt by the author to distance himself (and *La Luna*) from that phenomenon. There are several possible explanations for this attitude: the magazine contributor Javier Olivares, for instance, criticizes in a later issue the widespread tendency among his contemporaries to understand postmodernism as a form of superficial posturing, 'más cercano a teñirse el pelo, dejarse coleta o tomar una copa en la terraza de moda [...] que de una polémica rigurosa' [more to do with dyeing or growing one's hair, or having a drink at a fashionable establishment [...] than with a rigorous debate] (22: 7), a complaint he reiterates in a retrospective analysis of *la movida* published in 2007 (cf. Cadahía 2007: 48). Olivares's criticism of a widespread, if superficial, engagement with postmodernism suggests that the popularity and ubiquity of the term within Spanish cultural and countercultural circles was rendering it meaningless and affecting its prestige. Another possible reason for this disavowal of postmodernism could be the desire of those working on the magazine to be seen as up to date with the latest intellectual debates taking place not only within Spain, but also globally. Indeed, the term 'hyperreality' entered critical discourse in the 1970s and gained currency during the 1980s through the works of Jean Baudrillard and Umberto Eco.[12] But if Tono Martínez's vindication of 'hiperrealidad' stems from an engagement with the theories of these thinkers, then his article, which presents hyperreality as a new paradigm that replaces postmodernism, rather than (as both Baudrillard and Eco imply) a phenomenon that is characteristic of and results from it, distorts the concept as defined by them. It is impossible to tell whether such misrepresentation is deliberate or not: whether it is the result of a misreading on Tono's part, or of a deliberate appropriation and resignification of the term to his own ends. In any case, the embrace of 'hiperrealidad' as an alternative to or substitute for postmodernism in this article points to the desire of those working on *La Luna* to underline the magazine's independence from any one movement, concept or idea. By eschewing postmodernism in favour of something else, Tono Martínez is indirectly affirming the publication's distinctness and autonomy from a concept with which it was perhaps being, in the eyes of its editorial staff, too readily identified. However, paradoxically (and, it appears, unknowingly) Tono Martínez's choice of term further reinscribes *La Luna* within a postmodern constellation of meaning, as the new term he mobilizes within his text (hiperrealidad) is closely associated with the experience of postmodernity.

The impossibility of marginality

The ambivalent relationship of *La Luna* to postmodernism can be further traced in the magazine's frequent wavering between positions that vigorously challenge or mock some of the tenets of modern(ist) thought and cultural and artistic practice, such as the search for a singular, authentic self, discussed in the previous chapter, and what Paul Julian Smith (2006: 62) describes as the recuperation of modern(ist) concepts such as radical space (issue 12) or being modern (issue 14). Among examples of the former, in issue 6 we find a veiled attack on the figure of the bohemian. Miguel Cereceda's article 'El fin de la lampancia' (which is also the theme of this number) (6: 6–7) describes the 'lampante', a neologism used to refer to the marginal or marginalized, as unable to serve either the establishment or its opponents owing to his/her position as an outsider. And yet the 'lampante' is revealed as a figure which legitimizes both those who want to maintain the status quo and those who seek to destroy it. For the former, the 'lampante' represents a necessary 'other' that justifies the system's rules and order and control mechanisms; for the latter, s/he illustrates all that is wrong with the current order, and hence the need for revolutionary action. The text is accompanied by a series of images with made-up captions intended to illustrate 'la creciente tendencia a salir de la lampancia por parte de significados cabecillas de la misma' [the increasing tendency of abandoning impoverished bohemianism (*lampancia*) on the part of some of its more significant leaders] (6: 6). The former Communist Party member and radical leftist Andrés Sorel, for instance, is photographed outside the Ritz after, according to the caption, being named new government spokesperson, and the Retiro park puppeteer Paco Porras is portrayed as the proud recipient of a Guggenheim scholarship (6: 7). While Cereceda's article offers a serious and reflective consideration of the role and status of the 'lampante' within society, the images overtly mock these figures, whose bohemianism and apparent aloofness from the system are exposed as a mere pose. This caricature of the old-school bohemian is taken up again in the piece 'La Veleidad de la Pobreza', signed by Tonsky, Catania and Labarga (6: 8–9), in which they describe how bohemians tend eventually to grow up to discover the unglamorous effects of poverty. In a climate marked by generalized precariousness and instability, where even those who are not vocational 'lampantes' are faced with the constant threat of poverty, the figure of the bohemian appears as a useless and almost insulting anachronism, as a capricious stance that, ironically, only those of certain means can afford to adopt voluntarily. The article does not, however, call for an end to bohemianism, but rather for a new type of 'lampante' who does not regard him/herself as an indolent outsider, and hence as better or purer than the average citizen, but rather acknowledges his/her complicity with the system, while at the same time working hard and resorting to imagination and ingenuity in order to maintain at least a degree of independence within it.

There is an implicit self-reflexive dimension to the theme of bohemianism or 'lampancia' discussed in this sixth issue of *La Luna*. The magazine's editorial success (expanding its circulation beyond the city of Madrid to the whole of Spain from issue 3, and reaching a print run of over 30,000), did not translate into economic success, with members of the editorial team and contributors frequently remaining unpaid over long periods of time.[13] In this context, Luis García-Torvisco suggests that the theme of this issue should be read as 'una broma privada que mostraba la frustración de los creadores de una revista en la que todo el mundo quería participar, que organizaba las fiestas y los conciertos más sonados del momento, pero que seguía sin obtener beneficios económicos' [a private joke that revealed the frustration of the creators of a magazine in which everybody wanted to take part, that organized the most talked-about parties and concerts of its time, but that continued to fail to make an economic profit] (2012: 377). The caricature of the 'lampante', a figure identified, in the second text discussed, with the previous generation of 1960s *progres*, can thus be read as an attempt to undermine the glamour and cultural prestige of the modern(ist) bohemian, and also as an exercise of self-mockery in the face of the uncertain economic future faced by the magazine. Once again, then, the characterization of this editorial as postmodern rests not only, or even primarily, upon its overt attack on a quintessentially modern(ist) figure (that of the impoverished bohemian artist), but on its ability to challenge bohemianism while simultaneously tacitly acknowledging a degree of complicity with the figure of the 'lampante'.

Postmodern self-denunciation

The most radical example of this form of self-denunciation can be found in *La Luna*'s eighth issue, published in June 1984 but posing as a future issue of June 1987. This spoof number, which paints a picture of a near future that is at once dystopian and hilarious in its implausibility, with battles taking place across Madrilenian districts between grassroots groups and armed insurgents, and chaos spreading across Europe as increasing numbers of citizens boycott state institutions by refusing to pay tax and by burning ID documentation such as passports, driving licences and birth certificates, also contains a letter to the editor demanding the magazine's immediate disappearance. Signed by the editorial team member Gregorio Morales, '¡*La Luna* debe desaparecer!' (8: 70) claims that the magazine's overwhelming success over the past four years, which, we are told, has reached beyond Spain's borders, risks smothering the very individual talent it sought to promote:

> Aquí está el peligro, el inmenso y abrumador peligro; *La Luna* en sí misma, como revista, como espíritu, es la estrella [...]. De este modo, *La Luna* desglute [sic] a todos sus colaboradores y por otra parte los inviste a todos con un carácter uniforme. Desaparece así cualquier individualidad. (8: 70)
>
> [This is the danger, and immense and overwhelming danger; *La Luna*, in itself, as magazine, as spirit, is the star [...]. Hence, *La Luna* dissolves all its contributors and, on the other hand, covers them with a unifying varnish. Thus, all individuality vanishes.] (8: 70)

Morales concedes that during its initial two years, the magazine offered 'un reconfortante y refrescante cóctel de ideas' [a comforting and refreshing cocktail of ideas] that might have encouraged individual artists to embark on journeys of creative exploration. But four years on, he argues, *La Luna*'s success no longer inspires and promotes individual talent, but eclipses it. What began as an attempt to reflect 'una nueva y bulliciosa realidad creativa' [a new and bustling creative reality] now risks, by virtue of its success, annihilating the very diversity and heterogeneity it sought to foster. Hence, Morales concludes, *La Luna* must disappear immediately to pave the way for new forms of expression that reflect individual beliefs and sensibilities, rather than attempts to conform to *La Luna*'s conception of art. Despite its playful irreverence, Morales's piece should not be simply read as a joke. Its humorously overblown vision of *La Luna*'s success reveals an awareness of the limited, but very real, power that the magazine could (and eventually did) wield, in terms of its influence over Madrid's artistic and cultural spheres, and further, of the risks inherent to such power. Indeed, humour and irreverence are used here precisely in order to neutralize the perceived pitfalls to the magazine's success, and to the hegemony deriving from it. However, in spite of this early self-denunciation, *La Luna* did not manage to avoid the trappings of success identified in this article, as evidenced not only by its continued existence up to and beyond June 1987 or by its growing influence, which saw a parallel standardization of its format and contents, but also, and most importantly, by its role in transforming Madrid's *movida* into the dominant (and hence, to some extent, prescriptive) current and style of the time.

Despite the humorous tone of the letter, and the irreverent framework within which it is situated, the degree of self-awareness evidenced by Morales's text seems little short of nihilistic. Indeed, *La Luna*'s first editor, Borja Casani, retrospectively remarked that the magazine

> contiene en todo su planteamiento un aspecto radical y suicida, digamos, algo carente de futuro, algo que estaba en la propia colectividad en ese momento. Nadie estaba buscando sentar las bases de su profesionalidad. Es algo hecho por falsarios, por personas que están en un sitio donde no les corresponde estar... (Gallero 1991: 28).
>
> [contains, in its whole outlook, a radical, suicidal aspect, of something with no future, something which was felt collectively at the time. No one sought to establish his or her professional career. It [the magazine] is something done by impostors, by people who are in a position where they do not belong...] (Gallero 1991: 28).

Given that *La Luna*'s success is portrayed here as potentially dangerous for the very artists for whom it sought to provide a platform, it is hard to see how the magazine could have justified or indeed faced its long-term survival. Though such nihilism is frequently characterized as postmodern,[14] the clearest precedents to Morales' self-denunciation can be found in the historical avant-gardes, particularly in Dada and Surrealism. Dada's nihilistic streak is more obvious, with the movement's manifestos often denying or denouncing Dada.[15] The Surrealists, though never explicitly undermining their movement, did so indirectly, waging on-going disputes over the definition, scope and direction of Surrealism that resulted in a more or less constant stream of defections. The comparative lack of unity and sense of purpose of *la movida*, which never posited itself as an organized movement, mean that instances of nihilistic self-reflexive questioning are circumscribed to individual art works or cultural products, such as the aforementioned letter to the editor.

By purporting to be written in 1987, this spoof issue allows contributors to consider the present in retrospective terms, and the ensuing verdict is startlingly critical:

> Los ingenuos posmodernos se limitaron a darse de bruces con el tema: Ya no hay progreso, constataron haciendo alardes de servicio público, ya no hay ideas salvadoras. [...] Ha hecho falta que la sociedad salte en mil pedazos[16] para constatar por una parte que el individuo es sólo aquello que su voluntad y su memoria decide y por otra que el sistema es una estructura cuya permanencia está garantizada por su innegable capacidad de darle a cada uno la hostia que está pidiendo a gritos. (Jorge Marcel: 'Volver a donde nunca hemos estado', 8: 6)
>
> [The naïve postmoderns merely stumbled upon the issue: there is no longer progress, they established, as if demonstrating their public service-mindedness, there are no more redeeming ideas. [...] It has been necessary for society to explode in a thousand pieces in order to establish that, on the one hand, individuals are only that which their will and their memory decide, and that, on the other hand, the permanence of the system as structure is guaranteed by its undeniable capacity to administer to everyone the blow that they wish for so badly.] (8: 6)

In this extract, Marcel appears to attack postmodernism's failure to do more than state the obvious, and appeals to individuals' will and memory -mechanisms brought into question by postmodern thought- as possible ways out. Further, while 'the system' is often depicted as an inescapable set of constraints that conditions our thoughts and actions as individuals,[17] Marcel's irreverent allusion to its ability to 'darle a cada uno la hostia que está pidiendo a gritos' suggests the system may in fact constitute not only an unavoidable, but also necessary and useful regulatory mechanism. Elsewhere in the article, he takes postmodernism to task for its vindication of youth and novelty (the latter often revealed to be the result of a repackaging of old ideas) as the only value criteria. In what appears to be a direct reference to *la movida*, he argues that

> [l]a desmesurada potenciación del mito juvenil hasta la primera mitad de los ochenta produjo sin duda uno de los mayores desiertos culturales del siglo. [...] Ser joven y estar presenta en la ceremonia identificadora era más que suficiente para sentirse partícipe del proceso creador. (8: 6)
>
> [the disproportionate promotion of the youth myth up until the first half of the Eighties no doubt produced one of the biggest cultural deserts of the century. [...] Being young and in attendance at the ceremony of identification was more than enough to feel a part of the creative process. (8: 6)

Against this valorization of youth for its own sake, and within a context in which it is no longer possible to believe in initiatives driven by a social conscience, as these are regarded as symptomatic of a 'degastado paternalismo' [worn-out paternalism], the author proposes a return to radical individualism, an engagement with one's own personal passions.

The most striking aspect of Marcel's piece is its bleak perspective on Spain's 1980s cultural landscape as 'uno de los mayores desiertos culturales del siglo', which stands in stark contrast to the optimistic view of Madrid's cultural renaissance in *La Luna*'s first editorial. The author's assertion can be read as a warning to his contemporaries, perhaps as a means to avoid the danger of complacency by conjuring it. But in such a warning is also embedded the recognition that *la movida*'s insistence on superficiality, hedonism and ephemerality could only be sustained for so long without it becoming an empty gesture, repetitive and boring. Marcel thus touches on one of the key challenges faced by both *la movida* and *La Luna*: how to consolidate, or indeed define, the spontaneous creative energy originally emanating from a small number of individuals, but eventually irradiating over Madrid as a whole (and beyond), without betraying its very foundations (its ambiguity, its contradictions, its fluid and anarchic nature) in the process. The solution proposed here, the 'return to where we have never been' of the title, namely, a radical individualism, proved productive for many of the individuals identified with *la movida*, such as the film-maker Pedro Almodóvar, the punk and dance icon Alaska or the photographer Ouka Lele, who went on to establish successful careers over the following decades both in Spain and abroad. However, for *la movida* as collective urban experience, and for *La Luna* in particular, this emphasis on individualism resulted in internal conflicts and divisions that ultimately led to their demise. Both *la movida*, as a collective phenomenon, and *La Luna*, as a collaborative editorial project, simultaneously fed off and fostered individual talent; and yet their success led many of those who had made them possible to distance themselves in order to reaffirm their individuality, lest they be too readily identified with a loose movement (*la movida*) or an anarchic project (*La Luna*) over which no single individual could claim ownership or control.

La Luna's spoof issue represents the height of the magazine's approximation to postmodernism, even if postmodernism is denounced within it as naïve and insufficient. The magazine's playful distortion of chronological linearity and its construction of a vision of the near future that is at once dystopian and funny appear as unequivocally postmodern traits. In this issue, for the first and only time in its five-year existence, *La Luna* is not attempting to reflect or shape its surrounding reality, but deliberately manufacturing it, in line with Baudrillard's conception of postmodern reality as mediated simulacrum (1983: 23–26). The fact that this issue anticipates, indeed calls for, the demise of *la movida* and *La Luna* points to a postmodern recognition of the limits and contingency of any one movement or project. If plurality and flux are at the heart of the postmodern, then it follows that no category of thought, definition or classification, including postmodernism itself, can be conceived of as universal, static, and hence durable. Rather, the very premise underlying postmodern thought, a thorough questioning of the metaphysical presuppositions and epistemological conditionings that shape our understanding of the world, implies that, as Linda Hutcheon has noted, 'all is provisional and historically conditioned' (1988: 53). In other words, postmodernism's radical questioning of our modes of knowing and discursive practices presupposes its own eventual undoing, as such scrutiny is self-reflexively applied to postmodern insights, methodologies and practices, in much the same way as this issue prefigures (indeed, demands) *La Luna*'s demise.[18]

Simulation and the market as the new avant-garde

Simulation, a recurring postmodern motif (cf. Baudrillard 1983; Eco 1983; Sorkin 1992), is the theme of issue 13 of the magazine. In his 'Al principio fue la simulación', Jorge Lozano contends that simulacra are useful, not as reproductions of a reality that has been revealed to be illusory, but as tools that throw into question our very 'principle of reality' (13: 8–9). Lozano goes on to suggest that, in a context in which every 'original' has been itself unmasked as copy, as simulacrum, the quest for a universal, transcendental reality has given way to the question of 'who legitimizes the simulator', in other words, who (and how and why) decides the rules of the games (or simulacra) that constitute what we generally think of as reality. Using poker as a metonymy of the mechanisms that regulate the production of simulacra (and hence 'reality'), the author concludes that the rules of the game are in fact established through practice, and thus always subject to change. This depiction of reality as a game (or a series of games) whose rules are in a constant process of reformulation through practice is clearly reminiscent of Jean-François Lyotard's conceptualization of the language games or 'moves' that codify knowledge as 'never established once and for all (even if they have been formally defined). Rather, the limits are themselves the stakes and provisional results of language strategies' (1984: 17). The influence of Baudrillard's work on simulacra and simulation (1981; 1983) is also discernable, not only in the ideas expressed within the text, but also in its language, which is interspersed with phrases such as 'precesión del simulacro', a clear reference to the title of the first part of the French philosopher's *Simulations* (1983). Lozano's reference to 'una estética de la desaparición' could be read as a further postmodern intertextual reference, this time to Paul Virilio's 1980 book of the same title. Despite the obvious echoes of postmodern theory in the article, the author does not cite any of the aforementioned thinkers, choosing instead to use these allusions to weave and situate his own argument within a postmodern discursive praxis.[19]

Lozano's views are problematic on several levels: his characterization of the production of reality (understood here as a series of simulacra) as a game with ever-changing rules that players can mould fails to acknowledge the fact that not all players are equally positioned within the game; that is, that players have different levels and different kinds of resources at their disposal, and hence their ability to alter the rules of the game in their favour is not equal. His poker analogy implies that individuals' stake in the game is shaped by luck (the hand they are dealt) and talent (their ability to make the most of that hand), ignoring the socio-economic conditioning that means that certain players will always operate at an advantage, while others may be excluded from the game altogether, or have such a weak position as significantly to compromise their degree of agency within it.[20] Additionally, the author's identification of legitimization as the key question does not result in his addressing this issue in any depth: his assertion that those who play the game create its rules through practice does not explain the processes through which a new way of doing gains legitimacy, or fails to do so. If we extrapolate Lozano's argument to the sphere of artistic creation and cultural practice, the fields, after all, within which both he and *La Luna* operate, his words suggest that a work of art or cultural product legitimizes itself through its very coming into being, a view that echoes Lyotard's theorization of the postmodern artist who 'is in the position of a philosopher: the text he writes, the work he produces are not in principle governed by pre-established rules [...]. Those rules and categories are what the work of art itself is looking for' (1984: 81). While this may be a valid, and even useful, attempt at outlining the defining characteristic of postmodern works, it does raise the question of how (or, indeed, if) such oeuvres may be judged, and of how their value or merit ought to be assessed. In this context of confusion, the market is seen as a potential new arbiter of artistic worth and as a possible engine for creative innovation, as Paco Morales argues in this same issue of *La Luna*, in a piece entitled 'La vanguardia es el mercado'. This article notes that, while artistic innovation seems to be a thing of the past, the art market is tackling this deficit in originality by resorting to ever more creative means through which to repackage, promote and sell works. The avant-garde (*vanguardia*) is thus, according to Morales, no longer constituted by artists, but by a group of well-known art dealers with the power and know-how to launch the careers of newcomers.

This idea of the market as the new avant-garde is taken up again in issue 15, which adopts it as its theme and uses it as the title for an unsigned, manifesto-like proclamation (15: 6–7). This text advocates the recognition that all art is dependent on, and hence indissociable from, processes of industrial production and commercialization; hence the ability to communicate and market art becomes crucial (indeed, more important than the work itself) to guarantee its survival and create environments in which artists can thrive. This view of art as linked to industrial production processes is not new: Adorno and Benjamin had written extensively on the subject several decades before. Slightly newer perhaps is the optimism with which this state of affairs is greeted. However, what marks out this piece is not so much its reflection of a contemporary mood (the extensive and buoyant optimism with regard to postmodernism that characterized the early and mid-1980s), but the fact that its endorsement of some of the central premises of postmodern theory takes on a distinctively avant-gardist (and thus, arguably, modernist) form, that of the manifesto. While the text's structure as a list of succinct considerations and demands, and its irreverent tone and deliberately provocative intent are reminiscent of the manifestos of the early twentieth-century avant-gardes, its pragmatism stands in stark contrast to the utopianism characteristic of the historical avant-gardes. Despite this difference in outlook, the proclamation of the end of art's autonomy in the text is also made problematic by the implicit and paradoxical adoption by its anonymous subscribers of precisely the position of autonomy and authority explicitly and emphatically denied to the artistic sphere as a whole. Once again, the association of this piece with postmodernism rests not so much in its endorsement of one of the tenets of postmodern cultural theory — that the influence of mass production and commercialization practices over the work of art is an inevitable and not necessarily negative condition of our time — but on the oscillation between the postmodern viewpoint on the state of art and culture in Spain and the role of the market within those spheres, and its expression, which takes on a modern(ist) form, thus implicitly undermining the statement the text purportedly makes.

Leaving aside this tension between the statements made in the piece and the tone and form they adopt, or the inherent contradiction between its overt attack on artistic autonomy and the simultaneous adoption by its anonymous signatories of a position of authority, the text's tentatively optimistic proclamation of the new, enhanced role of market forces within the artistic and cultural spheres merits closer attention. This generally positive valorization of the role of the market echoes Jean-François Lyotard's *The Postmodern Condition*, in which he argues that Benjamin's and Adorno's reticence with respect to 'the contact between the industrial and mechanical arts, and literature and the fine arts' is symptomatic of 'an excessively humanistic notion of the Mephistophelian functionalism of sciences and technologies' that automatically exempts art and writing from the suspicion that concerns science and industry (1984: 76). Instead, Lyotard suggests that 'in the absence of aesthetic criteria, it remains possible and useful to assess the value of works of art according to the profits that they yield' (1984: 76); and that regulation of artistic practice through the market is preferable to political regulation, as it allows for greater diversity. However, Lyotard concedes the limitations of pure market regulation, which, though promising diversity, only really accommodates those tendencies that have 'purchasing power' (1984: 76).

The optimism underlying *La Luna*'s proclamation of the market as the new avant-garde is not only the reflection of a global mood, but also owes to specific contextual factors. The end of Franco's dictatorship paved the way for a rapid proliferation of independent art galleries in Madrid and elsewhere, which, thanks to easier international communications and to a renewed and increasing interest from abroad, managed in many cases to establish themselves as global players. Radio Futura's co-founder Herminio Molero, speaking in 1990, describes how '[e]n los años 70 en Madrid había tres galerías [...]. Hoy, cualquier galería modestita tiene sus relaciones con Milán, con Nueva York, con París. Los canales ya existen, están conquistados' [in the Seventies, in Madrid, there were three galleries [...]. Now, any small gallery has ties with Milan, New York, Paris. The channels already exist, they have been conquered] (Gallero 1991: 231); and the TV presenter and *movida* icon Paloma Chamorro describes a similar transformation when she declares '[n]o puedo dejar de pensar que soy un poco culpable de que haya doscientas noventa y nueve galerías en Madrid, en lugar de catorce como había antes' [I can't help but feel that I am a little to blame for the fact that there are now two hundred and ninety-nine galleries in Madrid, instead of the fourteen galleries there used to be] (Gallero 1991: 181). While the optimism generated by this development of a gallery circuit with a stake in the international art market is understandable, particularly given that those writing are trying to extricate themselves from and move beyond what they describe as the 'cultural wasteland' left behind by Francoism and by the 'cenutria, zafia, hortera y franquista' [uncultured, uncouth, vulgar and Francoist] (15: 7) Spanish bourgeoisie that emerged from the regime, the manifesto nonetheless fails to recognize and address the market's limitations (such as its exclusion or marginalization of non- or less profitable products or modes of expression) — a question that does, however, come to the forefront in successive issues of *La Luna*, as the magazine's own existence is thrown into question by internal divisions and economic troubles.

Distancing from and disillusionment with postmodernism

While the 'La vanguardia es el mercado' manifesto of issue 15 fails to acknowledge the illusory nature, identified by Lyotard, of the promise of market-led artistic diversity, the question re-emerges in Borja Casani's farewell editorial in the following issue of the magazine. In a sober, downcast tone that stands in stark contrast to the optimistic, playful and irreverently humorous quality of the preceding editorials, Casani's 'El estado de las cosas' (16: 5–7) considers *La Luna*'s trajectory over the preceding two years in an attempt to assess the present situation. Recalling the magazine's beginnings, Casani describes its original aim as an attempt to capture what was taking place at street level, and which the mainstream media chose to ignore. Almost immediately, however, he notes, the publication became associated with postmodernism, largely because of the title of its first editorial ('Madrid 1984. ¿La Posmodernidad?'). While Casani acknowledges *La Luna*'s role in disseminating postmodern theories within Spain, thanking a series of contributors for their help and their introductions to 'foreign guests' such as Lyotard, Baudrillard and Habermas,[21] he also goes on to attack the superficial popularization of the term within Spanish cultural circles, which, he states, many have adopted for opportunistic reasons. In the wake of the magazine's early enthusiasm for postmodernism, an enthusiasm that, judging by Casani's remarks, rapidly spread throughout Spain, diluting the complexity of the concept in the process, there now looms a realization of postmodernism's insufficiencies: 'Todo el mundo sabe ya que es imposible la marginalidad. La respuesta al sistema pertenece al propio sistema y fuera del sistema no se observa otra cosa que el infinito y desalentador desierto de la **indiferencia**' [Everyone already knows that marginality is impossible. Any response to the system is itself part of the system, and beyond the system we see nothing but an infinite and desolate desert of **indifference**] (16: 5) [Emphasis in the original].

Casani's assertion, which echoes the attack undertaken in issue 6 on the figure of the 'lampante' or marginalized bohemian, is arguably postmodern in the sense that it can be seen to have been influenced by the postmodern realization of the inextricable, if often subtle, links that bound all individuals and groups to the existing system of power relations. But this acknowledgement, which had seemed liberating in the first editorial of the magazine, inasmuch as it absolved artists and cultural practitioners from any transcendental imperative or utopian social goal, now appears as a dead end. While the initial issues of the magazine suggested that, even within a context in which no one can remain under the illusion of being independent from the system, it might at least be possible to negotiate, at an individual level, some degree of agency or autonomy within it (as seen in Tono Martínez's article in the second issue of *La Luna*), Casani's words here betray the weariness that comes from engaging in a lost battle — namely, that of constantly inventing and mobilizing new mechanisms through which to resist (or rather, defer) co-option; a battle that, we are told, if it were ever to be won, would only lead to indifference or invisibility.

The possibilities that the emergence of an active art market with a robust gallery circuit might open up to a new generation of artists, which occupied the previous issue of the magazine, are regarded with a new pessimism here: '[s]aber que el motor es el Mercado no es por más cierto, menos aburrido. La obsesión por conseguir grandes audiencias envilece el producto y lo convierte en uno más dentro de una superabundante oferta' [knowing that the market is the engine is not any less boring for being true. The obsession with securing large audiences tarnishes the product, turning it into one more within a super-abundant offer] (16: 7). There is, of course, a whiff of elitism in Casani's remarks, a sense of disappointment that the postmodern 'degree zero of contemporary general culture' has inaugurated an epoch of slackening (Lyotard 1984: 76), paving the way not only for a new generation of artists, but also for a large number of opportunistic hangers-on who are benefitting from what Casani terms 'la ceremonia de la confusión' (16: 7). In this context of widespread confusion and 'anything goes' attitudes, Casani appeals to myth as a way out of the present situation, a situation that threatens to lead to a sense of ennui (the tone of this editorial suggests that it has already done so). Myth, or the mythical dimension of artistic and cultural practice, is characterized by Casani as emanating from artists' personal investment in their work, an investment that needs to be passionate, sincere, and demonstrate a degree of independence, not only from 'the system' in the abstract, but also from the state subsidies which, Casani argues, are increasingly standing in for a largely indifferent public. Whereas the first editorial of *La Luna* invited the creation of a mythology of Madrid that could enable the city to become an international cultural centre, myth is no longer described as something that can be easily conjured or fabricated; indeed, myth, we are told, can never be the result of simulation, which, Casani warns, 'produce monstruos, pero no produce mitos' [produces monsters, not myths] (16: 7), thereby disavowing Jorge Lozano's earlier vindication of the productive (and perhaps even subversive) potential of simulation and simulacra in issue 13. What the difference between myth and myth making, on the one hand, and simulation, on the other, may be, is not explained, but rather suggested. For Casani, it seems, myth retains some truth-value: it presupposes a real involvement by the artist with the work of his/her making, and it is this personal engagement of the individual which validates the work, rather than any pre-existing criteria such as coherence or adherence to a particular style or canon. Simulation, on the other hand, is impersonal, requiring no such investment by the individual. Casani's mobilization of myth, understood primarily in terms of an individual's passionate involvement with a specific project, thus constitutes a new approach through which to judge works of art and cultural products in a postmodern context, and offers a potentially useful alternative parameter to that of their market-driven monetary value. But while Casani's emphasis of individuality appears as characteristically postmodern, his model nevertheless relies on subjective judgement (namely, establishing the level of engagement in a work by an artist), and hence ultimately reintroduces the issue of authority: who, and on what basis, ought to decide how much 'passionate engagement' by an artist is in evidence in any given artwork. His later disparaging reference to 'nuestra proverbial ignorancia' as the crux of Spain's problems suggests that the question of intellectual authority (or lack thereof) is at the heart of the current crisis.

Later in the article, we find a paragraph that reads like a rejection of many of the views expressed in earlier issues of *La Luna*:

> si en los últimos tiempos se ha producido sin duda un despertar sin precedentes en el campo de la cultura, no vale la pena ahogarlo con banales discusiones sobre si Madrid es o no la ciudad enana más alta del mundo o si hemos llegado o nos falta un palmo para llegar a la posmodernidad. Este país ha superado la "modernidad" sin digerirla, porque no hay que olvidar que estuvo largo tiempo **prohibida** y es inútil lamentarse ahora o intentar regresar a donde nunca hemos estado. (16: 7) [Emphasis in the original]
>
> [if, in recent years, there has been an unquestionable and unprecedented awakening in the field of culture, it is pointless to suffocate it with our banal discussion on whether or not Madrid is the tallest dwarf city in the world, or on whether we have arrived at, or we are some inches away from, postmodernity. This country has moved beyond "modernity" without digesting it, as we should not forget that it was **forbidden** for a long time, and it is pointless now to regret it or to attempt a return to a place where we have never been.] (16: 7)

This paragraph is intriguing for its apparent denunciation of some of the propositions and debates launched through *La Luna* (the description of Madrid as 'la ciudad más enana del mundo' in issue 1, or the attempt to 'volver a donde nunca hemos estado' proposed by Jorge Marcel in issue 8), which are here referred to as banal discussions that risk smothering the creative energy that led to the magazine's coming into being. However, Casani's words do not constitute an unequivocal admission of his publication's complicity in leading to the current situation of deadlock, inasmuch as they also link the perceived insufficiencies of the present to the Spanish context — a context marked by a four-decade dictatorship during which modernity was more or less effectively 'forbidden'. The implicit critique of the debates engendered by postmodernism that runs through this text (debates which, one senses, Casani has come to regard as entrenched, circular and pointless) is hence firmly framed within a specific socio-historical reality. And because his analysis, though using postmodern concepts such as simulation and simulacra, is carried out through the consideration of a specific reality, that of the present moment and future outlook for art and culture in Spain, this text ought not to be read merely as a general critique of postmodernism, but rather as a critique of its effects over the Spanish cultural landscape. Casani's subsequent call to engage with 'otras ciudades, otras ideas, otras lenguas, otros signos' constitutes, in my view, an implicit recognition of some of the pitfalls of postmodernism in Spain: for instance, the emphasis on the local, though contributing to Madrid's much-needed urban renewal, is seen here as leading to parochialism and self-complacent navel-gazing; and the success of the 'postmodern' label as leading to a proliferation of works and artists that paradoxically appear increasingly homogeneous in their adoption of heterogeneous styles and hybrid formats.

The trajectory which Casani describes in this piece, which is that of *la movida*, even if he does not directly use the term in the text, mirrors, in several ways, that of postmodernism both in Spain and on a global scale. *La movida*, like postmodernism, originated in part as a response to what is perceived as a restricted (and restrictive) order of things, namely, the (alleged) solemnity and sobriety of the 1960s generation of *progres*, who had grown up in opposition to (and hence, to an extent, also informed by) the Francoist regime in the case of *la movida*; in the case of postmodernism, the reaction was against the (apparent) shortcomings of modernist thought, such as its assumed position of autonomy with regards to mechanisms of power or its phallologocentrism. Both *la movida* and postmodernism quickly gained widespread currency, and before long, both phenomena came to be perceived as hegemonic, that is, as the dominant cultural movement or style (*la movida*) and the dominant current of thought (postmodernism) of their time. This development, though not new in itself, is particularly ironic in this instance, since *la movida* and postmodernism sought to challenge not only the hegemony of the movements that immediately preceded them, but the very notion of hegemony itself. Their success, in a conventional sense (spread, prestige and influence), thus constitutes proof of their failure to disrupt the dynamics of the artistic and cultural fields.

The bleak tone of this editorial seems to stem from this realization, which is also the realization that *la movida* (and hence *La Luna*) had run its course. By 1985, what had begun as an informal network of personal friendships and artistic collaborations centred in and around Madrid, and with no declared objective other than making the most of what the city had to offer, had become an unprecedented phenomenon within Spain and was attracting international media attention. In this context of *movida* frenzy, *La Luna*'s stated mission of granting visibility to new, emerging artists appeared increasingly redundant, and the magazine's editorial team faced the quandary either of winding up the project or of carrying on in the hope that *la movida*'s popularity would make *La Luna* a commercially viable enterprise. Casani would later refer to this crossroads in the publication's existence:

> Los últimos meses de *La Luna*, a principios del 85, desaparece el espíritu cavernícola, *underground*, donde nadie pensaba en otra cosa que en sostener disparates y lanzarlos como bombas. Entonces aparece un nuevo problema, que es cómo comercializar la cosa (Gallero 1991: 78).
>
> [The final months of *La Luna*, in early 1985, see the disappearance of the original caveman, underground spirit, where no one intended anything other than to utter nonsense and to throw it around like a bomb. At that stage, a new problem emerges, namely, how to commercialize it [the magazine].]

Casani's subsequent departure from *La Luna* in June 1985 suggests that he had little interest in the process of 'comercializar la cosa'. Instead, he chose to put into practice his call to look beyond Madrid and beyond *la movida* through a new editorial project, *Sur Exprés*.[22] Although Casani's departure triggered other desertions,[23] many of those working on *La Luna* decided to carry on, not necessarily because they wanted to 'cash in' on *la movida*'s popularity, as Casani's words above seem to imply, but rather, as several of the editorials of the magazine's second phase suggest, from a reluctance to accept that the party might be over, a refusal, as Tono Martínez put it, to 'celebrar el funeral de algo que no acaba sino de empezar' [hold a funeral for something that had only just begun] (25: 6).

Transitional phase: removida and further distancing from postmodernism

This second phase of *La Luna* (issues 21–44), primarily under the editorship of José Tono Martínez,[24] is characterized by a newfound critical zeal and a novel sense of purpose already manifest in Tono Martínez's first editorial at the helm of the magazine, 'Sálvese quien pueda' (21: 7–8). This piece is remarkable for several reasons: it includes the first explicit reference to *la movida* (21: 7) in the magazine, but this coincides with the launch of the alternative term *removida*:

> Lo que se avecina, lo que ya está aquí, es más bien la removida (algo que ya se ha producido en esta revista) de todos aquellos que desde la más supina ignorancia han jugado con las palabras, con las personas y con los conceptos suponiendo que la cultura, o lo que queráis, era algo que se confundía con las mismas personas que la invocaban. (21: 7)
>
> [What is approaching, and is already here, is rather the *removida* (which has already taken place in this magazine), that is the removal of all those who, from the greatest ignorance, have played with words, people and concepts, in the belief that culture, or whatever you want to call it, was something indistinct from those who invoked it.] (21: 7)

Tono Martínez's censorious reference to play (proclaiming the 'removal' of those who have played with words, people and concepts) contrasts with the vindication of play found (and displayed) in the early issues of the magazine — as seen, for instance, in the call to Madrilenians to 'adoptar el disfraz más feliz' [adopt the happiest disguise] (1: 7) and 'reírnos en un presente dudoso, embriagarnos pero guardando el tipo' [laughing at an uncertain present, becoming intoxicated while maintaining our form] (1: 7) in the editorial to the first issue, co-authored by Tono Martínez. Ironically, his condemnation of play, or of those who have engaged in it, is itself undertaken through wordplay. '*Removida*' literally translates both as 'removed' and 'stirred or shaken up', and the word's semantic ambiguity is used in the piece to allude to the recent exit of several members of the editorial team. But the term also plays on '*movida*', suggesting that this shake-up and/or removal of superfluous figures is in fact a continuation or a repetition of the original *movida* movement. Despite the serious tone of the article, with its solemn call for a new journalism that 'debe actuar como crítico y como máximo defensor de los derechos fundamentales frente al "trágala" del poder establecido' [must act as a critic and as the supreme defender of fundamental rights before established power] (21: 8), Tono Martínez, it seems, cannot resist playing with words. His ambivalence is further marked by the fact that, though he refers to the previous years as having seen 'el renacer cultural de este país, y de Madrid en particular' [the cultural reinaissance of this country, and, particularly, of Madrid] (21: 7), he simultaneously attacks *movida* participants (particularly, one senses in the quote above, some of his former colleagues) for their hybridizing approach, which, he concludes, 'conduce a un efecto distanciador de ruido' [leads to a distorting noise effect] (21: 7), as well as for their frivolous, 'anything goes' attitude (21: 8). Paradoxically, then, Tono Martínez endorses *la movida* (even if he disapproves of the term itself) while criticising two of its defining characteristics: its tendency to incorporate disparate cultural references, objects and genres to create pastiches, and its frivolity, largely fuelled by a mistrust of transcendentalism and authority. Tono Martínez's attitude points to a regression to some of the ideas that *La Luna* had originally set out to challenge, in particular to the notion that art works and cultural products should conform to certain standards of quality and taste, and that culture can (and should) have a political aim — namely, countering the abuses and excesses of established powers. This new tone and sense of purpose manifest themselves in *La Luna*'s abandonment of the uncompromisingly irreverent propositions found in the early issues of the magazine, as well as in its adoption of an increasingly standardized visual style and format during its second phase (end of 1985 to end of 1987).

This second phase of *La Luna* can be divided into two parts. There is an initial transitional period, characterized primarily by a desire to consolidate *la removida* as an alternative to the increasingly discredited *movida*, a move that involves attacking *movida* participants who are perceived to have sold out or jumped ship. In issues 21–32, the denunciation of those who 'basan su existencia en la total liquidación de los demás y, encima, basan su actitud en abstrusas teorías que nos inventan [sic] vender cíclicamente cada seis meses' [base their existence in the total liquidation of others and, moreover, base their attitude on obscure theories which they attempt to sell to us cyclically every six months] (Javier Olivares in 22: 7) runs parallel to a less and less convincing affirmation of the survival of the original, street-based creative effervescence at the heart of *la movida*:

> Nada está muerto hasta que no se hace puro polvo, y por el momento todavía corre sangre en nuestras venas, podemos ver más allá de nuestras narices y gritar palabras en el viento. No hay hermoso vencido que no pueda librar nuevas batallas. [...] El desprecio y el tedio no pueden correr el telón de un tiempo en que la gente ha sido bella y con un espíritu brillante y liviano, en que el cosquilleo de la risa franca, la capacidad de sacar dicha de la propia esencia, de hacer del trabajo un juego, de aceptar el hecho artístico como una elección libre y caprichosa del propio artista, a la manera de Marcel Duchamp, han creado una escena luminosa de al que sólo un necio no podía disfrutar (Jorge Berlanga in 23: 7)
>
> [Nothing is dead until it becomes mere dust, and, for the moment, there is still blood in our veins and we can see beyond our noses and shout words in the wind. There is no beautiful defeated that cannot wage new battles. [...] Disdain and tedium cannot make the curtain go down over a period in which people have been beautiful and have displayed a light and diaphanous spirit, a time in which the flutter of frank laughter, the capacity of deriving joy from one's own essence, of turning work into a game, of accepting the artistic event as a free and capricious choice from the artist, in the manner of Marcel Duchamp, have created a luminous scene that only a dunce could fail to enjoy.] (23: 7)

While Berlanga's words are ostensibly intended to reaffirm the vitality of *la movida*, the tone of this fragment is undeniably elegiac. Indeed, his reference to an 'hermoso vencido' points to a clear feeling of defeat, even if there is still a sense that not all may have been lost ('nuevas batallas'). Even more tellingly, his description of the glory days of *la movida* is undertaken here in the past tense ('ha sido', 'han creado', etc.). The piece is permeated by a nostalgia for the recent past which constitutes stronger proof of *la movida*'s decline than the overt criticisms in Casani's final editorial in issue 16.

Also symptomatic of the gradual demise of *la movida* is *La Luna*'s adoption of the alternative term *removida*, which first appears in issue 21 and is later defined by Javier Tímmermans in the following terms:

> la ya llamada "removida" que todavía no se ha vendido a ninguna institución pública, intenta mantener un nivel digno de creación y generación cultural, a la vez que las momias de turno se pasean por el extranjero a gastos pagados, por el Estado claro. (24: 12)
>
> [what is already known as *removida* has not yet sold out to any public institution, attempts to maintain a decent level of cultural creation and generation, at the same time as a number of mummies go on promenades abroad with all expenses paid for, of course, by the State.] (24: 12)

Tímmermans's characterization is revealing since his description of *la removida* implicitly positions it as an alternative, if not in clear opposition or contrast to, *la movida* itself: his claim that *la removida* has not (yet) sold out to any public institution is a veiled reference to the general perception that by the mid-1980s, *la movida* had been discredited by the readiness with which many of its participants accepted public subsidies. Similarly, the juxtaposition of hardworking *removida* artists and cultural practitioners with 'momias' that travel abroad at the state's expense seeks to distance *la removida* from the perceived excesses of *la movida*, if not from *la movida* itself.

Pervading the editorials of this transitional phase is an urge to fight an enemy within, namely those who are seen to be profiteering from their association with *la movida*, and who are often identified, sometimes by name, and in other occasions through fairly transparent allusions, with those who left the magazine along with Casani in 1985. For instance, in issue 30, Javier Olivares is scathing about the former contributors Marta Moriarty and Juan Carlos de Laiglesia,[25] whom he accuses of offering partisan accounts of *la movida* and contributing to its institutionalization (30: 8). This animosity towards former editorial staff extends beyond this transitional period, with, for example, José Tono Martínez accusing an unnamed group of former editorial team members of mediocrity and opportunism in issue 32 (17), in what appears as a veiled attack on Borja Casani's new project, *Sur Exprés*, launched a few months prior to this editorial. *La Luna*'s critique within this phase of *la movida* thus often becomes entangled with, and undistinguishable from, a personal settling of scores.

These editorials see a distancing of *La Luna* from postmodernism; but, in the same way as the magazine's endorsement was never unequivocal and wavered between optimism and scepticism, its rebuke is similarly ambiguous. Issue 23 contains an apparently explicit denunciation of postmodernism: 'Lo malo de las ideologías totalitarias (sean positivas o negativas) es que nunca son nuevas y sólo producen destrucción. Esa mezcla de liberalismo y nihilismo alegre que se llamó posmodernismo es un caso claro' [The problem with all totalitarian ideologies (be they positive or negative) is that they are never new and they always lead to destruction. That combination of liberalism and joyful nihilism called post-modernism is a clear case] (Carlos de Laiglesia in 23: 8).

This characterization of postmodernism as totalitarian contrasts with the liberating potential associated with the phenomenon in earlier issues of the magazine. But even more strikingly, despite his identification of postmodernism as a totalitarian ideology, de Laiglesia seems keen to underline its 'positive' aspects; note the remarkable parenthesis in the quote above, which establishes a problematic distinction between 'positive' and 'negative' forms of totalitarianism; as well as his benevolent description of postmodernism as a blend of liberalism and joyful nihilism. Even in this ostensibly frontal attack on postmodernism, there is a lingering hint of sympathy for the phenomenon. Further, in other pieces from this transitional period — most notably perhaps Jesús Ibáñez's 'Apología del terrorismo' (24: 9), which cites Deleuze, Guattari, Serres and Baudrillard — we see a continuation of the engagement with postmodern thought that had characterized the early issues of *La Luna*.

The magazine's uneven and ambiguous attitude towards postmodernism during this transitional phase is perhaps best captured in Jorge Berlanga's complaint:

> Uno empieza a estar harto de tanta peregrina polémica y tanta disertación de Perogrullo que bulle en el seso de la inteligencia neoprogre que nos invade. [...] Hay más respuestas a la vida en un baile de Fred Astaire que en los tomos de las obras completas de Savater. Es más brillante el grito de Tarzán que el discurso de un intelectual postlacaniano. [...] Mejor que dar notas es dar la nota, dar el espectáculo, y oponer la risa loca a la palabra insignificante. (26: 3)
>
> [One is beginning to tire of all the senseless controversies and of all the clichéd platitudes bustling in the brains of the neo-progressive intelligentsia that invades us. [...] There are more responses to life in a dance by Fred Astaire than in the complete works of Savater. Tarzan's scream is more brilliant than the discourse of any postlacanian intellectual. [...] Better to be of note than to dictate notes, to become spectacle, and to oppose mad laughter to the insignificant word.] (26: 3)

Berlanga's weariness with regard to postmodern thought seems to stem from the fact that, while advocating diversity, heterogeneity and the blurring of distinctions such as 'high' and 'low' culture and attacking modernism's elitism and phallologocentrism, postmodern thinkers nevertheless tend to couch their ideas in obscure discursive modes that remain elusive to all but a select minority of initiated intellectuals. This passage not only illustrates *La Luna*'s uneasy relationship with postmodern theories, dismissed here *en masse* as 'disertación de Perogrullo', but also points to one of the central contradictions at the heart of postmodern thought: the fact that it simultaneously denounces and relies upon narrative, reason and language. Berlanga's views, while condemning the debates and discourses emerging from postmodernism, are also, on another level, informed by it, inasmuch as his vindication of Fred Astaire and Tarzan as more vitally relevant than postlacanian discourse eschews 'high culture' in favour of popular forms and affirms sensual enjoyment over and above purely intellectual pursuits. However, in a final ironic twist to which the author appears oblivious, his call to 'oponer la risa loca a la palabra insignificante' falls prey to precisely the same contradiction that he identifies and attacks with regard to postmodernism, as his call to abandon language ('la palabra insignificante') in favour of irrational laughter is itself articulated through language.

My reading of issues 21–32 as transitional is based on their retaining some of the irreverence and the anarchic spirit that characterizes the early numbers of the magazine with Casani as editor. The clearest example of the provocative edge that can still be found throughout this period is the magazine's official candidacy to the general elections of June 1986, launched in issue 21 (October 1985) and featured intermittently up to issue 28 (May 1986). The magazine's candidacy intends to apply the Warhol-esque maxim that 'Todo el mundo debe ser diputado' [Everyone should become an MP] (21: 16) by allowing its (hypothetical) parliamentary seat or seats to be occupied by up to 32 individuals, who would serve for stints of between six weeks and three months each. Five of the 32 names on the magazine's candidates' list, we are told, will be drawn from its subscription pool; and readers are invited to submit half-page electoral programmes, which will be published in *La Luna*. The rationale of the magazine's candidacy is explained in issue 22 as follows: '¿Se va a conseguir algo? Indudablemente, no. Pero vindicar la inutilidad o el fracaso no deja de ser una forma irónica y graciosa de enfrentarnos al dramatismo y al supuesto rigor reclamado por nuestros próceres' [Will anything be achieved? Of course not. But vindicating uselessness or failure remains an ironic and funny way to confront the gravitas and supposed rigour demanded by our dignitaries] (22: 63). The initiative is thus simply a practical joke, but one with a clear critical intent: to undermine the aura of respectability and rigour with which politicians attempt to cloak their party-political (and personal) agendas. While political change (not only of a revolutionary nature, but even on a smaller scale, as implied by the modest 'algo' in the quote above) is seen as unattainable, those working on *La Luna* vindicate at least their right to present parliamentary politics as farce. This disenchantment with political process within barely a decade of Spain's transition to democracy may seem striking, but can be better understood if considered against the context of the controversy surrounding Spain's NATO membership that was taking place at the time.[26] The malaise surrounding NATO membership finds echo in *La Luna*'s pages, in the magazine's candidacy ('...a la OTAN decimos no y no. A no ser que nos inviten a copas durante los primeros tres años' [to NATO we say no, no. Unless they pay for all our drinks during the first three years] (26: 68), and in a poem of sorts published in issue 28, which describes the parliamentary vote regarding NATO membership as follows: 'Diez millones de "votantes"/mandamos 202 socialistas al PARLAMENTO/y, de éstos, 181, en ciertos momentos/se "mearon" en el juramento' [Ten million "voters"/sent 202 Socialists into PARLIAMENT/ from which 181, at given moments/chose to "piss" on their oath] (28: 32). These reactions testify to the impact the NATO referendum had on a generation that, despite its disinterest in formal politics, had nevertheless welcomed the advent of democracy, and in particular the personal and creative freedoms that came with it, with undeniable optimism and enthusiasm.

The final phase of La Luna: Taking itself (too) seriously

Such overt and sharp criticism of the Spanish political and cultural establishments intensifies during the second stage of Tono Martínez's editorship (issues 33–44;

November 1986 through to the end of 1987).[27] In contrast to earlier issues, in which the magazine's editorials, or contributions to a particular theme, spread over several pages and were made up of a series of often disparate articles by different authors, we now find short, half-page editorials signed by Tono Martínez. This format adheres more closely to the conventional press editorial, and underlines Tono Martínez's position of authority within the magazine, a gesture that seems at odds with *La Luna*'s initial aim of establishing an open, non-hierarchical (or as un-hierarchical as possible) editorial space. Indeed, despite the frontal attacks on questions such as the depoliticization of politics ('Vuelve el marxismo', 33: 3); the re-emergence of religious, social and sexual puritanism ('El Contraataque', 37: 13); or the power and influence of the Catholic church ('Con faldas y a lo loco', 43: 3), these pieces in fact constitute less powerful forms of critique than the more oblique forms of mockery and self-mockery found in earlier issues. Firstly, Tono Martínez's views often come across as obvious: given his age and status as a liberal professional involved in the arts, his attacks on social conservatism and the church are hardly surprising. There is also an element of preaching to the converted — a sense that readers of *La Luna* are bound to agree with what he has to say. Editorials in this second phase thus become increasingly predictable, losing the provocative edge that characterized earlier issues. Secondly, there is a sense of decreased agency in these pieces: whereas in earlier issues of the magazine there is a sense that, even if the trappings of the system cannot be eluded, there is still the possibility to act as an irritant, to claim a victory (admittedly small and largely symbolic) by refusing to take anything seriously, criticism here takes the form of a powerless lament. Thirdly, by taking the cultural and political establishments seriously, Tono Martínez is implicitly acknowledging (and thus arguably legitimizing) their power — for, while he is critical of how they operate, his attacks do not entail a radical questioning, of or contribute to undermine, their authority. In other words: by positioning himself and his editorials in clear and direct opposition to the establishment, it could be argued that Tono Martínez provides it with its necessary 'other', with an identifiable and potentially useful enemy that can be easily neutralized thanks to the predictability of its positioning and its attacks, which stand in and emerge from a symmetrical opposition to the political establishment of the day. Finally, these editorials are problematic because they assume a position of moral high ground, failing to recognize *La Luna*'s own implication in some of the attitudes or practices criticized,[28] and hence leaving the magazine open to the charge of hypocrisy. While *La Luna*'s trajectory is marked from its very first issue by tensions and contradictions, with ambiguity used as a deliberate strategy to provoke and confuse during its initial phase (issues 1–21), in these later editorials, which express unequivocal views and adopt a distinctly authoritative tone, such inconsistencies are harder to explain or accept, particularly as they see a parallel hollowing out of content within the magazine — not only in its editorial section, reduced from several pages to half a page, but also throughout the publication as a whole. The proliferation of often provocative and always highly personal opinion pieces found in preceding issues, which turned the magazine into a space of dialogue and debate, are replaced, from issue 32 onwards, by increasingly aseptic features on foreign and local films, bands and artists. The last four issues of

La Luna, edited by Javier Tímmermans, are no longer centred around a specific theme; there are no editorials or opinion pieces, and there are hardly any original works (short stories, photography, comics or reproduced paintings or sketches). Some artworks are reproduced, but this is done in the context of features on particular authors or artists, rather than as constituent parts of the magazine in their own right. By late 1987, *La Luna* has undergone a full transformation from *revista de agitación* to coffee-table title or *revista de tendencias* concerned with reflecting, rather than actively shaping, the cultural landscape.[29]

Towards a new definition of the avant-garde

La Luna's changing attitude towards postmodernism is perhaps best understood through the consideration of the magazine's shifting views on the concept of the avant-garde, which is, in turn, linked to its valorization of *la movida*. Its inaugural issue implicitly offers a notion of a popular avant-garde; it describes the transformation of social mores and creative practices taking place in Madrid as a street-level phenomenon, the result of a spontaneous reclaiming of the city's streets. This association of the avant-garde with Madrid and with urban life permeates the early issues of the magazine, as the second chapter of this book has shown. But over the first 15 issues *of La Luna*, there is a gradual shift from the (never explicitly articulated) 'la vanguardia es la calle' (or 'la vanguardia está en la calle') to 'la vanguardia es el mercado' (15: 6–7). This slogan is of course intended to shock, but it is more than just a provocative statement; nor should it be dismissed simply as a cynical admission of the commercial dimension of artistic and cultural production. Rather, the hopeful tone of the text accompanying this proclamation suggests a perhaps excessively naïve optimism (which fails to recognize the dangers of allowing the artistic and cultural fields to be determined solely, or primarily, by market forces) regarding the possibilities the art market could offer for the dissemination of works and the professionalization of creative activity.

This notion of the market as avant-garde is revised in issue 32, where José Tono Martínez writes that '[l]a vanguardia ya no es el mercado. La vanguardia es la "High Tech" [sic]' [the avant-garde is no longer the market. The avant-garde is "High-Tech"] (32: 6). This shift from a market-driven to a technology-driven avant-garde is not greeted with much enthusiasm;[30] rather, Tono Martínez warns that the current emphasis on process can result in a generalized sense of lack of purpose or direction. His remarks appear within an article that considers the legacies of futurism, and in which he concludes '[l]as puertas del museo de cera están abiertas: nos aguardan a nosotros antes que a ellos' [the doors of the wax museum are open: they will welcome us before they welcome them] ['ellos/them' referring here to the futurists] (32: 7). This bleak diagnosis of *La Luna*'s and *la movida*'s comparative status within the artistic canon seems symptomatic of a progressive crumbling of the initial unbridled enthusiasm about the possibilities of what was taking place in Madrid at the time; an impression that is further reinforced by the fact that 'High Tech' is seen here as a potential threat, rather than as an opportunity.

The final change in the magazine's definition of avant-garde appears in issue 40: 'hoy nos vemos obligados a decir "la Vanguardia es el Estado"' [today, we are forced to say 'the avant-garde is the State'] (40: 5). The phrasing of the statement ('nos vemos obligados') already signals the resigned pessimism that characterizes the outlook of the magazine's editorial members, not only with regard to the future of their own project, but also with respect to the state of the Spanish cultural landscape as a whole. Despite earlier proclamations, we are told in this piece, neither 'high tech' nor the market have materialized as viable alternatives capable of transforming the dynamics of the artistic and cultural fields — in the case of 'high tech', because of its insufficient implantation in Spain. The failure of the market is not considered or explained directly, though an oblique 'tal y como van las cosas en ciertos ambientes' (40: 5) suggests a crisis in Spain's art market, a crisis that Tono Martínez and Javier Tímmermans elsewhere attributed to the co-option efforts of local and national politicians, whose public subsidy policies, they claim, contributed to inflate artists' salaries, putting projects and initiatives that wished to remain independent at a disadvantage (Larson and Compitello 1997: 5). The interference of the state is also denounced in issue 40, though not for constituting a form of unfair competition, but for engendering a new class of 'ociosos serviles a cuenta de los presupuestos públicos' [servile idlers at public expense] (40: 5).

This perceived transformation of *la movida* from street-level, spontaneous and disorganized avant-garde to state-sanctioned vanguard illustrates the fact that the potentially liberating and productive mechanisms of postmodernism identified in the early issues of the magazine had failed to fulfil the expectations they had generated among *La Luna*'s team and many of their contemporaries. In the early days of *La Luna*, there is an (admittedly often wavering) hope that postmodernism might enable a popular, bottom-up avant-garde; that it could contribute to expand and consolidate what was already happening in Madrid. Postmodern thought is regarded in these initial stages as something that could provide *la movida* with a useful theoretical framework. Indeed, postmodernism's efforts to address and challenge modernism's alleged exclusions (such as its favouring 'metropolitan' artists and intellectuals at the expense of 'peripheral' ones, its disregard for non-canonical, 'low' or popular cultural forms, or its failure to acknowledge race, gender and ethnic bias) must have seemed like a golden opportunity to a generation who had grown up in an environment of '*jet lag* cultural' (Olivares in Cadahía 2007: 43) imposed by Francoism, and now had the opportunity not just to live and work freely, but to attract international attention to their work.

It is of course ironic, given *La Luna*'s general irreverence, self-declared disregard for hierarchies and taste for provocation, that those working on the magazine felt the need to legitimize or lend intellectual gravitas to their project, or, more broadly, to *la movida*; and it is even more ironic that postmodernism, which heralds the demise of legitimizing meta-narratives, should be the vehicle chosen to such ends. But it is precisely such paradoxes and contradictions which characterize both the magazine and much postmodern thought, and which, in the case of *La Luna*, generated creatively productive and intellectually stimulating frictions. Further, intellectual legitimization was sought, it appears, not only as a means to lend respectability to *la movida*, but also as a way to achieve the successful marketization of *movida* works within an art world in which, as we are told in issue 15, 'la cobertura teórico-comercial de la obra plástica tiene más importancia que la obra en sí, puesto que artistas hay millones y etiquetas consumibles muchas menos' [the theoretical-commercial wrapping of the work of art is more important than the work itself, for there are millions of artists and far fewer consumable labels](15: 6).

The contention that postmodernism offered *La Luna* a theoretical wrapping which rendered the *movida* works launched in and through the magazine more marketable should not, however, detract or distract from the genuine interest in the debates and theories emerging around the postmodern to which its pages testify. Postmodernism is not treated purely as a means to an end within the magazine; but its international prestige and resonance (and hence its legitimising and commercial value) are recognized. This realization might be regarded by some as cynical, but in my view it points to a characteristically postmodern awareness of the many vectors, including an amalgam of the commercial, industrial, theoretical, and political, that traverse and contribute to articulate the artistic and cultural fields. If there is a critique to be made of *La Luna*'s engagement with postmodernism, it is rather on the basis of the underlying belief that such postmodern awareness of being bound by (and thus inevitably complicit with) wider power systems could, in itself, grant a degree of autonomy within them, a distance that could allow for the emergence of a critical performative space, a hope that the magazine's trajectory from a *revista de agitación* in its beginnings to a *revista de tendencias* in its final years proved to be naïve.

La Luna's pages do not suggest the magazine explicitly and unequivocally supported postmodern ideas and practices, but rather, that its engagement with postmodernism throughout its five-year existence was hesitant and oblique. Moreover, the publication's relationship with and attitude towards postmodernism evolved over time, from an initial optimism about its liberating (and, indeed, visibility enhancing) potential to a progressive distancing and disillusionment, as the tensions and contradictions that postmodernism had contributed to identify (between, for instance, collective action and the right to individual difference; or between art and culture as products of the system, and as mechanisms that can highlight its inconsistencies) led to deadlock and paralysis. The fluctuating and evolving nature of the magazine's relationship towards postmodernism does not, however, preclude its characterization as postmodern, for such oscillations are typically postmodern. But given *La Luna*'s fluctuations between different attitudes and categories, including, as noted, between modern and postmodern ideas and values, such a characterization relies on an understanding of postmodernism as part of (or at least as contiguous to, and occasionally overlapping with) modernism, rather than as radically opposed to it — a conception of postmodernism that significantly differs from that of a number of Spanish critics and intellectuals (Subirats 2002: 75; Mainer 1988: 21–22; Cebrián in Gallero 1991: 4) who have insistently branded *la movida* as postmodern. While my analysis leads me to conclude that *La Luna* can be characterized as a postmodern cultural product, the magazine's own shifting and contradictory understanding and use of the term is very different from the clear and stable conception of postmodernism of these critics, who consider it negatively as an abandonment, or even an inversion, of modern values of intellectual clarity and rigour, political engagement, and social emancipation.

Going back to the tripartite division proposed at the beginning of this chapter of postmodernism understood as creative-aesthetic practice (or as style); as individual experience of a newfound freedom to express (and perhaps even make a living out of) one's individuality; and as collective phenomenon with (potentially) a political dimension, then, *La Luna* succeeded first and foremost in maximising the realm of individual experimentation and expression, placing self-definition at the centre of all concerns. This emphasis on individual experience contributed to a proliferation of creative manifestations of different types and scales — some of which, as this study has illustrated, testify to a quality and originality that has not yet been fully recognized. The first two poles, then, the creative-aesthetic (the formulation of a repertoire of styles and practices), and the experiential (the affirmation of one's individuality), appear as closely interrelated, with the emphasis on individual experience, individual identity, and self-definition leading to the emergence, and allowing for the coexistence of, a polyphony of often divergent voices, opinions, and styles. This polyphony, to which *La Luna*'s pages testify and which undoubtedly has postmodern echoes, nevertheless creates a tension between collective multiplicity and individual affirmation. In other words, the proliferation of expressions found in *La Luna*'s pages, though resulting in the first instance from individuals' desire and quest for self-expression, can (as presciently noted by Gregorio Morales in his letter in issue 8) eventually threaten the very individuality it sought to foster, as individual contributions risk being absorbed by, and becoming indistinct from, the larger framework (be that of *La Luna* or, more broadly, that of *la movida*) within which they emerge.

The third axis, the collective-political, proves similarly complex. On the one hand, the focus on individualism led to a reduced ability or willingness to compromise and act collectively. Issues arising from this include the failure to address or confront social problems such as domestic and sexual violence in a meaningful and cohesive manner, considered in the previous chapter; as well as the proliferation of internal conflicts within the magazine, which, as discussed in this chapter, contributed to its eventual demise. But while the experience of those working on *La Luna* suggest some of the limitations of a postmodern cultural and creative practice, this does not mean their activities were entirely ineffectual on a political level. Their urban reimaginings helped create a more participatory urban culture in Madrid, and their parodic resignification of national and gender identity clichés contributed to neutralize their power, or at least to question their role and relevance in the present. The key political achievement of *La Luna* can thus not be entirely extricated from its creative-aesthetic and individuality-affirming facets, as it resides precisely in its success in establishing itself (at least temporarily) as a diverse and participatory space, which allowed readers to glimpse a more inclusive culture, one in which previously marginalized groups (women, homosexuals, drug users) were not just allowed, but indeed expected, to take part.

Notes to Chapter 4

1. This fragment is taken from Ramírez's essay 'Catecismo breve de la postmodernidad (notas provisionales)', originally published in *La Luna* (issue 24: 20–22), and reprinted in the 1986 edited volume *La polémica de la postmodernidad* (Madrid: Ediciones Libertarias), pp. 15–25.
2. In terms of postmodernism's break or continuity with respect to modernism, Hutcheon (1988), Jameson (1991), Jencks (2011) and even, although somewhat ambiguously, Lyotard (1984), suggest some degree of continuity and contiguity between modernism and postmodernism, while others, such as Gianni Vattimo (1992), suggest postmodernism constitutes a clear break form modernism. As for the mass media, while Baudrillard (1983) regards them as key for the production and dissemination of simulacra, Vattimo has a more positive view of the media, which, he argues, may offer a possibility for emancipation. The anxiety with respect to the status of art and culture — not least the cultural production that these critics and scholars themselves engage in — within a postmodern context is often implicit, taking the form, for instance, of revisions to the literary canon. Linda Hutcheon, however, tackles the question explicitly, arguing that 'we cannot exempt our own "discriminating scholarly discourse"' from critical scrutiny (1988: 21), but concludes that the imperative to contextualize (and thus recognize the contingency of) our critical praxis does not entail an abdication; for Hutcheon, '[i]f we accept that all is provisional and historically conditioned, we will not stop thinking, as some fear; in fact, that acceptance will guarantee that we never stop thinking — and rethinking' (1988: 53).
3. In issue 15, for instance, in an unsigned manifesto-like proclamation, it is claimed that four decades of Francoism have left Spain's cultural landscape 'como un erial comparable con la Alemania post-nazi' [a wasteland much like post-Nazi Germany] (15: 7), and in issue 27 Javier Olivares declares: 'Tenemos la obligación de apostar fuerte con el fin de avanzar cinco años cada doce meses. Ese es el retraso que llevamos y eso es lo que tenemos que recuperar para que el pasado de nuestro futuro no sea tan desolador' [We are duty-bound to invest strongly in order to advance five years every twelve months. That's how far behind we are, and we need to catch up if we want a future less desolate than our past] (27: 12).
4. Vattimo recognizes the problematic nature of his hypothesis, which may be seen as a reworking of the essentialist cliché of Spaniards (and, more generally, 'latinos', among whom he includes Italians) as different from (i.e. more passionate and hedonistic and less disciplined than) their Northern European neighbours. As he himself notes in this piece, it is his awareness of the risks inherent in such a discourse that led him to include these remarks as a prologue, published only in the Spanish edition of the text.
5. The organized censorship apparatus that had operated during Francoism was dismantled following the regime's end and the formal transition to democracy (1975–1977), but there were specific instances of authoritarian practices beyond that period, such as the incarceration of Albert Boadella from the theatre company *Els Joglars* in December 1977, and upon his return to Spain in 1979 (cf. <http://www.elsjoglars.com/produccion.php?idPag=latorna_cas>); or the ban on Pilar Miró's 1979 film *El crimen de Cuenca*, embargoed by the Ministry of the Interior on the eve of its release in December 1979, and finally authorized for release in 1981 (cf. Díez Puertas 2003: 223–24).
6. Other examples of collaborative working include the *Cascorro Factory*, a comic production and distribution operation set up by the visual artist Ceesepe and the photographer Alberto García-Alix, and later joined by El Hortelano, Agust and Ouka Leele; *La liviandad del imperdible* (later *Kaka de Luxe*), a group of teenage aspiring artists including Olvido Gara (better known by her artistic name Alaska) and Enrique Márquez (El Zurdo); or PREMAMÁ (Prensa Marginal Madrileña). For more details on these collectives, see Lechado 2005. Additionally, film-makers such as Pedro Almodóvar and Iván Zulueta have referred to the collaborative working methods of their films of this period (*Pepi, Luci, Bom...* and *Arrebato*, respectively), which relied on friends and acquaintances to make up the cast, often for little or no pay (cf. Zulueta in Gallero 1991: 167; and Almodóvar in Strauss 1996: 12–20).
7. Martín-Begué explains the resistance of many of his contemporaries to the *movida* label in the following terms: 'En el fondo, todos renegamos de la movida, porque a nadie le gusta que le

encasillen' [In the end, we all repudiate *la movida* because no one likes to be pigeonholed] (Gallero 1991: 154); and Pérez-Villalta echoes this, stating that '[s]iempre fuimos muy individualistas. Hubo intentos de agruparnos, pero fracasaron por cuestiones puramente internas' [we were always profoundly individualistic. Attempts were made to group us together, but they always failed for purely internal reasons.] (Gallero 1991: 307).

8. The fragment is entitled 'El Cernícalo', and includes an introduction by the translator, Vicente Molina Foix.
9. Sádaba makes a similar argument in an article on individual identity in issue 5 of *La Luna* (5: 7), and discussed in the previous chapter. In that piece, the author argues that the multiplicity of selves that coexist within any one being can either be suppressed (at the price of becoming imbeciles) or acknowledged, the more sensible approach for Sádaba, even if it may lead to the verge of insanity. The suppression of the multiplicity of selves mentioned in that article can be seen as analogous to the repression of internal chaos the author alludes to here, with similarly negative results.
10. I am thinking, for instance, of slogans such as 'L'imagination prend le pouvoir!' [Imagination takes power]; 'or 'Dessous les pavés, c'est la plage' [Under the paving stones, the beach] (cf. Besançon 1968).
11. For instance, following its legalization in 1977, the Spanish Communist Party (PCE) abandoned its long-standing pledge for the restoration of a Republic in Spain, recognizing the parliamentary democracy that resulted from the transitional process; and in its IX Congress, held in 1978, it distanced itself from Leninism. Similarly, the Spanish Socialist Workers' Party (PSOE) renounced Marxism in 1979.
12. Umberto Eco describes hyperreality as 'instances where the American imagination demands the real thing and, to attain it, must fabricate the absolute fake; where the boundaries between game and illusion are blurred, the art museum is contaminated by the freak show, and falsehood is enjoyed in a situation of "fullness", of *horror vacui*' (Eco 1983: 8); while Jean Baudrillard defines the hyperreal as 'the generation by models of a real without origin or reality', a consequence of the precession of simulacra (Baudrillard 1983: 2).
13. Javier Tímmermans, co-founder and third editor of *La Luna*, stated that '[a] pesar del éxito, la publicación nunca fue rentable, de hecho nunca tuvimos, ni nos interesó, lo que hoy llamaríamos una política comercial seria' [despite its success, the publication was never profitable, indeed, we never had, or were interested in, what you would nowadays call a proper business policy] (Cadahía 2007: 55).
14. Will Slocombe notes that '[n]ihilism, postmodernism and poststructuralism are frequently confused, primarily because of the way in which they each construct truth', and goes on to argue that 'both postmodernism and poststructuralism affect how nihilism is constructed, rather than being nihilistic themselves' (2006: 77).
15. Tristan Tzara's 'Dada Manifesto 1918', for example, proclaims 'DADA MEANS NOTHING' (Ades 2006: 36), and in 'Dada is a Virgin Germ', he writes 'Dada is against the future, Dada is dead, Dada is idiotic' (ibid: 66).
16. This is a reference to the dystopian landscape of generalized social anarchy and civilian skirmishes across Madrid and beyond described within this spoof issue.
17. See for instance Foucault's work on the imbrication of power, knowledge and discourse in titles such as *Madness and Civilization*, *The Order of Things*, and the three volumes of his *History of Sexuality*.
18. Critics such as Peter Dews, for instance, have questioned the extent to which 'a philosophical position which assumes the classical forms of critique to be necessarily and oppressively identitarian can itself continue to perform a critical function' (1987: xvi). In other words, postmodernism's on-going interrogation of the legitimacy and authority of critical discourses and epistemological models arguably ultimately undermines, or at least throws into question, its own validity as an interpretative approach.
19. Of course, it could be argued that Lozano's use of borrowed ideas and phrases without explicit acknowledgement is simply opportunistic, but given the obviousness of his allusions, it seems rather more plausible that he is engaging in a postmodern game of intertextual cross-referencing.

20. It is worth mentioning that this blindness with regards to the asymmetry of power relations has been raised in relation to some thinkers associated with postmodernism, such as Michel Foucault, whose insistence on the ubiquity and dispersion of power has, according to some of his critics, the effect of de-politicising politics (cf. Moi 1985a: 95).
21. Casani credits *La Luna* contributors Jorge Lozano, José Luis Brea, Javier Sádaba, Jesús Ibáñez and Miguel Cereceda, who, he writes, had been thinking about and working on postmodernism for some time, with helping to introduce the debate to the magazine's readers.
22. Borja Casani launched *Sur Exprés* in the spring of 1987 (the first issue is dated '15 de abril–15 de mayo 1987'). This new arts monthly, set up to portray more global cultural and artistic trends, ran for 12 issues, with its final edition appearing in October 1988.
23. In an article published in *El País* on 13/09/1985 about *La Luna*'s editorial schism, artistic director José Luis Tirado, deputy editor José Manuel Costa and staff member Carlos García Calvo are mentioned as leaving the publication alongside Casani. The article can be accessed at <http://elpais.com/diario/1985/09/13/cultura/495410407_850215.html>.
24. Jorge Berlanga acts as guest editor in issue 26, Javier Olivares appears as editor in issue 27 and Juan Ramón Yuste is the editor of issue 31.
25. Marta Moriarty (née Marta Villar), co-founder of Galería Moriarty alongside Borja Casani and his wife Lola Moriarty (née Lola Fraile), is not listed as a member of the *La Luna*'s editorial staff in the magazine's content pages, but she regularly contributed to its feminine section *Luz de Boudoir/Somos unas señoras* in the first 14 issues of *La Luna*. Juan Carlos de Laiglesia was one of the founding members of *La Luna* and was one of the publication's 'jefes de redacción' (section editors) in issues 1–20. Although his name is not mentioned in the aforementioned *El País* article about *La Luna*'s editorial schism, he no longer appears as a member of staff after the split (though he penned an article for, and is listed as a contributor in, issue 23).
26. The Spanish Socialist Workers' Party (PSOE) had made its pledge to bring Spain out of NATO one of its cornerstone policies during the electoral campaign that led to its 1982 victory; but within three years in government, reneged on this promise and legislated in favour of Spain's continued membership. In an attempt to appease its left-wing bases, the PSOE organized a consultative referendum on the issue, held on 12 March 1986. The 'yes' camp (in favour of continued membership) won with 52.5 per cent of the vote, against 39.8 per cent voting for Spain's exit from NATO. However, because of the non-binding nature of the referendum, as well as the (some argue deliberately) confusing phrasing of the referendum question and the fact that the PSOE actively campaigned for a 'yes' vote, many one-time Socialist supporters came to see the consultation as a farce.
27. Issues 31 and 32 are difficult to ascribe to either phase of this second period of the magazine, as they are special numbers devoted to specific topics relating to current events. Issue 31, guest-edited by Juan Ramón Yuste, is devoted to photography; while issue 32 focuses on post-futurism, offering an overview of historical futurism to coincide with the exhibition 'Futurismo e futurismi', held in Venice at the time.
28. One clear example of such double standards can be found in the magazine's criticism of public subsidies to the arts, which fails to acknowledge that, while *La Luna* did not technically rely on such support mechanisms, it did count government bodies and institutions among its key advertisers. Further, Borja Casani retrospectively admitted that the magazine's unsubsidized status was due to the local authorities' initial reluctance to support the project, rather than a result of a conscious and deliberate editorial policy (Ripoll 1988).
29. Javier Tímmermans, one of the co-founders of *La Luna* and its last editor, describes the decadence of the magazine as follows: 'Los únicos números de *La Luna* que no han dado pérdidas son los tres últimos, que dirigí yo. Reconozco que tuve que emplear técnicas de periodismo amarillo. Miguel Bosé en portada, o Marta Sánchez; la primera portada de Marta Sánchez en su vida. Tuve que poner carnaza.' [The only issues of *La Luna* that did not incur losses were the three final ones, which I edited. I admit I had to use sensationalist techniques. Putting [singers] Miguel Bosé or Marta Sánchez in the cover, Marta Sánchez's first ever cover. I had to resort to cheap titbits.] (Tímmermans in Gallero 1991: 177).
30. In issue 40 of *La Luna* Tono Martínez credits Eduardo Subirats with informing this change in perception (40: 5).

CHAPTER 5

Conclusion: Towards a New Critical Approach to *la movida*

This book set out to invite a rethink of how we understand and conceptualize *la movida*, in the belief that the 1970s and 1980s urban youth movement is more complex than the familiar narratives of *la movida* suggest, either as a banal, thoughtlessly hedonistic moment in Madrid's history, or as a response to the trauma of Francoism and the *desencanto* ensuing from the transition to democracy; or as a golden age for counterculture. Despite the fact that *La Luna* never explicitly aligned itself with *la movida*, the magazine has come to be seen as one of the movement's most emblematic cultural products. However, the relationship between *La Luna* and *la movida* is more complex and fraught than that of a movement and its main or official organ of expression, not least because both *la movida* and the magazine emerged as fairly anarchic enterprises that lacked the sense of purpose and unity of other artistic and cultural movements. Some *movida* participants have argued that *La Luna* is not so much a product of *la movida* as a vehicle for its co-option and assimilation into the cultural mainstream:

> *La Luna* es un producto literario y rápidamente se institucionaliza. [...] Es entonces cuando empiezan a hacerse ecos los periódicos, y el término posmodernidad centra el debate de los intelectuales. Hasta que no salió *La Luna*, yo no había oído hablar de posmodernidad... (Miguel Trillo in Gallero 1991: 54–55)
>
> [*La Luna* is a literary product and is rapidly institutionalised. [...] It is then that the newspapers start to react to it, and the term postmodernity takes to the centre of intellectual debate. Until the launch of *La Luna*, I had not heard any talk about postmodernity...] (Miguel Trillo in Gallero 1991: 54–55)

This view of *La Luna* as a product that enables or facilitates the institutionalization of *la movida* relies upon a periodization of the movement that situates its highpoint in the late 1970s and early 1980s (that is, before the appearance of the magazine). The photographer Miguel Trillo, the painter Sigfrido Martín Begué (cf. Gallero 1991: 148) and the film-maker Pedro Almodóvar (cf. Cervera 2002: 14) locate the 'explosive moment' of *la movida* during the years of the government of Unión de Centro Democrático (UCD) (1977–1982) rather than under the first Socialist government (1982–1986). This periodization of *la movida* throws into question *La Luna*'s status as a *movida* product, suggesting instead a reading of the magazine as a publication that reacted to the movement, rather than actively contributing to shaping it.

In contrast, for *La Luna*'s first editor, Borja Casani, the process of gaining visibility is a central element of *la movida*; the process of becoming visible (a process in which the magazine plays a pivotal role) coincides, in Casani's view, with the height of *la movida*, rather than with its demise. As the fourth chapter of this book brought to light there is, nevertheless, an awareness on the part of the magazine's editorial team of the dangers inherent in their efforts to make visible (and make sense of) *la movida*, a realization that, by attempting to communicate to a wider audience what was taking place within Madrid's countercultural circles, they inevitably open up what they are trying to communicate to (mis)interpretation and manipulation. As Stephen Duncombe notes in relation to fanzine culture:

> In insignificance lies a certain freedom. [...] Being ignored by the media and the culture industry was part of what stimulated people to create *zines*; remaining ignored is often the only way to keep control over the independent culture that is created. (Duncombe 1997: 155)

The tension Duncombe identifies between independence (or control) and visibility is central to the relationship between *La Luna* and *la movida*, as well as, more broadly, to the evolution of *la movida* from a spontaneous, countercultural urban movement to an internationally renowned cultural phenomenon. Faced with a choice between insignificance (or invisibility) and the risk of misinterpretation or manipulation, those working on *La Luna* opted to take their chances. And they were not alone; during the early 1980s, Trillo, Begué and Almodóvar all willingly contributed to *La Luna*'s pages and took advantage of the space and visibility the publication granted them. Their retrospective postulation of the more underground period of *la movida* (i.e. pre-1982) as its authentic heart or culminating moment thus seems symptomatic of nostalgia for a time when, as Almodóvar wrote elsewhere, they were all younger, thinner, and naive about the price of things or the pressures of the market (Almodóvar 1991: 7). The suggestion, by some *movida* participants, that *La Luna* initiated or facilitated the process of popularization, neutralization and co-option of *la movida* ought not to overlook the fact that they as individuals benefited from (and often sought) the exposure the magazine offered, and were hence complicit, wittingly or unwittingly, in such processes.[1] This understandable quest for visibility by *movida* artists throws into question familiar narratives that posit the movement as a radically underground, chaotic happening that became co-opted and transformed by external forces (whether the mainstream media or the Socialist government of the time), suggesting instead a degree of agency and complicity on the part of its protagonists. The dual nature of *La Luna* as both a product of *la movida*, and as a vehicle that contributed, or may have contributed, to its institutionalization, is thus not unique to the publication, but also extends to the ample body of works that sought an audience and durability beyond the here and now of Madrid's nightlife. However, because of its status as a media product, *La Luna* illustrates this problematic division or tension between visibility and co-option particularly vividly. The fact that *La Luna* may have facilitated the institutionalization of *la movida* does not counter its status as one of the movement's most iconic cultural products, but rather highlights a tension that runs through *la movida* as a whole.

While it would be problematically reductionist to equate *La Luna* with *la movida*, since the former is but one of the many cultural products resulting from the latter, many of the insights derived from the analysis of the Madrilenian magazine in the preceding chapters apply to *la movida* as a whole. *La Luna* constitutes a particularly useful vehicle through which to approach *la movida* for four reasons. Firstly, the magazine incorporated a wide variety of materials (stories, opinion pieces, reviews, artworks) in different formats (photography, comics, collage, text) and from a broad range of artists linked to *la movida* (Pedro Almodóvar, Ouka Lele, Ceesepe, El Hortelano, Juan Ramón Yuste, Pablo Pérez-Mínguez, Alberto García-Alix, among others), and hence it can be read retrospectively as an invaluable archive of *movida* works and chronicles. Secondly, *La Luna*'s status and constitution as a periodical reflects the sense of urgency and immediacy of those working in 1980s Madrid, as well as their combination of ambition and amateurism. Thirdly, the magazine's serialized nature and its transformations over its five-year run offer a glimpse into the evolution of *la movida* from a chaotic, disorganized underground or countercultural movement to an established and internationally renown cultural phenomenon. And finally, the publication's ambiguous status as both a cultural product of *la movida* and a media product that may have contributed to its theorization and institutionalization is indicative of the tension between independence and visibility that spans *la movida* from its beginnings.

The analysis of *La Luna* in Chapter 2 documents the magazine's efforts to reimagine Madrid and to transform the ways in which its readers thought about and engaged with the city. The magazine encourages a sense of community and belonging that is not postulated on origin (having been born in Madrid) and hence exclusive, but on participation in and enjoyment of the city. Critics such as José Carlos Mainer (1988; 2000), Tom Lewis (1994), Eduardo Subirats (2002) and María del Mar Alberca (2003) have argued that this emphasis on enjoyment or hedonism, which they regard as one of the more distinctive features of *la movida*, is largely predicated upon a rampant consumerism. However, as the second chapter illustrates, many works from this period featured in *La Luna* are in fact concerned with the potential for experimentation and sensual pleasure inherent to the city's streets, encouraging the reclaiming of urban space as a site for enjoyment that ought to be open and accessible to all. It is undeniable that, for many, the frequenting of bars, cafés and parties characterized their experience of *la movida*; but this penchant for nightlife and excess is not exclusive to the Spanish movement, but has characterized bohemian subcultures since at least the nineteenth century. If *la movida* is often slated as consumerist, it seems that it is not only owing to its well-documented hedonism, but also for its fascination with consumer culture. The language of advertising is frequently incorporated into works associated with *la movida*, as, for instance, in Pedro Almodóvar's first feature-length film *Pepi, Luci, Bom y otras chicas del montón* (1980) or in Ouka Lele's untitled duo of images, published in issue 9/10 of *La Luna* (57–59; Figures 5.1 and 5.2). But such incorporations cannot be read as mere endorsements of consumerism or of consumer culture; rather, as these examples illustrate, the strategies and visual languages of advertising are often used to comic and parodic effect.[2]

FIGS. 5.1 (left) and 5.2 (right). Ouka Leele's Madrid 1983 © Ouka Leele

The destabilization of gender, sexual and national identity categories in *La Luna*'s pages, considered in the third chapter, and which is also found in other *movida* works,[3] calls into question the alleged apolitical nature of the phenomenon. Scholars who are critical of *la movida*, such as Alberca, have argued that for its participants 'las bases de su comportamiento y su expresión se encontraban en un rechazo total de la política' [at the heart of their behaviour and expression was a total rejection of politics] (2003: 290). While *movida* participants showed no interest in formal politics, and in fact frequently mocked parliamentary politics, as seen in *La Luna*'s candidacy in the general election of 1986, their challenge to firmly established and widely accepted identity paradigms had a political dimension. The mobilization and parody of gender and national clichés found in *La Luna* contributed to neutralize their power, revealing, in the process, both the historically determined and ideologically charged nature of identity categories, and the limited, but significant, degree to which individuals can help perpetuate or transform such paradigms. As noted in Chapter 3, this approach is not without its limitations, as the focus on discourse and representation risks detracting or distracting from the tangible, specific problems (discrimination, violence, etc.) arising from, or partly enabled by, the discursive practices challenged in the magazine. However, *La Luna*'s attempts to transform the social collective imaginary by querying how men and women, heterosexuals and homosexuals, Spaniards and non-Spaniards, see and define themselves and each other, constitutes a necessary and useful first step towards a more equal and more liberal society. That such efforts have not been acknowledged to have political implications has to do with a narrow definition of the political as parliamentary process, as Paul Julian Smith notes (2006: 65); and it is also symptomatic of the tendency, within some anti-Francoist opposition circles, to regard the plight of women and homosexuals as personal, rather than political, issues, and as such secondary to the revolutionary struggle — a stance of which *movida* participants such as *La Luna*'s editor Borja Casani (cf. Gallero 1991: 26) or the journalist and founder of the magazine *Madrid Me Mata* Moncho Alpuente (Ripoll 1988: 54–55) were deeply critical.

The fourth chapter of this book analysed *La Luna*'s engagement with postmodern ideas and practices, in an attempt to qualify and contextualize the characterization of *la movida* as a postmodern phenomenon. The textual evidence considered in that chapter suggests that the magazine's relationship with postmodernism is more complex and nuanced than the unproblematic postulation of *la movida* as a localized postmodern manifestation, or as a Spanish version of postmodernism, favoured by critics such as Eduardo Subirats, José Carlos Mainer, or Juan Luis Cebrián, would have us believe. The early issues of *La Luna* show an undeniable fascination with postmodernism, which is regarded optimistically as opening up the possibility for a peripheral city such as Madrid and an originally underground phenomenon such as *la movida* to take centre stage. Yet even in these early stages, the publication refrains from identifying itself as postmodern, or from unequivocally endorsing postmodernism; its adscription to the global phenomenon is, at best, tentative and by implication — a trait which itself can be regarded as characteristically postmodern. However, this wavering support for postmodernism soon gives way to a realization of its limitations, as those working on the magazine come to realize that postmodernism's rejection of legitimizing metanarratives cannot, in and of itself, guarantee any degree of autonomy or independence for artists and cultural practitioners from wider networks of power.

This chapter further suggests that the clear-cut conceptual opposition between modernity/modernism and postmodernity/postmodernism postulated by some of the aforementioned Spanish critics is problematic in a Spanish context, which, as Helen Graham and Antonio Sánchez have noted, is marked precisely by a juxtaposition of processes and paradigms:

> in recent times, accelerating after 1978, Spain has experienced a rapid process of belated modernization (political democratization and the social-infrastructural development of civil society), but at the same time — precisely because this modernization process has necessarily meant assimilation to a wider European economic and cultural environment — it displays all the social and economic decentring and cultural fragmentation typical of the postmodern era (Graham and Sánchez 1995: 408)

The synchronicity or parallel nature of modernization processes and postmodernism within Spain identified by these authors explains, at least in part, the initial enthusiasm and readiness with which postmodernism was greeted in *La Luna*'s pages, as the magazine's engagement with postmodernism can occasionally come across as part of a wider attempt to 'catch up' with the rest of Europe in cultural terms. Additionally, postmodernism's valorisation of difference and its canonical re-evaluations (through, for instance, its vindication of 'low' and popular culture) provided *movida* artists with an opportunity to overcome their marginality both in geographical terms (as artists from a peripheral European country) and in terms of their status, within Spain, as countercultural or underground figures. The almost immediate success of both *La Luna* and *la movida* in Spain and beyond (in the case of the latter), suggests that their mobilization of postmodern themes (simulation, chaos and carnival) and practices (parody, pastiche, citation, self-reflexive mocking) within a postmodern context (albeit one that was precariously so) paid dividends in the short term. However, in the long run, the association of *la movida* with postmodernism has proven detrimental for the Spanish phenomenon, leading to a reductionist view of *la movida* as a Spanish version of postmodernism, or as a movement that facilitated Spain's entry into postmodernity.

The analysis of *La Luna*'s contents in the preceding chapters demonstrates that *movida* artistic and cultural products are conceptually complex, visually rich and innovative. The tendency to minimize or deny the creative-aesthetic dimension of *la movida* is due, at least in part, to enduring prejudices as to what constitutes a valid or legitimate cultural product, that is, a creation meriting critical attention. The works of individuals such as the multidisciplinary visual artist Rodrigo Muñoz Ballester, the photographer Juan Ramón Yuste, the writers Juan Madrid and Eduardo Haro Ibars, or the intellectual musings of, among others, Javier Sádaba, Jorge Lozano and José Luis Brea testify to the diversity and the originality of those working in 1980s Madrid. If their work has not received due critical attention, it would seem that this is largely because it was first (and in some cases, solely) published in a magazine, an ephemeral format still widely regarded as less prestigious than more durable formats such as the book. Further, the success and media ubiquity of a handful of *movida* figures (Pedro Almodóvar and Olvido Gara 'Alaska' are two paradigmatic examples) since the mid-1980s has tended to overshadow many others whose work, though less visible, is equally deserving of critical attention — not only because of its calibre, but also because their evaluation can help challenge existing preconceptions of *la movida* as a short-lived liberating movement or moment that left nothing (or nothing of any consequence) in its wake (cf. Ilie 1995: 28).

La movida cannot be characterized as a superficial, inconsequential moment in or of Madrid's recent history, nor as a response to the trauma of Francoism and the *desencanto* ensuing from the transition to democracy, nor as a golden age for counterculture. It was both all and none of those things, inasmuch as elements from those narratives are present within the phenomenon, but are not enough, in isolation, to make sense of it. While banality, frivolity and hedonism feature heavily in *La Luna*, such attitudes are not always (if ever) thoughtless, but rather have a strategic value that is often not immediately obvious — in terms, for instance, of challenging the perceived elitism and transcendence that dominated in contemporary Spanish cultural circles; as well as a means to indirectly question or mock gender and national stereotypes.

The notion of *la movida* as a traumatic response to Francoism and the transition, in which direct references to the past are obliterated, yet return in repressed form as nihilistic attitudes and practices (cf. Vilarós 1998) does not account for the reappropriation and resignification by *movida* artists of popular culture elements that, by the 1970s and early 1980s, had become associated with Francoism through their use by the regime's propaganda apparatus. The psychoanalytic model is helpful in that it identifies the oblique manner in which *movida* artists and cultural practitioners engage with the past, but where that narrative sees this as a symptom of repression of a traumatic experience, I regard this as indicative of a tiredness or a loss of faith with formal politics in the wake of the politics of consensus that characterized the transitional process in Spain, but that also finds resonance within a global postmodern context in which ideology and politics appear as increasingly diffused constructs. The reverse of this apathy towards party politics is an often-overlooked interest in the everyday, in the affirmation of personal freedoms and the right to difference, and in the local practices and allegiances that can help sustain such freedoms and enrich daily life.

The narrative that posits *la movida* as a new dawn for Spanish (counter)culture, while acknowledging these aspects and emphasizing its liberating effects (a feature not always considered by either of the previous interpretative approaches), nevertheless fails to address the tensions and contradictions that characterize, indeed articulate, the movement. This discourse is unhelpful not only because it contributes to a dangerous mythologizing of the period, but also because it simplifies what this work has shown to be a complex phenomenon-cum-construct — a simplification that, though intended to have the opposite effect to that of those who dismiss *la movida* outright on the grounds of its superficiality, nevertheless entails a not entirely dissimilar obliteration of some of its key features.

The engagement, within *La Luna*'s pages, with urban space, with the city of Madrid, considered at length in the second chapter, and with personal and collective identities and identity categories, analysed in the third chapter, underlines *la movida*'s emphasis on the quotidian, the local and the experiential. Such a focus is not entirely new: urban space and the de- and reconstruction of identity are preoccupations which feature in twentieth-century avant-garde movements such as Surrealism and Situationism. Given the echoes and influences of such movements upon *la movida*, it is tempting to posit the Madrilenian movement as part of a wider European or Western avant-garde or countercultural tradition, that is, as a last collective attempt at transforming art and life from the margins of the artistic-cultural establishment. However, the efforts within *La Luna* to effect change (through the reimagining and reclaiming of Madrid's streets, and through a parodic dismantling and reassembling of identity categories and clichés) are punctuated throughout by irony, contradiction and self-reflexivity — as seen, for instance, in the magazine's self-implication in its mockery of the figure of the bohemian *lampante* in issue 6, or in its self-denunciation in a spoof letter to the editor published in issue 8.

La Luna's mocking and undermining of its own position, moves which are themselves not constant or stable, but vary in degree and frequency throughout the magazine's existence, can only be understood when considered in the context in which the publication emerges: a postmodern context within which the historical avant-gardes have been assimilated into the academy; and, which has seen the failure of utopian projects such as the 1968 movement (its French version inspired largely by Situationism), and the renunciation, within Spain, to the more radical aspirations (such as the restoration of a Republic or the constitution of a Marxist-socialist state) held by many anti-Franco activists in the early stages of the transitional process (cf. Andrade Blanco 2012; Morán 1991). Within this context, then, any belief in a movement's independence or autonomy from the constraints of the system of power relations, or, indeed, in its ability actively, freely and single-handedly to effect change within it, has been shattered. There is nonetheless a sense, at least during the first phase of *La Luna*, that it may be possible to negotiate one's position within the system — and the magazine's frequent self-questioning, ambiguity and self-mockery can be understood as strategies aimed precisely at enabling such a temporary and at least partly self-determined positioning. Such a strategy is not without its pitfalls: as was argued in Chapter 2, the refusal to take anything (including itself) too seriously and the resistance to adopting a clearly defined position with regard to anything render *La Luna* inoperative when faced with specific problems such as domestic violence or rape, which are at best tiptoed over, and at worst dangerously trivialized. Further, such an approach involves a strenuous balancing act that, as the magazine's internal conflicts and eventual demise illustrate, cannot be sustained over an extended period of time.

The speed with which *la movida* gained visibility and widespread popularity, and its parallel co-option or institutionalization by the cultural, media and political establishments of its day are often read as signs of its inherent corruptibility, with critics such as Pedro Pérez del Solar arguing that *la movida* 'undid itself to become a mass media spectacle for internal and external consumption' (2000: xx).[4] In contrast to this diagnosis, which places the onus of institutionalization solely on *la movida*, I would suggest that the processes that led to the co-option, neutralization and eventual demise of the phenomenon in fact speak less about *la movida*'s shortcomings, as about the difficulty (if not the impossibility) of changing or resisting the dynamics that structure the artistic and cultural fields. Following Libbie Rifkin's assertion that theories that posit 'institutionalization as a necessary and final fall from grace [for avant-garde and countercultural movements] [...] cannot do justice to the struggle over identity and value that marks every stage' of such processes (2000: 130), I propose that we view *la movida*'s institutionalization as a dialectic process, one that facilitated the neutralization and eventual demise of the Madrilenian phenomenon, but which also, in the process, led to changes within the socio-cultural context within which it had emerged.

Even those critics who dismiss *la movida* as a superficial, inconsequential incident inflated by the media admit that the phenomenon had some positive, socially liberating effects. Juan Luis Cebrián, for instance, concedes that it led to 'una aireación de los espacios cerrados de algunos círculos intelectuales' [an airing of the closed up spaces within some intellectual circles] (Cebrián in Gallero 1991: 4); while for José Carlos Mainer, *movida* participants at least '[h]an sabido convertir Madrid y Barcelona (sobre todo, la primera) en dos ciudades divertidas' [have managed to turn Madrid and Barcelona (particularly the former) into two fun cities] (1988: 21). Javier Escudero goes one step further, arguing that

> el mayor legado de la movida reside no tanto en la importancia de sus contribuciones artísticas sino en haber abierto el camino a una nueva época

> estética e ideológica, la posmodernidad, en la que se practica un tipo de arte más lúdico, que se sirve continuamente de la ironía, la parodia y el pastiche, incorporando a su génesis los géneros 'bajos', las voces marginales (la mujer, el homosexual, el travestí o el delincuente). (1998: 159)
>
> [the greatest legacy of *la movida* is not so much in the importance of its artistic contributions, but rather in its role in opening up the path for a new aesthetic and ideological period, postmodernity, in which a new form of more playful art is practised, one which constantly mobilises irony, parody and pastiche, and which incorporates, in its genesis, 'low' genres and marginal voices (women, homosexuals, transgender, criminals).] (1998: 159)

Escudero's words point to *la movida*'s role in enabling the aesthetic and ideological transition to postmodernity within Spain, thus crediting the movement with having effected (or at least facilitated) change within the context from which it emerged. Crucially, he places such transformations not only at the aesthetic, but also at the at the social level, noting *la movida*'s incorporation of marginalized voices into mainstream cultural discourse, hence throwing into question, if implicitly, its alleged lack of political engagement. Indeed, *la movida*'s contribution towards the overcoming of a *franquismo sociológico* that survived the regime itself has been underlined in recent years by critics such as Alberto Mira (2004) and Gema Pérez-Sánchez (2007), for whom the movement played a crucial role in changing attitudes towards gender roles, sexual orientation and sexual practices. While such reassessments of *la movida* contribute to a welcome and necessary dismantling of certain clichés with regard to the phenomenon, this emphasis on its liberating effects risks overlooking its creative innovations and aesthetic specificities. Escudero's words quoted above exemplify precisely this tendency to minimize *la movida*'s artistic and cultural production, which the author considers as secondary to its legacy. This dissociation of *movida* works from the movement's social effects is problematic, as it fails to account for how and why *la movida* managed to transform its socio-cultural landscape. In other words, *la movida*'s effectiveness at facilitating or accelerating social change is predicated upon its ability to capture the public's attention and imagination — a process in which its artistic and cultural products play a central role. If there is still an enduring sense that *la movida*'s creative legacy is scant or irrelevant, this is largely the result of a failure (or an unwillingness) to look beyond established narrative formats such as the feature film or the novel, two forms that are relatively neglected by *movida* participants, with the exception of Pedro Almodóvar's early films,[5] and to consider less conventional items, such as fanzines, magazines, comics, pop music or, indeed, musical and artistic performance.[6]

Any meaningful reassessment of, or approximation to, *la movida* thus entails an exercise in archaeology — both in the Foucauldian sense of resisting the urge to ignore or minimize its contradictions and complexities in order to construct a neat interpretative model, and in the literal sense of unearthing and studying the wealth of often hard to trace ephemera through which *movida* art works and ideas were first (and often exclusively) articulated and circulated. This book is conceived as a (necessarily limited) example of precisely such an exercise of archaeology. Underlying this work is a desire to propose an alternative discourse on *la movida* — one that hopes to offer a more subtly nuanced account of the period. Given the fascination that *la movida* continues to exert over the Spanish popular imaginary (evidenced, as mentioned in the Introduction, by the release, over the past decade and a half, of a series of anthologies on the period), and given the palpable influence it has exerted over subsequent generations, such as the so-called 'generación X',[7] or their younger 'siblings' of the 'generación nocilla',[8] the critical reappraisal of *la movida* appears as a necessary step in any attempt at understanding Spain's contemporary cultural landscape.

Notes to Chapter 5

1. Trillo himself, though retrospectively noting the normalizing role of *La Luna*, took advantage of the platform the magazine offered, publishing his work in issue 6 (33). Olvido Gara, 'Alaska', a *movida* icon who was critical of *La Luna*'s role with regard to *la movida* (cf. Gallero 1991: 372), though not appearing in the magazine herself (presumably because she did not need the exposure, given her established status as a TV personality thanks to her presenting role in *La bola de cristal*), did not seem to object to the features the publication dedicated to her band mates Carlos Berlanga (issue 17: 7–11) and Nacho Canut (issue 19: 44–45).
2. A similar example of such parody can be found in Radio Futura's 1980 single 'Enamorado de la moda juvenil', which, as Santiago Auserón notes, was misunderstood at the time of its release: 'tenía un sarcasmo evidente que poca gente entendió' [was evidently sarcastic in a way that few people understood] (*La Luna* 4: 8).
3. Examples of the parodic reformulation of elements associated with gender and national identity can be found in a number of works of this period, including, for instance, Las Costus's series *El Valle de los Caídos*, which entails a pictorial reproduction of the statues of General Franco's eponymous mausoleum in El Escorial, but with their artist friends (many of them well-known *movida* figures, such as Olvido Gara, 'Alaska') assuming the role of virgins and virtues. These figures are portrayed against colourful, pop-inflected backgrounds, a transposition that further contributes to the re-signification of the originals, whose ominous symbolic charge is playfully subverted. The street performances of painter José Pérez Ocaña, 'La Ocaña', whose drag attire involved traditional female garments such as the Spanish mantilla and the fan, highlight the connections between gender and national identity. Ocaña's mobilization of such traditionally feminine and traditionally Spanish items served not only to query the gender of his alter ego 'La Ocaña', but also contributed to the re-signification of the mantilla itself, as the traditionally feminine attributes this item symbolizes, such as demureness and piety, were undermined through his gender subversion, as well as by the hyperbolic and kitsch nature of his performances.
4. Other scholars such as Tom Lewis (1994) and José Carlos Mainer (2000) have expressed similar views.
5. The apparent or relative absence of writers in *la movida* is raised in José Luis Gallero's volume of interviews on the period, and Tómas Cuesta comments that '[p]uede que, en última instancia, el único escritor [de la movida] fuera [Eduardo] Haro Ibars' (1991: 331).
6. There are, of course, some notable exceptions, such as Michael Preston Harrison's 2009 PhD dissertation, *Comics as Text and Comics as Culture. Queer Spain through the Lens of a Marginalized Medium* (University of California, Irvine). and Héctor Fouce's 2002 doctoral thesis, '"El futuro ya está aquí": Música pop y cambio cultural en España. Madrid 1978–1985'. Fouce's work aims to trace a collective imaginary of *la movida* through an analysis of pop songs of the period. It is worth noting that Fouce's work appears in the context of media and communication studies (his thesis was written and examined within Universidad Complutense's journalism department), rather than within the Spanish literature, culture or history departments. Given that media studies and journalism are widely regarded as more vocational and less "academic" than the other disciplines mentioned (i.e. with less cultural or symbolic capital), such an adscription could be read as symptomatic of some of the elitist prejudices which, as I have argued, still surround *la movida* in some Spanish academic circles.

7. The label 'generación X' is frequently applied to a group of Spanish writers who started publishing in the early and mid-1990s, including Ray Loriga, José Ángel Mañas, and Lucía Etxebarría, among others. Although the term was borrowed from the title of Douglas Coupland's 1991 book *Generation X*, the works of these writers, decidedly urban and, as Christine Henseler writes, 'steeped in colloquial speech and popular media culture' (2011: 1), are undoubtedly influenced by *la movida*, as both Henseler and Gema Pérez-Sánchez have noted (cf. Henseler 2011: 61).
8. 'Generación nocilla', 'generación afterpop' or 'mutantes' are some of the terms used to refer to authors such as Agustín Fernández Mallo (whose 2006 novel *Nocilla Dream* led to the coinage of the first of these labels), Isaac Rosa, Mercedes Cebrián, or Vicente Luis Mora, among others. In the prologue to the 2007 anthology of new Spanish narrative *Mutantes*, Juan Francisco Ferré describes these writers as 'educados en la escuela de la imagen y los medios, y en la escuela de la globalización, y en la escuela del recalentamiento informativo y el enfriamiento global de las estructuras humanas de relación' (2007: 11). This emphasis on visuality, the role of the media and mediatisation, and globalization is already present in *la movida*. Indeed, the imprint of *la movida* is noticeable in the very labels used to describe this group of emerging writers: in 'generación nocilla' through the pop-inflected mobilisation of an everyday foodstuff brand; and in 'generación afterpop', the prefixing of 'pop', a term often applied to *la movida*, invites an ambiguous reading of this new generation as both an overcoming and a continuation of *la movida*'s pop style and ethos.

BIBLIOGRAPHY

Ades, Dawn. 2006. *The Dada Reader. A Critical Anthology* (London: Tate Publishing)

Adorno, Theodor. 1991. *The Culture Industry. Selected Essays on Mass Culture* (London: Routledge)

Afinoguénova, Eugenia and Jaume Martí-Olivella (eds). 2008. *Spain Is (Still) Different. Tourism and Discourse in Spanish Identity* (Lanham: Lexington Books)

Alberca García, María del Mar. 2003. 'La configuración de una imagen de España para la democracia: juventud, vanguardia y tradición', in *Madrid de Fortunata a la M-40. Un siglo de cultura urbana*, ed. by Edward Baker and Malcolm Alan Compitello (Madrid: Alianza Editorial), pp. 283–308

Almodóvar, Pedro. 1991. *Patty Diphusa y otros textos* (Barcelona: Anagrama)

Andrade Blanco, Juan Antonio. 2012. *El PCE y el PSOE en la transición. La evolución ideológica de la izquierda durante el proceso de cambio político* (Madrid: Siglo XXI)

Balibrea, Mari Paz. 2001. 'Urbanism, Culture and the Post-Industrial City: Challenging the "Barcelona Model"', *Journal of Spanish Cultural Studies*, 2.2 (2001): 187–210

Basualdo, Ana. 1984. '"La Luna" en el cielo de Madrid', *La Vanguardia*, 31 January 1984, p. 34.

Baudrillard, Jean. 1983. *Simulations*, trans. by Paul Foss, Paul Patton and Philip Beitchman (New York: Semiotext(e))

Bauman, Zygmunt. 1997. *Postmodernity and its Discontents* (Cambridge: Polity Press)

Bech, Henning. 1997. *When Men Meet: Homosexuality and Modernity* (Cambridge: Polity Press)

Benjamin, Walter. 1999. *Illuminations*, trans. by Hannah Arendt (London: Pimlico)

Bersani, Leo. 1995. *Homos* (Cambridge, MA: Harvard University Press)

Besançon, Julien. 1968. *Les Murs ont la parole. Journal mural mai 68* (Paris: Tchou)

Bürger, Peter, 1984. *Theory of the Avant-Garde*, trans. by Michael Shaw (Manchester: Manchester University Press)

Butler, Judith. 1990. *Gender Trouble. Feminism and the Subversion of Identity* (New York: Routledge)

Cadahía, Emma (ed.). 2007. *La Luna de Madrid y otras revistas de vanguardia de los años 80* (Madrid: Biblioteca Nacional)

Castells, Manuel. 1983. *The City and the Grassroots. A Cross-Cultural Theory of Urban Social Movements* (London: Edward Arnold)

Certeau, Michel de. 1984. *The Practice of Everyday Life*, trans. by Steven Rendall (Berkeley: University of California Press)

Cervera, Rafael. 2002. *Alaska y otras historias de la movida* (Barcelona: Random House Mondadori)

Dews, Peter. 1987. *Logics of Disintegration. Post-Structuralist Thought and the Claims of Critical Theory* (London: Verso)

Domingo, Javier. 1989. '*La Luna*, el *Madriz*, *El Paseante*... y otras especies de los 80' in *Madrid, años ochenta*, ed. by Rafael Sierra (Madrid: Ayuntamiento de Madrid, Área de Cultura, Educación y Deportes, Dirección de Servicios de Educación y Juventud), pp. 301–28

Drolet, Michael (ed.). 2004. *The Postmodern Reader. Foundational Texts* (London: Routledge)

Duncombe, Stephen. 1997. *Notes from the Underground. Zines and the Politics of Alternative Culture* (London: Verso)

Eco, Umberto. 1983. *Faith in Fakes*, trans. by William Weaver (London: Secker & Warburg). Revised and published as *Travels in Hyperreality*, 1995

Escudero, Javier. 1998. 'Rosa Montero y Pedro Almodóvar: miseria y estilización de la movida madrileña', *Arizona Journal of Hispanic Cultural Studies*, 2 (1998): 147–61

Ferré, Juan Francisco (ed.). 2007. *Mutantes. Narrativa española de última generación* (Córdoba: Berenice)

Fincher, Ruth and Jane M. Jacobs (eds). 1998. *Cities of Difference* (New York: Guilford Press)

Fontes, Ignacio and Manuel Ángel Menéndez. 2004. *El parlamento de papel. Las revistas españolas en la transición democrática* (Madrid: Anaya y Asociación de Prensa de Madrid)

Foucault, Michel. 1979. *The History of Sexuality*, trans. by Robert Hurley, 3 vols, I. *An Introduction* (London: Allen Lane)

—— 1985. II. *The Use of Pleasure* (Harmondsworth: Viking)

—— 1986. III.*The Care of the Self* (London: Penguin)

—— 2002 [1967/1984]. 'Of Other Spaces', in *The Visual Culture Reader*, ed. by Nicholas Mirzoeff (London: Routledge), pp. 229–36

—— 2003 [1967]. *Madness and Civilization*, trans. by Richard Howard (London: Routledge)

Fouce, Héctor. 2002. '"El futuro ya está aquí". Música pop y cambio cultural en España. Madrid 1978–1985' (unpublished doctoral thesis, Universidad Complutense de Madrid)

Friedan, Betty. 1963. *The Feminine Mystique* (New York: W. W. Norton)

Fusi, Juan Pablo. 2000. *España. La evolución de la identidad nacional* (Madrid: Temas de Hoy)

Gallero, José Luis. 1991. *Sólo se vive una vez. Esplendor y ruina de la movida madrileña* (Madrid: Ediciones Ardora)

García Torvisco, Luis. 2012. 'La Luna de Madrid: Movida, posmodernidad y capitalismo cultural en una revista feliz de los ochenta', *MLN*, 127 (2012): 364–84

Graham, Helen and Antonio Sánchez. 1995. 'The Politics of 1992', in *Spanish Cultural Studies. An Introduction*, ed. by Helen Graham and Jo Labanyi (Oxford: Oxford University Press), pp. 406–18

Habermas, Jürgen. 1993. 'Modernity versus Postmodernity', in *A Postmodern Reader*, ed. by Joseph Natoli and Linda Hutcheon (Albany: State University of New York Press), pp. 91–104

Harrison, Michael Preston. 2009. 'Comics as Text and Comics as Culture. Queer Spain through the Lens of a Marginalized Medium' (unpublished doctoral dissertation, University of California, Irvine)

Harvey, David. 1989. *The Condition of Postmodernity. An Enquiry into the Origins of Cultural Change* (Oxford: Blackwell)

Hassan, Ihab. 1987. *The Postmodern Turn. Essays in Postmodern Theory and Culture* (Columbus: Ohio State University Press)

Henseler, Christine. 2011. *Spanish Fiction in the Digital Age. Generation X Remixed* (New York: Palgrave Macmillan)

Hooks, Bell. 2000. *Feminist Theory: From Margin to Center* (Cambridge, MA: South End Press)

Hutcheon, Linda. 1988. *A Poetics of Postmodernism. History, Theory, Fiction* (Oxford: Routledge).

—— 1993. 'Beginning to Theorize Postmodernism', in *A Postmodern Reader*, ed. by Linda Hutcheon and Joseph Natoli (Albany: State University of New York Press), pp. 243–72

Irigaray, Luce. 1985. *This Sex Which is Not One*, trans. by Catherine Porter and Caroline Burke (Ithaca: Cornell University Press)

JAMESON, FREDERIC. 1991. *Postmodernism, or The Cultural Logic of Late Capitalism* (London: Verso)

JENCKS, CHARLES (ed.). 2011. *The Postmodern Reader* (Chichester: Wiley & Sons)

JOGLARS, ELS. 'Caso *La Torna*', Els Joglars', official website of the theatre group Els Joglars, <http://www.elsjoglars.com/produccion.php?idPag=latorna_cas> [accessed 10 May 2013]

JONES, AMELIA. 1995. '"Clothes Make the Man": The Male Artist as a Performative Function', *Oxford Art Journal*, 18.2 (1995): 18–32

KINDER, MARSHA. 1987. 'Pleasure and the New Spanish Mentality: A Conversation with Pedro Almodóvar', *Film Quarterly*, 41.1 (1987): 33–44

KRAUSS, ROSALIND. 1981. 'The Photographic Conditions of Surrealism', *October*, 19 (1981): 3–34

La Luna de Madrid, 1–48. Madrid, 1983–1988

La Révolution Surréaliste, 11 (March 1928)

LABRADOR, GERMÁN. 2009. *Letras arrebatadas. Poesía y química en la transición española* (Madrid: Devenir Ensayo)

LARSON, SUSAN and MALCOLM A. COMPITELLO. 1997. 'Todavía en la luna: A Round Table Discussion with Darío Álvarez Basso, Antonio Bueno, Pierluigi Cattermole Fioravanti, Ignacio Martínez Lacaci, Javier Timmermans de Palma y José Tono Martíniez', *Arizona Journal of Hispanic Cultural Studies*, I (1997): 153–68

LARSON, SUSAN. 2003. '*La Luna de Madrid* y la movida madrileña: un experimento valioso en la creación de la cultura urbana revolucionaria', in *Madrid de Fortunata a la M-40*, ed. by Edward Baker and Malcolm A. Compitello (Madrid: Alianza), pp. 309–25

LECHADO, JOSÉ MANUEL. 2005. *La movida: una crónica de los 80* (Madrid: Algaba)

LEEUWEN, THOMAS A.P. VAN. 1998. *The Springboard in the Pond: an Intimate History of the Swimming Pool* (Cambridge, MA: MIT Press)

LEFEBVRE, HENRI. 1991. *The Production of Space*, trans. by Donald Nicholson-Smith (Oxford: Blackwell)

——2003. *The Urban Revolution*, trans. by Robert Bononno (Minneapolis: University of Minnesota Press)

LEWIS, TOM. 1994. 'Aesthetics and Politics', in *Critical Practices in Post-Franco Spain*, ed. by Silvia López, Jenaro Talens and Darío Villanueva (Minneapolis: University of Minnesota), pp. 160–82

LOMAS SAMPEDRO, ESTHER. 2008. 'El Madrid postmoderno: identidades en proceso de cambio en el postfranquismo' (unpublished doctoral dissertation, Stony Brook University)

LYOTARD, JEAN-FRANÇOIS. 1984. *The Postmodern Condition: A Report on Knowledge*, trans. by Geoff Bennington and Brian Massumi (Minneapolis: University of Minnesota Press)

MAINER, JOSÉ CARLOS. 1988. '1975–1985: Los poderes del pasado', in *La cultura española en el posfranquismo. Diez años de cine, cultura y literatura (1975–1985)*, ed. by Samuel Amell (Madrid: Playor), pp. 11–26

—— 1994. *De Postguerra (1951–1990)* (Barcelona: Grupo Grijalbo-Mondadori)

MAINER, JOSÉ CARLOS and SANTOS JULIÁ. 2000. *El aprendizaje de la libertad 1973–1986. La cultura de la Transición* (Madrid: Alianza Ensayo)

MCDONOUGH, THOMAS. 2001. 'Fluid Spaces: Constant and the Situationist Critique of Architecture', in *The Activist Drawing. Retracing Situationist Architecture from Constant's New Babylon to Beyond*, ed. by Catherine de Zegher and Mark Wigley (New York: The Drawing Center), pp. 93–104

——(ed.). 2002. *Guy Debord and the Situationist International: Texts and Documents* (Cambridge, MA: MIT Press)

MEDINA DOMÍNGUEZ, ALBERTO. 2001. *Exorcismos de la memoria. Políticas y poéticas de la melancolía en la España de la transición* (Madrid: Ediciones Libertarias)

MELERO, JAVIER and JUAN CARLOS MELERO. *La Luna de Madrid* (blog), <http://lalunademadrid.wordpress.com> [accessed 26 February 2015]

MIRA, ALBERTO. 2004. *De Sodoma a Chueca. Una Historia cultural de la homosexualidad en España en el siglo XX* (Barcelona: Egales Editorial)

MOI, TORIL. 1985. *Sexual Textual Politics. Feminist Literary Theory* (London: Routledge)

—— 1985A. 'Power, Sex and Subjectivity: Feminist Reflections on Foucault', *Paragraph*, 5 (1985): 95–102

MORÁN, GREGORIO. 1991. *El precio de la transición* (Barcelona: Planeta)

MOREIRAS MENOR, CRISTINA. 2002. *Cultura herida. Literatura y cine en la España democrática* (Madrid: Ediciones Libertarias)

MORET, XAVIER. 1992. 'El franquismo era feísmo. Daba la impresión de que a todo el mundo le olían los calcetines', interview with Manuel Vázquez Montalbán, *El País*, 26 October 1992, <http://elpais.com/diario/1992/10/26/cultura/720054002_850215.html> [accessed 25 June 2013]

MULVEY, LAURA. 1975. 'Visual Pleasure and Narrative Cinema', *Screen*, 16.3 (1975): 6–18

NICHOLS, WILLIAM J. and ROSI SONG (eds). 2014. *Toward a Cultural Archive of La Movida. Back to the Future* (Lanham: Fairleigh Dickinson University Press)

PAETZOLD, HEINZ. 2000. 'The Philosophical Notion of the City', in *The City Cultures Reader*, ed. by M. Miles, Tim Hall and Iain Borden (London: Routledge), pp. 204–20

PAVLOVIC, TATJANA. 2003. *Despotic Bodies and Transgressive Bodies. Spanish Culture from Francisco Franco to Jesús Franco* (New York: State University of New York Press)

PAYNE, STANLEY G. 1987. *Historia de España. La España contemporánea. Desde el 98 hasta Juan Carlos I* (Madrid: Playor)

PEGRUM, MARK A. 2000. *Challenging Modernity. Dada between Modern and Postmodern* (New York: Berghahn)

PÉREZ DEL SOLAR, PEDRO. 2000. 'Imágenes del desencanto: Historieta española 1979–1986' (unpublished doctoral dissertation, Princeton University)

PÉREZ-SÁNCHEZ, GEMA. 2007. *Queer Transitions in Contemporary Spanish Culture: from Franco to 'la Movida'* (New York: State of New York University Press)

PREGO, VICTORIA. 1995. *La Transición* (13-part documentary produced by Radio Televisión Española and first broadcast in 1995)

PUTMAN, JOHN J. 1986. 'Madrid: The Change in Spain', *National Geographic*, February 1986: 142–80.

RESINA, JOAN RAMÓN (ed.). 2000. *Disremembering the Dictatorship: The Politics of Memory in the Spanish Transition to Democracy* (Amsterdam: Rodopi)

——2008. *Barcelona's Vocation of Modernity. Rise and Decline of an Urban Image* (Stanford: Stanford University Press)

RICHMOND ELLIS, ROBERT. 1997. *The Hispanic Homograph. Gay Self-Representation in Contemporary Spanish Autobiography* (Urbana: University of Illinois Press)

RIFKIN, LIBBIE. 2000. 'Making It / New: Institutionalizing Postwar Avant-Gardes', *Poetics Today*, vol. 21, no. 1, (2000): 129–50

RIPOLL, ANTONIO J. (ed.). 1988. *La gloriosa movida nacional* (Avilés: Casa Municipal de Cultura)

ROSS, ANDREW. 1989. *No Respect. Intellectuals and Popular Culture* (London: Routledge)

SÁNCHEZ, ANTONIO. 2007. *Postmodern Spain* (Oxford: Peter Lang)

SHEPPARD, RICHARD. 2000. *Modernism-Dada-Postmodernism* (Illinois: Northwestern University Press)

SLOCOMBE, WILL. 2006. *Nihilism and the Sublime Postmodern. The (Hi)Story of a Difficult Relationship from Romanticism to Postmodernism* (New York: Routledge)

SMITH, PAUL JULIAN. 1994. *Desire Unlimited: The Cinema of Pedro Almodóvar* (London: Verso)

——2006. *Spanish Visual Culture. Cinema, Television, Internet* (Manchester: Manchester University Press)

SONTAG, SUSAN. 1982. 'Notes on "Camp"', in *A Susan Sontag Reader* (Harmondsworth: Penguin), pp. 105–19

SORKIN, MICHAEL. 1992. 'See You in Disneyland', in *Variations of a Theme Park. The New American City and the End of Public Space*, ed. by Michael Sorkin (New York: Hill and Wang), pp. 205–32

SPITZ, BOB. 1985. 'The New Spain', *Rolling Stone*, June 1985: 33–37

STAPELL, HAMILTON. 2010. *Remaking Madrid: Culture, Politics, and Identity after Franco* (Basingstoke: Palgrave Macmillan)

STRAUSS, FRÉDÉRIC. 1996. *Almodóvar on Almodóvar*, trans. by Yves Baigneres (London: Faber and Faber)

SUBIRATS, EDUARDO (ed.). 2002. *Intransiciones. Crítica de la cultura española* (Madrid: Biblioteca Nueva)

TONO MARTÍNEZ, JOSÉ (ed.). 1986. *La polémica de la posmodernidad* (Madrid: Ediciones Libertarias)

TUSELL, JAVIER and ÁLVARO SOTO (eds). 1996. *Historia de la transición 1975–1986* (Madrid: Alianza Editorial)

UGARTE PÉREZ, JAVIER. 2008. *Una discriminación universal: la homosexualidad bajo el franquismo y la transición* (Barcelona: Egales Editorial)

URRERO, GUZMÁN. 2003. 'Movida, carnaval y cultura de masas', *Cuadernos Hispanoamericanos*, 636 (2003): 15–29

USOZ DE LA FUENTE, MAITE. 2013. 'Sex and the City: Urban Eroticism in Rodrigo Muñoz Ballester's *Manuel* Series', *Hispanic Research Journal*, 14. 5, (2013): 394–408.

VAQUERO, JOSÉ MANUEL. 1983. '"Cuadernos del Norte", iniciativa cultural periférica', *El País*, 16 January 1983, <http://elpais.com/diario/1983/01/16/cultura/411519605_850215.html> [accessed 31 March 2013]

VATTIMO, GIANNI. 1990. *La sociedad transparente*, trans. by Teresa Oñate (Barcelona: Ediciones Paidós)

—— 1992. *The Transparent Society*, trans. by David Webb (Cambridge: Polity Press)

VÁZQUEZ MONTALBÁN, MANUEL. 1981. *Asesinato en el comité central* (Barcelona: Planeta)

VILARÓS, TERESA. 1998. *El mono del desencanto: Una crítica cultural de la transición española, 1973–1993* (Madrid: Siglo XXI)

VILLENA, LUIS ANTONIO DE. 1999. *Madrid ha muerto. Esplendor y caos en una ciudad feliz de los ochenta* (Barcelona: El Aleph)

VIRILIO, PAUL. 2009. *The Aesthetics of Disappearance,* trans. by Philip Beitchman (Los Angeles: Semiotext(e))

WALKER, IAN. 2002. *City Gorged with Dreams. Surrealism and Documentary Photography in Interwar Paris* (Manchester: Manchester University Press)

WIGLEY, MARK, CONSTANT, ET AL. 1998. *Constant's New Babylon : the Hyper-Architecture of Desire* (Rotterdam: Witte de With, Center for Contemporary Art 010 Publishers)

ZEGHER, CATHERINE DE and MARK WIGLEY (eds). 2001. *The Activist Drawing. Retracing Situationist Architecture from Constant's New Babylon to Beyond* (New York: The Drawing Center)

'La ruptura del equipo de "La Luna de Madrid" provoca una nueva orientación', unsigned article, *El País*, 13 September 1985, <http://elpais.com/diario/1985/09/13/cultura/495410407_850215.html> [accessed 30 May 2013]

INDEX

1968 movement 61, 116, 117, 151
96 lágrimas 4

Adorno, Theodor 69 n. 30, 113, 126, 127
Ajoblanco 2
Alaska (Olvido Gara) 3, 95, 124, 142 n. 6, 150, 154 n. 1 and 3
Almodóvar, Pedro 3, 11, 13, 16, 22 n. 6 and 8, 55, 85–91, 97, 104 n. 1, 105 n. 17, 124, 142 n. 6, 145, 146, 147, 150, 153
Alpuente, Moncho 149
Antoñete 105, n. 19
apolitical 6, 83, 148
Aranda, Vicente 104 n. 4
Aranguren, José Luis 55
architecture 13, 15, 28–35, 54, 57, 58, 66 n. 2 and 3, 67 n. 8, 68 n. 23, 112
  modernist architecture 31, 32
  postmodern architecture 31, 32, 34, 35
Atienza, Pedro 96, 97, 106 n. 22
Auserón, Santiago 154 n. 2
Autorretratos 71, 73, 76
avant-garde 11, 18–20, 26, 27, 60, 89, 101, 107, 110, 111, 113, 114, 116, 122, 125–27, 138, 139, 151, 152

Barber, Llorenç 117, 118
Barcelona 2, 3, 22 n. 6, 69 n. 32, 92, 152
Baudelaire, Charles 33, 35, 60
Baudrillard, Jean 119, 124, 125, 128, 135, 142 n. 2, 143 n. 12
Bauman, Zygmunt 110
Bech, Henning 48
Bellmer, Hans 75
Benjamin, Walter 33, 68 n. 20, 69 n. 30, 89, 93, 126, 127
Berlanga, Carlos 154 n. 1
Berlanga, Jorge 102, 133, 135, 144 n. 24
Bersani, Leo 88, 105 n. 15
Blanco, Manuel 66 n. 2,
Bogarde, Dick 67 n. 14
bola de cristal, La 22 n. 11, 154 n. 1
Bosé, Miguel 144 n. 29
Bravo Villasante, Carmen 80
Brea, José Luis 72, 104 n. 5, 144 n. 21, 150
bricolage 79, 98
bullfighting 21, 71, 92, 93, 95, 96, 100, 104
Bürger, Peter 20
Butler, Judith 83, 84, 105 n. 15

camp 79, 83, 85, 86, 88, 91, 93, 95, 97, 101, 105 n. 13
Campano, Javier 77
Canut, Nacho 154 n. 1
Casa de Campo 38, 88, 89, 90,
Casani, Borja 3–5, 10, 11, 16–19, 23 n. 23, 24 n. 27, 54, 57, 66 n. 2 and 4, 67 n. 16 and 17, 68 n. 27, 101, 103, 106 n. 29, 110–14, 119, 122, 128–31, 134, 136, 144 n. 21, 22, 23, 25 and 28, 146, 149
Cascorro Factory 2, 3, 142 n. 6
Castells, Manuel 64
Catholic 71, 92, 100, 137
Cebrián, Juan Luis 2, 22 n. 4, 107, 140, 149, 152
Ceesepe 2, 3, 22 n. 8, 68 n. 25, 142 n. 6, 147
censorship 4, 103, 113, 142 n. 5
Cereceda, Miguel 120, 144 n. 21
Certeau, Michel de 59, 60, 69 n. 29
Chamorro, Paloma 3, 68 n. 28, 95, 127
Chávarri, Jaime 2, 3 n. 17
co-option 7, 18, 57, 60, 65, 113, 128, 139, 145, 146, 152
comics 1–4, 11, 13, 22 n. 5, 25, 53, 54, 57, 65, 67 n. 11, 68 n. 23, 112, 138, 147, 153, 154 n. 6
Concurso Rock Villa de Madrid 62
Constant (Constant Nieuwenhuys) 34, 35, 66 n. 7, 67 n. 8
consumerism 5, 6, 147
copla 71, 93, 96–98, 100
Costus (Enrique Naya/Juan Carrero) 3, 154 n. 3
Cuadernos del Norte 10, 23 n. 24
Cuadernos para el Diálogo 4
Cuesta, Tomás 3, 5, 154 n. 5

Dada 11, 49, 54, 60, 88, 105 n. 14, 116, 122, 143 n. 15
Dalí, Salvador 45, 68 n. 21
  Cannibalism in Autumn 68 n. 21
dérive 34
desencanto 1, 2, 6, 145, 150
desencanto, El (film) 2, 21 n. 3, 23 n. 17
Dezine 4
dictatorship 1, 2, 4, 5, 8, 68 n. 22, 69 n. 33, 105 n. 9, 114, 127, 130
Divine 107
doubling 75, 77, 104 n. 8
Duchamp, Marcel 86–88, 102, 133
Duncombe, Stephen 146

Eco, Umberto 119, 143 n. 12
edad de oro del pop español, La 22 n. 11, 68 n. 28
Éluard, Paul 48, 67 n. 18, 68 n. 20

Erice, Víctor 45
Escher, Maurits Cornelis 45
Escudero, Isabel 82, 83, 97
Escudero, Javier 152, 153
essentialism 99, 100
European Economic Community / European Union 63, 69 n. 35, 99, 100, 106 n. 24
everyday 6, 7, 26, 28, 33, 35, 38, 40, 42, 48, 51, 57–61, 66 n. 3, 69 n. 29 and 30, 79, 84, 85, 92, 93, 99, 103, 151

fait divers 49–52, 68 n. 20
fanzine 1–4, 11, 17, 71, 101, 112, 146, 153
femininity 13, 22 n. 13, 79, 80–83, 85
feminism 80–82, 84, 89
flamenco 21, 71, 93, 96, 97, 100, 106 n. 22
flânerie 33
  flâneur 33–35
flux 49, 65, 70, 71, 76, 91, 100, 101, 124
Foucault, Michel 25, 26, 31, 38, 40, 66 n. 5, 143 n. 17, 144 n. 20
Fouce, Héctor 2, 22 n. 13, 103, 154 n. 6
Franco, Francisco 1–3, 5, 6, 8, 10, 21 n. 3, 61, 69 n. 33, 127
Francoism 2, 5, 6, 17, 21 n.2, 62, 68 n. 22, 100, 114, 118, 127
  Francoist 2, 4, 35, 38, 61, 100, 103, 105 n. 9, 127, 130
  anti-Francoist 2, 4, 22 n. 10, 68 n. 24, 69 n. 31, 149
  Francoist elite 2
  Francoist past 2, 4, 63
  Francoist propaganda 71, 88, 92, 99
  Francoist regime 103, 130
freedom 2, 6, 10, 20, 22 n. 4, 42, 48, 49, 59, 63, 80, 90, 113, 117, 119, 136, 141, 146, 151
Friedan, Betty 105 n. 12
Futurism 138, 144 n. 27
  Futurist 54, 138
  futuristic 11, 35

Galería Moriarty 9
Gallero, José Luis 1–5, 9–11, 13, 16, 18, 19, 22 n. 12, 23 n. 18, 23 and 26, 68 n. 27, 69 n. 28, 102, 108, 112, 114, 122, 127, 131, 140, 142 n. 6, 143 n. 7, 144 n. 29, 145, 149, 152, 154 n. 1 and 5
García Torvisco, Luis 8, 121
García-Alix, Alberto 2, 3, 78, 142 n. 6, 147
gaze 40, 48, 73, 87, 93, 105 n. 20
gender 8, 70, 71, 79–88, 90–93, 96, 101, 104 n. 2, 105 n. 11, 106 n. 21, 109, 139, 141, 148, 150, 153, 154 n. 3
Generación nocilla 154, 155 n. 8
Generación X 154, 155 n. 7
Gilbert, Lola (Lola Montez) 80
glam 18, 93, 97, 98, 100, 103, 106 n. 22
global 21, 35, 59, 61, 71, 93, 98, 101–04, 108, 118, 127, 130, 144 n. 22, 149, 151, 155 n. 8
  globalization 99, 103, 155 n. 8
  globalized 99, 100, 104
Gómez de la Serna, Ramón 102
González, Felipe 7
Gorospe, Jaime 105 n. 10
greguería 102
Guio, Francisco 105 n. 19

Habermas, Jürgen 109, 128
Hagen, Nina 80
Haro Ibars, Eduardo 3, 17, 55, 68 n. 24, 115–17, 150, 154 n. 5
Harrison, Michael Preston 22 n. 13, 67 n. 11, 154 n. 6
Harvey, David 109, 111
hedonism 5, 6, 107, 124, 147, 150
heterotopia 38, 42
  heterotopic 25, 26, 38, 40, 48, 90
homophobia 92
homosexuality 22 n. 12, 105 n. 18
hooks, bell 105 n. 12
Hortelano, El 3, 142 n. 6, 147
Hoy no me puedo levantar 22 n. 11
Humanes, Alberto 36
Hutcheon, Linda 77, 88, 105 n. 15, 108, 109, 124, 142 n. 2
hybrid 4, 49, 130
  hybridization 60, 104
  hybridizing 98, 103, 132
hyperreality 118, 119, 143 n. 12

Ibáñez, Jesús 135, 144 n. 21
identity 19–21, 26, 56, 59, 62, 65, 66, 70–75, 77–79, 81, 85, 86, 89, 90–92, 99, 100–02, 104 n. 1, 107, 114, 141, 148, 151, 152, 154 n. 3
  editorial identity 15, 17, 54, 57, 71, 101, 102
  individual identity 73, 78, 100, 141, 143 n. 9
  national identity 22 n. 13, 71, 92, 98, 100, 148, 154 n. 3
  Republican identity 69 n. 31
individualism 6, 17, 72, 123, 124, 141
institutionalization 18, 134, 145–47, 152
Interview 15–17, 102
Irigaray, Luce 83, 84

Jameson, Frederic 109, 142 n. 2
Jones, Amelia 87
jungla de Madrid, La 49–51, 53, 58, 65, 90

Kaka de Luxe 3, 142 n. 6
Kinder, Marsha 86
kitsch 86, 93, 98, 101, 154 n. 3
Krauss, Rosalind 75, 104 n. 8

Laigleasia, Juan Carlos de 23 n. 23, 100, 134, 135, 144 n. 25
Larson, Susan 1, 7, 8, 23 n. 15, 55, 63, 65, 113, 139

Latino 92, 99, 101, 142 n. 4
Lefebvre, Henri 25, 27, 28, 30, 31, 33, 69 n. 29
Lenclos, Ninon de 80
Ley de Peligrosidad y Rehabilitación Social 38
Littérature 49, 68 n. 20
liviandad del imperdible, La 3, 4, 142 n. 6
Lollipop 4
Lozano, Jorge 125, 129, 143 n. 19, 144 n. 21, 150
ludic 31, 35, 76, 91, 109, 111, 153
  homo ludens 35
luna de Madrid, La 1, 3, 4, 7–9, 23 n. 19, 20 and 25, 25, 64, 66 n. 1, 70, 107, 109
Lute, el (Eleuterio Sánchez) 72, 104 n. 4
Luz de Boudoir 13, 21, 71, 79, 84, 85, 91, 92, 105 n. 13, 144 n. 25
Lyotard, Jean-François 6, 108, 109, 125–29, 142 n. 2

machismo 80, 92
Madrid 1–5, 9–11, 16, 17, 19, 20, 22 n. 6, 11 and 13, 23 n. 22, 25–33, 35, 36, 38, 40, 42, 45, 47, 48–58, 61–69, 86, 91, 92, 102, 103, 104 n. 5, 106 n. 27, 108, 110–12, 114, 115, 118, 119, 121, 122, 124, 127–32, 138, 139, 141, 143 n. 16, 145–47, 149–52
Madrid, Madrid, Madrid 62
Madrid me mata (magazine) 4, 64, 149
Madrid me mata (bar) 22 n. 11
Madrid, Juan 17, 49–55, 58, 68 n. 22 and 24, 90, 150
Madriz 3, 64, 65
Mainer, José Carlos 5, 108, 140, 147, 149, 152, 154 n. 4
Makoki 3
Man Ray 75, 86
Mansilla, Pedro 5, 15
Manuel 36–49, 53, 57–59, 67 n. 9–11
Marcel, Jorge 123, 124, 130
Marisol 45, 47
Martín Begué, Sigfrido 114, 145
Martínez-Acha, Juan Ramón 4, 19, 23 n. 18
Mayrata, Ramón 13, 26
McNamara, Fabio / Fanny (Fabio de Miguel) 3, 22 n. 7, 86, 107
Medina, Alberto 2, 6
Mediterranean 93, 99, 101, 106 n. 23
Mena, Pedro de 42
Mira, Alberto 153
modern 8, 20, 33, 34, 35, 62, 64, 69 n. 32, 87, 95, 98, 104, 107, 108, 110, 111, 112, 113, 115, 117, 118, 120, 121, 126, 140
  modernism 76, 108, 109, 111–13, 135, 139, 140, 142 n. 2, 149
  modernist 2, 31, 32, 35, 65, 66, 72, 101, 107, 126, 131
  modernity 2, 20, 72, 76, 105 n. 9, 108, 109, 112, 118, 130, 149
  modernization 2, 31, 63, 72, 111, 112, 149
Moi, Toril 83, 144 n. 20
Molero, Herminio 127
Molina Foix, Vicente 143 n. 8
Molina, Miguel de 97, 106 n. 22
Morales, Gregorio 26, 121, 122, 141
Moreiras Menor, Cristina 6
Moreno Ruiz, José Luis 105 n. 19
Moriarty, Lola (Lola Fraile) 144 n. 25
Moriarty, Marta (Marta Villar) 80–82, 85, 134, 144 n. 25
movida, la 1, 3, 5–9, 17–19, 21, 22 n. 11 and 14, 23 n. 22, 23 and 26, 55, 60–65, 67 n. 11, 68 n. 28, 71, 75, 90, 91, 95, 98, 99, 103, 105 n. 9, 107, 108, 113, 114, 119, 122–24, 127, 130–34, 138, 139–41, 142 n. 7, 145–54, 154 n. 1, 3, 5 and 6, 155 n. 7 and 8
  removida, la 132–34
Muñoz Ballester, Rodrigo 17, 36, 37, 39–47, 66 n. 1, 67 n. 9 and 11, 150
Murillo, Bartolomé Esteban 93
Muro, Paz 93
myth 98–100, 114, 115, 123, 129
  mythology 111, 115

national 62, 63, 70, 71, 92, 98–101, 139, 148, 150
  nationalism
  Catalan nationalism 2, 22 n. 6
NATO referendum 136, 144 n. 26
New Babylon 35, 66 n. 7, 67 n. 8
nihilism 122, 134, 135, 143 n. 14
Noviciado 36, 37

Ocaña, La (José Ángel Ocaña) 2, 154 n. 3
Olivares, Javier 20, 63, 64, 119, 133, 134, 139, 142 n. 3, 144 n. 24
Ortiz, Lourdes 26
Ouka Leele (Bárbara Allende) 3, 11, 12, 17, 55, 124, 142 n. 6, 147, 148

Panero, Leopoldo 21, 23 n. 17
Panero, Leopoldo María 10, 17, 23 n. 17
parody 17, 21, 70, 84, 85, 88, 91, 92, 96, 101, 105 n. 15, 106 n. 25, 148, 150, 153, 154 n. 2
  parodic 79, 84–86, 88, 91–95, 97, 100, 141, 147, 151, 154 n. 3
pasodoble 95, 106 n. 21
pastiche 98, 102, 133, 150, 153
Patón, Vicente 9, 12, 27, 30–33, 66 n. 1 and 2
Patty Diphusa 11, 13, 16, 21, 23 n. 21, 58, 71, 85–92, 102, 105 n. 17
Peinado, Pablo 67 n. 15
Pepi, Luci, Bom y otrás chicas del montón 3, 142 n. 6, 147
Peraita, Jesús 78
Péret, Benjamin 68 n. 20, 89, 105 n. 16
Pérez del Solar, Pedro 152
Pérez Villalta, Guillermo 114, 143 n. 7
Pérez-Mínguez, Pablo 3, 68 n. 25, 93, 147
Pérez-Sánchez, Gema 7, 8, 22 n. 14, 153, 155 n. 7
performative 18, 20, 70, 79, 101, 140
  performativity 78

peripheral 99, 114, 139, 149, 150
Permanyare Producciones 10
Perrin, Dominique 51
photography 17, 54, 75, 93, 104 n. 8, 138, 144 n. 27, 147
Plan Especial Villa de Madrid 62
Plan General de Ordenación Urbana de Madrid 62, 69 n. 32
Pop Art 103
popular culture 21, 30, 62, 93, 103, 149, 150
postmodern 6, 8, 9, 21, 31–35, 66 n. 4, 69 n. 32, 71, 72, 76, 77, 95, 99, 102–10, 112–30, 135, 139–41, 142 n. 2, 143 n. 19, 149–51
  postmodern city 20, 47, 53, 56, 57, 58, 61, 70, 89, 90
  postmodernism 2, 6, 8, 21, 24 n. 28, 32, 49, 65, 66, 71, 76, 77, 93, 99, 103, 105 n. 15, 107–20, 123, 124, 126, 128, 130–35, 138–41, 142 n. 2, 143 n. 14 and 18, 144 n. 20 and 21, 149, 150
  postmodernity 16, 19, 107, 109–12, 115–20, 130, 145, 149, 150, 153
PREMAMÁ 142 n. 6
psychoanalysis 76
  psychoanalytical 6, 21 n. 3
Puerta del Sol 27, 28
punk 3, 80, 93, 103, 124

queer 7, 8, 22 n. 13, 67 n. 11, 71, 104 n. 1, 154 n. 6
  queering 87, 91
  queerness 86

Racionero, Luis 100, 106 n. 23
Radio Futura 127, 154 n. 2
Ramírez, Juan Antonio 108, 142 n. 1
rape 88–91, 105 n. 16, 152
Rastro 2, 3, 17, 69 n. 28
Recortables 27–29, 55, 57, 58, 66 n. 1
representation 22 n. 14, 42, 73–78, 83, 87–89, 91, 92, 148
  representational spaces 25, 36
  representational practices 92
  representations of space 25, 27, 28, 35, 63
  self-representation 70, 71, 73–79, 87, 90, 101
Resina, Joan Ramón 5, 8, 69 n. 32,
Révolution Surréaliste, la 49, 50, 68 n. 20, 75, 105
Richmond Ellis, Robert 86, 89, 90
Rifkin, Libbie 18, 152
Ripoll, Antonio J. 1, 17, 144 n. 28, 149
Ripoll, José Ramón 96, 97, 106 n. 22
Rrollo, el 2, 3, 22 n. 5
  Rrollo enmascarado, El 22 n. 5
Rrose Sélavy 86, 87

Sádaba, Javier 5, 72, 102, 104 n. 5, 116, 117, 143 n. 9, 144 n. 21, 150
Sánchez, Marta 144 n. 29
Sardi 98, 106 n. 22
Satie, Erik 45
Savater, Fernando 55, 68 n. 24, 135
self-portraits 73, 77, 78, 86
Serna, Pablo de la 97
Serrano, Cristóbal 97
Sheringham, Michael 59, 60, 69 n. 29 and 30
simulation 16, 21, 125, 129, 130, 150
  simulacra 125, 129, 130, 142 n. 2, 143 n. 12
  simulacrum 76, 124, 125
Situationism 69 n. 29, 151
  Situationist(s) 34, 35, 61, 63
Smith, Paul Julian 1, 6–8, 23 n. 26, 24 n. 28, 25, 57, 62, 67 n. 11, 102, 104 n. 1, 120, 149
Somos unas señoras 21, 71, 79, 84, 85, 91, 144 n. 25
Sontag, Susan 79, 83
Sordera, Los 96, 106 n. 22
Soriano, José 95, 106 n. 21
Spanish Communist Party (PCE) 21 n. 2, 62, 69 n. 31, 117, 120, 143 n. 11
Spanish Socialist Workers' Party (PSOE) 10, 69 n. 31, 143 n. 11, 144 n. 26
  socialist(s) 136, 152
  Socialist government 7, 145, 146
  Socialist party 63
Spanish transition 1, 5, 6, 7, 10, 61, 62, 69 n. 34, 117, 118, 142 n. 5, 145, 150
  transitional process 2, 22 n. 4, 69 n. 31, 143 n. 11, 151, 152
Spanishness 21, 71, 92, 95, 99, 101
Stapell, Hamilton 61–65
Star 2
Suárez, Antonio 76, 77
subconscious 76, 82, 116
Subirats, Eduardo 5, 72, 73, 104, 104 n. 5, 107–09, 140, 144 n. 30, 147, 149
subvenciones [subsidies to the arts] 7, 23 n. 14, 139
Surrealism 60, 68 n. 20, 69 n. 29, 75, 76, 116, 122, 151
  Surrealist(s) 11, 45, 48–54, 60–62, 67 n. 17, 68 n. 20, 75, 76, 89, 104 n. 8, 105 n. 9 and 16, 122
Surréalisme au Service de la Révolution, Le 49, 68 n. 20

Tierno Galván, Enrique 61, 65, 69 n. 33
Tímmermans, Javier 7, 13, 18, 19, 23 n. 18 and 23, 134, 138, 139, 143 n. 13, 144 n. 29
Tirado, José Luis 11, 144 n. 23
Tono Martínez, José 7, 9, 18, 19, 23 n. 23, 35, 59, 60, 66 n. 4, 68 n. 27, 98, 99, 106 n. 23, 110, 111, 116, 117–19, 128, 131, 132–34, 136–39, 144 n. 30
totality 49, 61, 107
Trillo, Miguel 145, 146, 154 n. 1
Triunfo 4

urban space 19, 25, 26, 31, 34, 48, 53, 57, 59, 61, 65, 70, 89, 90, 107, 147, 151
Utray, Javier 8, 9, 106 n. 26

Valle de los Caídos, El 3, 154 n. 3
Vallhonrat, Javier 78

Vattimo, Gianni 109, 112, 142 n. 2 and 4
Velázquez, Diego 45
  Las Meninas 45
Víbora, El 3
Vicente, Fernando 55, 68 n. 25, 93, 94
Viejo Topo, El 4, 22 n. 9
Vilarós, Teresa 2, 6, 7, 21 n. 3, 150
Village Voice 15, 16, 102
violence 49–53, 58, 68 n. 21 and 22, 84, 85, 89, 90, 92, 105 n. 9, 148
  domestic violence 84, 92, 141, 152
  sexual violence 89, 141
  terrorist violence 2
Visconti, Luchino 67 n. 14

Warhol, Andy 15, 16, 86–88, 136
  Altered ego 86, 87

youth 28, 57, 62, 102, 123
  youth culture 56, 62, 102, 103
  youth movement 1, 145
Yuste, Juan Ramón 14, 17, 73, 74–78, 104 n. 7, 144 n. 24 and 27, 147, 150

Zulueta, Iván 22 n. 12, 142 n. 6
Zurdo, El (Enrique Márquez) 3, 142 n. 6